Brooklyn's Green-Wood Cemetery

✳

NEW YORK's BURIED TREASURE

Green-Wood Cemetery's main gates, 1908.

Brooklyn's
Green-Wood Cemetery
NEW YORK's BURIED TREASURE

Written and Photographed by

JEFFREY I. RICHMAN

THE GREEN-WOOD CEMETERY

BROOKLYN

2008

SECOND EDITION

ISBN 0-9663435-0-6

Design by Jerry Kelly and Jeffrey I. Richman

Printed in the United States of America
by Capital Offset, Concord, New Hampshire

Table of Contents

Preface

I'VE COME FULL CIRCLE. Born in Brooklyn, I soon moved to Long Island and grew up there. Having lived my entire life in the New York metropolitan area, I've always been fascinated by New York City's history. That interest has led to my passion for Brooklyn's Green-Wood Cemetery.

In the early 1970's, while studying law at New York University, I was introduced by a fellow student to Jack Finney's classic book *Time and Again*. The story of one man's time travel back to nineteenth century New York City, it was illustrated with photographs of that time and place. Thereafter, I was hooked on nineteenth century New York.

It was a few years later that I began collecting stereoscopic views of New York City. Side by side photographs pasted on cardboard, they had their heyday in the nineteenth century, providing tours of the world to Victorians in the comfort of their parlors. When viewed in a stereoscope, these views were miraculously transformed into three-dimensional scenes. The more I searched for New York views, the more I came across scenes of a place called Green-Wood Cemetery. These cemetery views were relatively inexpensive, so I started buying them.

By 1987, I had a pretty extensive collection of photographs of Green-Wood. Studying these views, I had a good idea of what Green-Wood had looked like in the 1860's and even around 1900, but no idea whether it even existed anymore. That all changed that year when I joined a photographic tour of Green-Wood. I was amazed at this incredible place, its monuments, its vistas, its parklike setting in the midst of urban Brooklyn. I was enchanted.

And I've been fascinated by Green-Wood Cemetery ever since. I haunted book stores and shows, buying items that related to the cemetery or the people buried there. I began to write a book about Green-Wood, and Adrienne Hale encouraged me and diligently edited several versions of my writing. Thanks also to Elizabeth Emmons and Karen Kalikow, who read the manuscript and made it better. My late wife Judy deserves special thanks for tolerating my Green-Wood obsession while stepping over those book piles and boxes without too many complaints.

Richard J. Moylan, president of Green-Wood Cemetery, wisely recognized the importance of preserving its history for posterity. The committee of trustees with whom I met, Malcolm Mackay (now Vice Chairman of the Board of Trustees), C. Payson Coleman (now Chairman of the Board), and Ann Walker Gaffney encouraged me in this project with their love of history. Thanks are due all of the Green-Wood Cemetery trustees for their generous support for this project.

Much has changed at Green-Wood since the publication of the first edition of this book in 1998. The Green-Wood Historic Fund was founded that year, and has brought new spirit to the task of preserving this remarkable place. Its program, "Saved in Time," has had remarkable success in getting key monuments at Green-Wood adopted and fixed up. Art Presson, superintendent of the grounds, has made the hills and dales come alive with gardens and plantings. Most importantly, media coverage, documentaries, and special events such as "Angels and Accordions," have begun to put Green-Wood increasingly on the map as a destination for visitors interested in history, art, or just a quiet walk. I started working for the cemetery as a consultant and have just become its fulltime historian.

Just a few notes about this book. This book is not meant as a biographical dictionary of the individuals interred at Green-Wood—there are now almost 560,000 of them, and no single book could come close to mentioning them all. Rather, it is meant to give the reader a brief history of the cemetery and a few of the fascinating people who are now its permanent residents. Names of individuals who are interred at Green-Wood Cemetery or who were, in a few instances, cremated there, appear in bold when they first appear in a story. Chapters are meant to give a sense of an era; the stories within each chapter are not (except for the last chapter) in chronological order. Recent photographs of the cemetery, unless otherwise attributed, are by the author.

It's now more than twenty years since I first walked the glorious grounds of Green-Wood Cemetery. I've spent many days since that first visit wandering the cemetery, leading tours, researching, and reading. Certainly there is more than enough that I have learned since then to fill many more volumes. But, with the exception of a few corrections and some updating of images (it really is a great credit to the cemetery's leadership that so much has changed in just ten years), this is the book as written. It should be noted that, in 2006, Green-Wood was honored with its designation as a national historic landmark, one of only five cemeteries in all of America which have been so designated.

Following in the footsteps of Nehemiah Cleaveland and Effie Brower, two nineteenth century Green-Wood historians, I dedicate this book to the famous, the infamous, and the obscure who deserve to be remembered, who form the unique mix that is Green-Wood Cemetery.

A good book devoted to Green-Wood Cemetery, a book that records for posterity the story of this extraordinary place and its people, is long overdue. I have tried to make this book, published by Green-Wood Cemetery, that good book. I hope you enjoy it.

Jeffrey I. Richman
May, 2008

Introduction

EVERYBODY LOVES a great story, and Brooklyn's Green-Wood Cemetery has many of New York's great stories to tell. Everyone who was anybody in nineteenth century New York wanted to be buried there, and they were. As *The New York Times* succinctly put it in 1866, "It is the ambition of the New Yorker to live upon Fifth Avenue, to take his airings in the [Central] Park, and to sleep with his fathers in Green-Wood." They came by the thousands and the hundreds of thousands, first as tourists, then as permanent residents: Civil War generals, murder victims, victims of mass tragedies, inventors, artists, the famous, and the infamous. And they have continued to come to Green-Wood for over a century and a half now, bringing their lively stories and dark secrets with them. This book, by telling those stories, resurrects a vital part of New York's past.

Today, New Yorkers are close enough to nineteenth century New York to be enchanted by it. Every day they see street names, statues, and buildings that survive from that era. And New Yorkers are passionate about their history. Walt Whitman predicted more than a century ago that "there will come a time here in Brooklyn and all over America, when nothing will be of more interest than authentic reminiscences of the past." That time has come, and book-buyers have made best-sellers of many books about old New York, including such classics as *Time and Again*, *The Great Bridge*, and *When Brooklyn Was the World*.

No place today has a greater connection to, and more to say about, nineteenth century New York and where we have come from than Green-Wood Cemetery. This book is about Green-Wood Cemetery, its birth, its evolution, and the factors that make it such a special place. But the story of this cemetery is about more than its roads, its trees, and its monuments. It is also about the people who have chosen it as their final resting place; without them, there would be no cemetery. The men and women who shaped New York are buried here, and Green-Wood provides a unique window to their stories. Green-Wood Cemetery is a means of presenting the very best, both in narrative and illustration, of New York's past.

Green-Wood Cemetery is, in its own right, an extraordinary place. It and Niagara Falls were the great tourist attractions of nineteenth century America. Green-Wood, which developed an unparalleled national reputation and influence, is important in the development of America's rural cemeteries, public parks, and planned communities. Its grounds are a remarkable survivor of nineteenth century landscape design. The buildings and structures within its borders are a unique collection of architectural styles. Its funereal monuments, many of them notable works of art, have fascinating tales associated with them.

Green-Wood's story is further enriched by the most spellbinding tales of some of the almost 600,000 people who are interred here. Hundreds of books are devoted to individuals who are buried at Green-Wood Cemetery, and material from many of those books has been used for this work.

But Green-Wood's glory is not limited to a bygone era. Though much of this book reclaims the history of "lost New York," Green-Wood continues to attract the famous and the infamous: musical theater lyricist Fred Ebb, Seafarers Union president Paul Hall, renowned musician Leonard Bernstein, controversial Southampton Diet Doctor Stephen Berger, and artist/Warhol protegé Jean Michel Basquiat are but a few recent arrivals. And Green-Wood continues to be a popular tourist attraction—the public continues to respond to its call. Virtually every weekend, from early spring to late fall, groups tour this remarkable place and hear its stories. A wide range of organizations, from architectural students to senior citizens, from Civil War buffs to social clubs, from the Brooklyn Center for the Urban Environment to the Brooklyn Historical Society to the Municipal Arts Society, sponsor tours of Green-Wood's grounds.

This is a book about New York's animated and lively past; it is not a book of cemetery walking tours. Though this book discusses Green-Wood Cemetery, and addresses changing attitudes toward death, it is really about lives. It is about the noteworthy and absorbing individuals for whom Green-Wood is a final resting place, the men and women who made New York the great city that it is, and their funny, outrageous, tragic, triumphal, creative, scandalous, murderous, and heroic lives. The great visual delights of this gem, its parklike beauty, its trees and ponds, its sculpture and buildings by the leading artists and architects of their time, are featured in this book, as well as some of the great art that the people who reside at Green-Wood created during their lives. This book is for everyone who enjoys a good story about New York, its people, and their legacy.

Brooklyn's Green-Wood Cemetery

※

NEW YORK's BURIED TREASURE

Obelisks along Coreopsis Path.

CHAPTER ONE

Welcome to Green-Wood Cemetery

THE BACKGROUND

THE EARLY nineteenth century was a time of enormous growth in New York City. The Erie Canal, opening in 1825 and connecting New York City with the produce, natural resources, and markets of the West, launched an economic boom that drew immigrants to New York City from throughout the world. Industrialization created an urban center, attracting thousands from the countryside. And, as New York's population soared, problems with burial of the dead increased.

As the 1830's began, New York City had been a population center for about two hundred years. During those years, its citizens had relied on traditional churchyard burial or interment in vaults beneath churches. However, after generations of use, those facilities were filling up. Burying grounds were not able to keep pace with the population explosion and the parallel increase in death; annual interments in New York City had reached 10,000 and were steadily rising. Churches were located in settled areas, where there was no room to expand their burial yards, already "glutted with inhabitants." As late as 1822, there were twenty-two burying grounds south

South Street From Maiden Lane, *drawn and engraved by* WILLIAM J. BENNETT *(1787–1844) in 1828, shows the forest of masts along South Street that signaled new heights for New York's economic activity.*

of City Hall in Manhattan. These yards were too close to the hubbub of business and were not well-kept. As Joseph Story told the crowd of two thousand at the consecration of America's first rural cemetery, Mount Auburn, in 1831, old burial grounds were bleak, unattractive places:

> Why should we deposit the remains of our friends in loathsome vaults or beneath the gloomy crypts and cells of our churches, where the human foot is never heard, save when the sickly taper lights some new guest to his appointed apartment . . . ? Why should we expose our burying-grounds to the broad glare of day, to the unfeeling gaze of the idler, to the noisy press of business, to the discordant shouts of merriment, or the baleful visitations of the dissolute?

As cholera and yellow fever epidemics claimed thousands of New Yorkers in the 1820's, suspicions arose that burying the dead in the same ground from which the city's wells drew drinking water might be creating a "miasmata" which was spreading these diseases. Though the scientific basis for this link was not known (in 1832, on the mistaken theory that the sale of fresh fruit and vegetables contributed to the spread of disease, New York City enacted a law that banned their sale during that year's cholera outbreak), action was taken. Beginning in 1823, laws barred all burials in graves or vaults south of Canal, Sullivan, and Grand Streets. By 1851, all interments south of 86th Street, except those in private vaults and cemeteries, were outlawed.

Added to these concerns was the problem of the impermanence of burial in New York City. The Commissioners' Plan of 1811, which imposed a grid street plan on New York City, did not exempt already-existing churchyards. As a result, churchyards were destroyed for the placement of new streets and avenues. And, as the city stretched to the north, residents moved to newly-fashionable neighborhoods, and their churches followed. When this happened, many old church buildings and churchyards were sold to commercial developers. These developers, concerned more with building quickly than with the sensibilities of New Yorkers, dug up unclaimed bodies, the "crumbling coffins and mouldering remains . . . thrown rudely into the glare of day," loaded them on carts, and moved them off to potters fields or worse. George Templeton Strong, the great New York City diarist, was well-aware that a "final resting place" in his hometown was often not that at all in the mid-nineteenth century:

> . . . for in this city of all cities some place is needed where a man may lay down to his last nap without the anticipation of being turned out of his bed in the course of a year or so to make way for a street or a big store or something of that kind.

Given these conditions in New York City, a radical solution to the burial problem was needed. Fortunately, such a solution was at hand.

THE RURAL CEMETERY

THE IDEA of the rural cemetery, with its roots in the ancient Greek Kerameikos (a burying ground outside Athens), spread through

View From Battle Hill, *from* Green-Wood Illustrated in Highly Finished Line Engraving, From Drawings Taken on the Spot, by James Smillie, with Descriptive Notices by Nehemiah Cleaveland *(1847). Both Smillie and Cleaveland chose Green-Wood Cemetery as their final resting place.*

Europe and America in the late eighteenth and early nineteenth centuries. Starting in 1765 with Père-Lachaise, a rural "city of the dead" on the outskirts of Paris, France, the rural cemetery evolved in England with the addition of romantic landscape features such as trees, shrubs, lawns and ponds connected by winding paths in Liverpool Cemetery (1825) and London's Kensal Green Cemetery (1830).

Introduced to the United States in the 1830's, the rural cemetery was an exciting advance for Americans, offering burial in a spacious and romantic setting convenient to urban centers. It provided ready access to lawns, trees, and ponds for city dwellers, offering an escape for those who struggled daily with the difficulties of urban living.

Not only did the rural cemetery hold out prospects of space, permanence, and security while protecting health, it also provided an opportunity to associate with nature, a benign force (in contrast to seventeenth and eighteenth century ideas of nature as a harsh and forbidding power against which human beings struggled for survival) that looked increasingly attractive as an antidote to urban ills. English novelist Charles Dickens well-understood the connection in the Victorian mind between nature and death. In 1842, when he saw the wonder of Niagara Falls for the first time, he wrote:

> . . . then, when I felt how near to my Creator I was standing, the first effect, and the enduring one—instant and lasting—of that tremendous spectacle, was Peace . . . calm recollections of the Dead, great thoughts of Eternal Rest. . . . What voices spoke . . . what faces, faded from the earth . . . what Heavenly promise glistened in those angels' tears!

Americans of the late eighteenth and early nineteenth centuries associated the city with poor sanitation, dirty water, and overcrowded housing. As NEHEMIAH CLEAVELAND (1796–1877), Green-Wood's nineteenth century historian and chronicler, observed, the rural cemetery offered city dwellers an escape from the blighted city:

> Here, if alive to gentle influences, you will pause a moment. You will shake from your feet the city's dust, and leave behind you its cares and follies. You are within the precinct of a great, primeval temple, now forever set apart to pious uses.

The first rural cemetery in the United States was Mount Auburn Cemetery, established by the Massachusetts Horticultural Society in 1831 in Cambridge, just across the Charles River from Boston. Five years later Laurel Hill Cemetery, on the outskirts of Philadelphia, became the second. Green-Wood Cemetery, in the newly-created City of Brooklyn, just across the East River from New York City, was the third in 1838.

At the time that these rural cemeteries were being organized, a different type of cemetery had only recently emerged in New York City: the nonsectarian cemetery. The New York Marble Cemetery (1830) and the New York City Marble Cemetery (1832), which still exist on what is now the Lower East Side, did not adjoin a church and were not affiliated with any single church. This was a departure from the tradition of burial in the yard of the village church (and more recently the city church) that a family had attended for generations. These new "marble" cemeteries were not rural, they were not on large tracts, but they were different from their predecessors in that they were nondenominational Christian. Unfortunately, they were also small, and could therefore serve few. But no suitable location for a large rural cemetery could be found in Manhattan.

Green-Wood Cemetery, circa 1860, looking southeast from Ocean Hill. Nature and God could be experienced here.

Profound changes in attitudes towards death in America determined Green-Wood Cemetery's characteristics. In the seventeenth and eighteenth centuries death was a grim and feared presence leading all but the chosen few to hell and damnation. But by the time Green-Wood was in its planning stages, death was widely seen as peaceful and beautiful, with eternal and heavenly reunion accompanied by salvation and deliverance.

Also central to the conception of Green-Wood Cemetery was the widespread belief that nature and God were connected. By the time of Green-Wood's founding, Western thought had been revolutionized by Jean Jacques Rousseau's idea that humans were noble savages living in an unspoiled and hospitable landscape. A visit to Green-Wood

A rare old snow scene of Green-Wood Cemetery, circa 1865, looking west from Ocean Hill.

would be a sojourn with an idealized maternal nature, a return to "Mother Earth," a meeting with a benign God. Green-Wood would be a place where the picturesque landscape's hope and resurrection replaced the churchyard's Calvinist doom and terror.

These concepts were expressed in Green-Wood Cemetery's name. Early on, as the rural cemetery in Brooklyn was being planned, it was suggested that it be named the "Necropolis," Greek for "The City of the Dead." That idea was promptly rejected; "Necropolis" connoted a "fixed, set rule with formalized art and refinement," "an ideal of city form and show," a "depository for the dead." Rather, this place would be called "Green-Wood," a "place of quiet repose," of benign and civilized nature expressing "noble sentiments and refined taste," where healing truths abounded in "rural quiet," free of the crime, disease, poverty, constant change and immorality of the industrialized city. Green-Wood Cemetery was to be a spiritual place of moral instruction, where visitors, in an atmosphere full of life and Christian cheer, would have a religious experience contemplating earthly and other worlds. Green-Wood would be, as Harriet Martineau said of Mount Auburn Cemetery, a place for resurrection of the living:

> A visitor from a strange planet, ignorant of mortality, would take this place to be the sanctum of creation. Every step teems with the promise of life. Beauty is about to "spring up out of the ashes, and life out of the dust," and Humanity seems to be waiting, with acclamations ready on its lips, for the new birth.

It was also important that its name include "cemetery." The term "cemetery," derived from the Greek "koimeterion" ("sleeping place"), was adopted by early Christians anxious to show that death was but a temporary rest, not the finality that the Greeks and Romans believed it to be.

Henry E. Pierrepont was the man whose vision was crucial to Green-Wood Cemetery's creation.

"Cemetery" only came into common usage in the 1830's, when "rural cemetery" began to replace "burial ground" and "church-yard." This new term was meant to connote a place of rest and repose. Oak Hill Cemetery in Newburyport, Massachusetts, was dedicated with these words: "Let it ever be, what its name indicates, a cemetery, a place of rest, a *lodging-chamber*, where the sleep of the grave may be slept undisturbed, till the morning of the Resurrection shall break it."

As Gary Wills notes in *Lincoln at Gettysburg*, ideological factors provided an important impetus for rural cemeteries: "an escape from the theological gloom of church-yards, a return to nature, a pantheistic identification of dissolution with initiation." Much of the doctrine shaping the rural cemetery was derived from Transcendentalism. Led by Ralph Waldo Emerson, the Transcendentalists believed that God, a benevolent and mystical force, was present in nature. Nature allowed essential goodness, not outdated concepts of hell and damnation, to come to the fore.

Further, the rural cemetery would be a place where the real and the ideal met. The horizon, where heaven meets earth, could be seen there. The heavens themselves were reflected in the ponds of the rural cemetery. To the nineteenth century mind, the rural cemetery was a borderland between city and nature, life and death, mortality and eternity, past and future.

BROOKLYN'S EMERGENCE

THE FINAL FACTOR that made Green-Wood Cemetery a reality was the incorporation of the City of Brooklyn. In 1834, as New York City struggled with its burial problem and rural cemeteries began to emerge in the United States, newly-born Brooklyn needed "to lay out streets, avenues and squares," and it created a commission for that purpose. HENRY EVELYN PIERREPONT (1808–1888) was one of the men who served on that commission.

THE SOLUTION

IN 1832, Henry Pierrepont traveled to Mount Auburn Cemetery, on the hills of Cambridge overlooking Boston, and came away convinced that it should be the model for Brooklyn's cemetery. The next year he was off to Europe to study its cities and cemeteries, visiting Père-Lachaise in Paris and the Campos Santos in Italy. Pierrepont firmly believed that New York needed a rural cemetery and that Brooklyn's Gowanus Hills were the place for it.

Henry Pierrepont was a man of vision. He made sure that the commission's plans for Brooklyn included eleven public parks. It was Pierrepont who insisted that a large tract of land be set aside for a rural cemetery and that the projected streets and avenues of the new city stop at its borders.

THE OPPORTUNITY

PIERREPONT'S IDEAS for a cemetery, however, lay dormant until the Depression of 1837. This depression, which prompted HORACE GREELEY to urge the legions of unemployed to "Go West, young man, and grow with the country," was a boon for Henry Pierrepont's plans. It caused a substantial drop in real estate prices, creating a unique opportunity to buy land for Brooklyn's rural cemetery.

The Pierrepont Monument was designed by famed church architect Richard Upjohn. It is made of brownstone, Upjohn's favorite building material. Gothic Revival in style, it is an open-air church.

THE EARLY YEARS

ON APRIL 18, 1838, by act of New York State's Legislature, "The Green-Wood Cemetery" was incorporated "for the purpose of establishing a public burial ground in the City of Brooklyn," and was authorized to purchase up to 200 acres. Its name, Green-Wood, was chosen as one "indicating that it should always remain a scene of rural quiet, and beauty, and leafiness, and verdure." Though it was initially established as a joint stock company under the misapprehension that that was the only structure possible, within a year it was converted to a nonprofit corporation "eminently and essentially philanthropic ... from which even the appearance of individual profit is excluded." Its Act of Incorporation dictated that the trustees were to be elected by its lot owners and all of its income was to be applied to the acquisition, preparation, and maintenance of its grounds. Land that had been used primarily as pasture and woodland was purchased from old Brooklyn families: the Wyckoffs, Ibbotsons, Deans, Sacketts, Schermerhorns, Bennetts, and Bergens.

DAVID BATES DOUGLASS (1790–1848) was chosen as Green-Wood Cemetery's landscape architect and first president. An experienced civil engineer who had surveyed the area and was intimately familiar with it, Douglass rode on horseback over the heights of Brooklyn with Henry E. Pierrepont until he found "the best locality in the vicinity for a cemetery, and probably the finest in the world." The land they chose had several

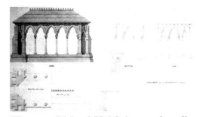

These are Richard Upjohn's recently rediscovered architectural drawings for the Pierrepont Monument. Courtesy of Norman Brosterman.

No man did more to assure the existence of Green-Wood Cemetery than Henry Pierrepont. He spent the years from 1833 to 1838 helping to set up the cemetery, donated the original fence that marked the cemetery's borders, was the first vice president and the second president of Green-Wood, and in 1842 purchased lots one through eight there. For his efforts in nurturing the cemetery, he was honored with a choice location for his family plot atop one of its few man-made hillocks. The names carved into the monuments on that hillside are a roll call of the leading families of New York and Brooklyn. Henry E. Pierrepont was the last survivor of the men who created Green-Wood Cemetery.

Henry Pierrepont was the son of HEZEKIAH B. PIERREPONT (1768–1838) and ANNA MARIA CONSTABLE PIERREPONT (1782–1859). In 1804, Hezekiah purchased sixty acres of the Benson, De Bevoise, and Remsen farms on Brooklyn Heights, and by 1819 had given up all other businesses to devote himself to the sale and development of the Heights and the over 500,000 acres which he owned in northern New York State. Henry's mother was the daughter of New York State's largest landholder.

1838 was a particularly good time to acquire land for a rural cemetery. Land prices, in the wake of the Panic of 1837, were depressed. But when Green-Wood's agents attempted to buy 200 acres from the old farmers who owned the land, they were met with skepticism. The cemeteries these farmers knew were no more than an acre or two. Some of them, having heard a rumor that the land was being bought up because there was a treasure buried on it, hesitated to sell. But eventually they all came around, and the cemetery purchased the land that it needed. Reaching its current size of 478 acres later in the nineteenth century, Green-Wood remained until the turn of the twentieth century the largest landscaped cemetery in the world, more than four times the size of its predecessor, Mount Auburn Cemetery.

This circa 1860 photograph, by Beer & Co., published by Green-Wood Cemetery, is of the west side of Ocean Hill, looking north. Note the stones at the left side of the road; they are glacial rubble removed from the surface and used to form the road bed. Such rocks can still be seen on the edges of the cemetery's paved roads. Courtesy of Jeffrey Kraus.

advantages: its proximity to New York City ("sufficiently remote to be beyond the range of city improvements, yet so near as to be of convenient access"), its panoramic view of New York Harbor, and the variety offered by its hilly surface and ponds.

This land had been shaped 17,000 years earlier, when the glacier crept southward, then halted at the moraine which runs east-west through what is now Green-Wood Cemetery. As the glacier began to recede, it left behind ponds, hills, and rock rubble. These features made the land unattractive for commercial or residential development, but inexpensive and well-suited for a rural cemetery.

Douglass had no intention of grossly changing the land; rather, he planned to grade and groom the original 178 acres to meet the cemetery's needs. Consistent with the attitude of the time, nature was not to be allowed to take its own course, but was to be improved upon, to be made more "natural." Rock rubble was taken from the hills and used for the beds of carriage roads. Variety was prized as hills, glacial ponds, forests, dells, and valleys were manicured and lawns were planted. Circular, oblong, and triangular family plots were created; rows of gravestones, such as those found at the Congressional Cemetery in Washington, D.C., or the later Arlington National Cemetery, were scorned. Curved paths and roads

One of the reasons that Green-Wood Cemetery was established on the heights of Brooklyn was the New York Harbor view that that location afforded. However, Green-Wood's founders could not have envisioned this spectacular skyline vista from the cemetery. Photograph by Ken Taylor.

Arbor Water and the Receiving Tomb at Green-Wood Cemetery, circa 1895. Nature here is manicured and controlled by man. Note the variety of architectural styles, including Romanesque, Egyptian, and Greek Revival, of these hillside mausoleums.

added to the land's mystery, surprising and delighting visitors whose leisurely walk or carriage ride was driven forward by the desire to know what was just around the bend. Picturesque trees, framing the distant scene, were planted. (But Douglass never took the picturesque concept as far as the eighteenth century Englishmen who "planted" a dead tree in London's Kensington Gardens for its scenic effect.) The names of features, roads and paths at Green-Wood were chosen to enhance this experience of

At the request of Green-Wood Cemetery's Board of Trustees, David Bates Douglass's remains were brought there and interred beneath this monument.

being in the presence of life, not death: Sylvan Water, Grassy Dell, and Sassafras Avenue were typically-uplifting choices. Under Douglass's direction, Green-Wood Cemetery became the finest of the first generation of American landscapes in the English picturesque garden tradition.

THE STRUGGLE TO SURVIVE

YET, despite the forces that prompted Green-Wood Cemetery's birth, it was far from an overnight success. Rather, it was soon forced into a struggle for survival. After two years of landscaping work, its first burials occurred on September 5, 1840, when Sarah Hanna, John Hanna, Richard Hanna, and Sarah Draper, who had been removed from New York's Marble Cemetery, were reinterred in Green-Wood's lot 233 at the base of Ocean Hill. But fewer than 400 burials followed in the next three years. Some prospective lot-buyers were reluctant to commit their money to the new idea of burial distant from the church where they worshipped. Others were reluctant to have their family buried at Green-Wood because it would mean separation from their already-interred ancestors.

Green-Wood Cemetery was able to survive and prosper for several rea-

David Bates Douglass squeezed careers as civil engineer, landscape architect of rural cemeteries, soldier, and teacher into his lifetime. He graduated from Yale College, then went to the Military Academy at West Point to train as an engineer, and later was named commander of that post. During the War of 1812, he commanded sappers and miners and took part in the Battle of Niagara. After the war, he returned to West Point, where he taught philosophy and engineering. He also worked on a survey of the defenses of Long Island Sound and as the astronomical surveyor to determine the border with Canada near Detroit. In 1831, he left the army to become an engineer of the Morris Canal, where he introduced inclined planes as an alternative to locks. He taught architecture and civil engineering at the University of the City of New York (later known as New York University), and designed its building on the east side of Washington Square.

In 1835, Douglass became the chief engineer of the great Croton Aqueduct project that brought running water to New York City. He selected its watershed, located the route of the aqueduct, and planned the system. Douglass, at the suggestion of Henry E. Pierrepont, delivered a public lecture in the autumn of 1835 in which he urged that a rural cemetery be established in Brooklyn. After helping to select the site for Green-Wood Cemetery, Douglass, in the winter of 1838, began to survey and lay out its grounds. Construction of the cemetery began under Douglass's supervision in May, 1839. By October of that year, lots were advertised for sale. Douglass served as Green-Wood's architect and first president until 1841, then resigned to become president of Kenyon College, but came east again four years later to lay out rural cemeteries in Albany and Quebec. He also designed the supporting wall for Brooklyn Heights, the water system for Brooklyn, and some of the landscape features of Staten Island. In 1848, Douglass became professor of mathematics at Hobart College, where he taught until his death.

This engraving shows Green-Wood Cemetery in its early years, about 1847.

sons. As the first rural cemetery in the New York metropolitan area, it offered without competition (Woodlawn Cemetery in the Bronx would not begin to offer a rural cemetery alternative until 1865) a convenient location (less than three miles from Manhattan, with service by mid-century provided by four ferry lines) for burial in a park-like setting. Green-Wood survived and prospered because it appealed to the civic pride of Brooklynites and New Yorkers, who bought plots so that this local effort would succeed. Appeals such as that of the *Long Island Star* in the 1840's that "in order to ensure the success of an enterprise which in after years will redound to the praise and be the pride of their City, every individual must do something and that soon, to foster its existence," won out.

Green-Wood Cemetery also had some success in marketing large plots to churches and fraternal organizations. The Dutch Reformed Church, Christ Church, First Presbyterian Church of Brooklyn, First Unitarian Congregational Church of Brooklyn, Howard Colored Orphan Asylum,

Green-Wood Cemetery's prospects for survival were greatly helped by the work of JOSEPH A. PERRY (1807–1881). In 1842, when Green-Wood was still struggling to survive, Perry, Henry E. Pierrepont's son-in-law, gave up his business career to take over management of the cemetery. During the first year of his stewardship, twenty tombs were constructed and 162 interments occurred. In the years before his death in 1881, Perry guided the cemetery as it grew from 175 to 460 acres, while improving its facilities and beautifying its grounds.

On Perry's monument, the following inscription is carved:

The Trustees of the Green-Wood Cemetery have erected this monument in recognition of the eminent services of Joseph Alfred Perry, who, for more than forty years, and until his death, was its faithful and efficient comptroller. To Mr. Perry's untiring energy, sound judgment, and personal care, the proprietors of Green-Wood Cemetery are chiefly indebted for the development of the sacred City of the Dead.

Joseph Perry, who managed Green-Wood Cemetery's financial affairs for the first forty years of its existence.

Joseph Perry is buried beneath this monument, on a hillside just inside the cemetery's main gates.

Sons of Temperance, Widows and Orphans Fund Society, Odd Fellows, American Seamens' Friend Society, New York University, and Columbia College all purchased plots. In turn, these groups sold graves to individuals who otherwise could not have afforded family plots at Green-Wood. But these sales to organizations were not as great as Green-Wood's founders had hoped. Certainly their greatest disappointment occurred when New York City's prestigious Trinity Church agreed to buy twenty acres, but later withdrew in favor of creating its own cemetery at 155th Street in Manhattan.

The prospects for Green-Wood's survival were certainly helped by the good publicity it was able to generate. In the cemetery's early years it offered a final resting place to the well-known McDONALD CLARKE, "the Mad Poet of Broadway" (who died in 1842), and the meteorically-popular Indian Princess DO-HUM-ME (who died in 1843). Both, it was hoped, would attract attention, visitors, and ultimately buyers. In 1846, with Green-Wood's existence assured, and receipts starting to match expenses, the New York State Legislature authorized the cemetery to purchase an additional 125 acres beyond the original 200 acres that had been initially authorized.

But Green-Wood Cemetery's ultimate marketing coup occurred a few years later, when it wrested the body of the most respected New Yorker of his time, Mayor and Governor DE WITT CLINTON (1769–1828), from his "final resting place" in the Little Albany Cemetery, obtaining permission from one of his relatives to have him reinterred at Green-Wood. The attendant publicity from a mammoth publicly-subscribed bronze statue of Clinton, which was displayed temporarily in front of the City Hall in New York City before joining him at Green-Wood, and the resulting good will, helped to assure the cemetery's success.

Green-Wood Cemetery was established to serve residents of New York City and the City of Brooklyn. As shown in this detail from an 1855 print, its sales office was on the west side of Manhattan's Broadway, just south of Exchange Alley, in the low building second from the right.

The Dutch Reformed Church purchased this large area of Cedar Dell for reinterments and relocation of old gravestones, as well as for new burials.

The public excitement at the news that De Witt Clinton's remains were coming to Green-Wood Cemetery was so great that this print, View From Ground Appropriated For the Clinton Monument, *was marketed to illustrate nothing more than the empty plot where he was to be buried.*

No. 23. VOL. I.   NEW YORK, SATURDAY, JUNE 4, 1853.   PRICE SIX CENTS.

THE COMMERCIAL CENTRE.

The City Hall Park unveiling of the Clinton statue, which was destined for Green-Wood, was the front page story in New York's Illustrated News *on June 4, 1853.*

As Green-Wood Cemetery emerged from its early years, it became a source of national pride with an international reputation. Lady Emmeline Wortley, after coming from England to visit Green-Wood, was clearly envious: "When will London have any thing even *approaching* to this magnificent cemetery." Green-Wood's national reputation is demonstrated by the decision of Dixon Hall Lewis, a States' rights United States Senator from Alabama, to be buried in Brooklyn. Nor was this an isolated occurrence: Green-Wood's lots were sold to individuals throughout America. Of all the rural cemeteries, Green-Wood was widely considered to be the most varied, refined, and attractive. In 1866, *Harper's Weekly* called Green-Wood "the largest and most beautiful burial-place on the continent." In tribute, rural cemeteries throughout the country were named "Greenwood"; those in New Orleans, Louisiana, Hamilton, Ohio, Jackson, Mississippi, Dallas, Texas, and Galena, Illinois, are a few examples.

After the Great Fire of 1835 destroyed the statue of Alexander Hamilton in the Merchants Exchange, there was virtually no public sculpture in New York City. Green-Wood soon had the finest collection of mid-nineteenth century American sculpture anywhere: one commentator said of its monuments and tombs that "[i]n beauty of design and costliness they surpass any similar collection in the New World."

Green-Wood Cemetery also served as a model for the planned suburban communities that emerged later in the nineteenth century. As one writer has recently observed, "The dead were the first to move to the suburbs." Green-Wood's revolutionary use of "zoning," of page after page of rules imposed on lot owners in the cemetery (don't use veneers; make foundations solid and deep; maximum curb around a plot one foot high by one foot wide; no pets to be buried there; no shrubs or trees to be planted with-

This booklet, Green-Wood Cemetery's Rules and Regulations of 1872, *was eighty-three pages of do's and don'ts.*

A good example of the variety of monuments at Green-Wood Cemetery.

Someone in the family of Elias Howe, the inventor of the sewing machine, felt strongly about their dog Fannie, erecting this monument, with its heartfelt verse, to the dog with the "limpid eyes."

Rex's owners memorialized him with this monument.

out permission; avoid "tame and uninteresting" monuments; don't use posts and chains: they were likely to rust and to be used as swings by children; the trustees reserved the right to remove "any injurious or offensive structure or monument"), emphasized the need for variety and permanency. The spectacular array of its funereal monuments is not happenstance, but is largely the result of these rules that encouraged dissimilarity.

Rural cemeteries, which by virtue of their size were able to offer separate family plots, provided new opportunities for expressions of status, virtue, and refinement. Individuals, no longer interred with their congregation, could now be buried with their family. In Green-Wood's lots, typically 14 by 27 feet, there was even room for memorials to the family pet, the emerging symbol of domesticity. The ample space of rural cemetery plots gave lot owners a chance to individualize their new "home." They surrounded their plot with an iron or bronze fence or a stone curb to set their family's area apart. They decorated within that space with shrubs, statuary, planters filled with flowers, and even cast iron furniture.

With consumerism glorified in the post–Civil War boom, noted architects and sculptors were hired to help make the neat and well-tended family plot a statement of taste and morality. Prime locations on street corners or atop hills were coveted as places for the ostentatious display of social distinction. As one observer of Green-Wood said, "All classes come here, but the cemetery is characteristic of the living city beyond. Wealth governs everything here as there." Those who tastefully decorated their plots (their "eternal homes"), just as those who adorned their dwellings, were seen as contributors to the community's morality.

It was not long before Green-Wood Cemetery became immensely popular. As early as 1839, David Bates Douglass, supervising the first efforts to convert Brooklyn pastures into a rural cemetery, noted that "visitors begin to be attracted from the city in considerable numbers daily." With virtually no public parks in existence, Green-Wood, within a few years, became a fashionable place for family outings. It was no morbid graveyard; rather, as the *Long Island Star* reported, its miles of carriage roads offered "a delightful ride through shady groves, occasionally affording distant and extensive views." The *Daily News* was just as enthusiastic about Green-Wood's virtues:

> What merchant in New York—What professional man—What mechanic, but would feel better, physically and morally, to forget the season, the cares and toils incident to his pursuits, amidst the beauties of the Green-Wood Cemetery.

As the 1850's began, Green-Wood was attracting 100,000 visitors per year; by 1860, the yearly total was up to 500,000. At the middle of the nineteenth century, America's rural cemeteries rivaled Niagara Falls as the country's greatest tourist attractions. The written guides to New York City all recommended a visit to Green-Wood. Photographs of Green-Wood were sold throughout the country, as were guidebooks and maps describing its attractions. Cars of the Brooklyn City Railroad carried tourists

A plot at Green-Wood, 1868, with some of the comforts of home, including cast iron lawn furniture.

Four of the more elaborate tombs at Green-Wood Cemetery.

A bird's-eye view of Green-Wood Cemetery in 1852, looking west toward New York Harbor.

Detail of an elaborate cover of a Green-Wood Cemetery guide. At center is the cemetery's first entrance; four of the early tombs and monuments frame it in this illustration.

A map of the Tour, 1847.

every few minutes from the Fulton Ferry, and stages ran up the hills from the Hamilton Avenue Ferry.

Once inside the cemetery, generations of visitors were taken by carriage on "The Tour," a specified route past the famed attractions of the cemetery, with no extra charge for a stop to visit loved ones.

Some of these tourists, however, did have a complaint: "the funerals stream[ed] in, in an almost continuous procession," got in the way, and spoiled the festive mood. And the cemetery had its own concerns: despite the efforts of Green-Wood's own Sunday police, who were instructed that the "grounds are sacredly devoted to the interment of the Dead" and were ordered to "conduct violators to the gate," tourists often broke the rules by lounging on the grass, smoking, picnicking, talking loudly, laughing, and picking flowers, and hackmen sometimes failed to obey notices not to "speed" in their carriages over four miles per hour. This tension between recreational use and religious contemplation was a constant problem for Green-Wood and other rural cemeteries.

In 1856, one newspaper described Green-Wood Cemetery as "the best kept park in the United States." At that time, no city in the United States had a spacious rural park. Green-Wood's great success in attracting tourists was cited by those who argued for public parks: if thousands went to Green-Wood, thousands would certainly flock to a park. As Andrew Jackson Downing, the noted landscape architect who pushed for the birth of Central Park, said:

> Judging from the crowds of people in carriages, and on foot, which I find constantly thronging Green-Wood and Mount Auburn, I think it is plain enough how much of our citizens, of all classes, would enjoy public parks on a similar scale.

At the same time that Green-Wood was gaining great popularity with tourists, it also became the fashionable place to be buried. Over 100,000 people were buried there in its first twenty-five years of operation, and an

A carriage on the Tour, circa 1870. Courtesy of Jeffrey Kraus.

An advertisement for the Green-Wood Carriage Service, circa 1885. Visitors could tour the cemetery, see its sights, and stop to pay their respects to their loved ones.

Tourists who weren't interested in taking the Tour could stroll the grounds or row around Arbor Water. Photograph circa 1870. Note Green-Wood's main gates in the background.

Green-Wood Cemetery maintenance workers, circa 1870. In the cemetery's early years, many workers lived on its grounds. Up until the relatively recent advent of gas-powered trimmers, maintaining the grounds was very labor-intensive, and all trimming was done by hand, using a scythe.

Tourists and mourners flocked to Green-Wood Cemetery, circa 1865.

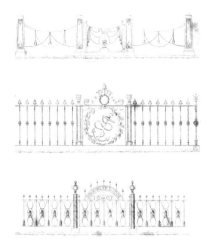

These drawings of cast iron fences at Green-Wood appeared in Green-Wood Illustrated, *published in 1847. Cast iron could be customized by foundries: the posts of the fence surrounding the monument to war hero Colonel Vosburgh were cast in the shape of bayoneted rifles and those for the Firemen's Monument were molded as fireplugs.*

In this circa 1865 photograph by Beer & Co., published by Green-Wood Cemetery, the recently-completed main gates appear in the distance, with workers' housing at the far right. The grassy area in the foreground, and the ground on which those houses stood, became gravesites only a few decades ago. Courtesy of Jeffrey Kraus.

even greater number of graves had been purchased for future use. The *New York Herald* felt that "no doubt . . . some people in good health" were anxious to meet their Maker so "that they may have the enjoyment of being buried as soon as possible in that beautiful location." By 1866, *The New York Times* was speaking with admiration of the position Green-Wood had assumed as a leading New York institution in the less than thirty years since its birth:

> Green-Wood is as permanently associated with the fame of our city as the Fifth Avenue or the Central Park. It is one of the institutions to be served up to strangers, and no guest has been courteously entertained until he has been driven through its winding avenue and looked down upon the bay and city from its commanding heights. It is the ambition of the New Yorker to live upon Fifth Avenue, to take his airings in the [Central] Park, and to sleep with his fathers in Green-Wood.

Reaching its current size of 478 acres in the nineteenth century, Green-Wood Cemetery remained until the turn of the century the largest landscaped cemetery in the world, and was more than four times the size of its predecessor, Mount Auburn Cemetery.

In this Memorial Day, 1899 photograph, promenaders enjoy a sunny holiday along Green-Wood Cemetery's Landscape Avenue.

ITS EVOLUTION

GREEN-WOOD CEMETERY has changed over the years. In the 1850's, the main entrance was moved from 26th and 27th streets to Fifth Avenue and 25th Street so that mourners did not have to be affronted by the open taverns there. The original wooden fence surrounding the cemetery was replaced by longer-lasting iron. The entrance gates by the great architectural firm of Richard Upjohn & Son were built during the

The Shelter House, seen in this circa 1890 photograph, was torn down years ago.

Civil War. Structures for workers' housing and several visitors' shelters, built in the early years, were torn down. The erection of the Chapel (which replaced Arbor Water) at the beginning of the twentieth century, by leading society architects Warren and Wetmore, demonstrated that Green-Wood, generations after its founding, still had great prestige.

Other changes have occurred over the years. Under the guise of World War II's patriotic scrap metal drive, almost all of the cast iron fences surrounding individual lots, which were so prevalent in the cemetery during the mid-nineteenth century, and which added interest but also

Both cast iron and metal bar fences were common in the cemetery until World War II. This view, dating circa 1890, gives some idea of the extent to which fences surrounding family plots proliferated in the cemetery.

The recently reinstalled fountain in Valley Water, one of four Green-Wood Cemetery ponds.

Though this spectacular cast iron gate remains, the fence that accompanied it was removed years ago.

This is the last phase of Hillside Mausoleum, offering an alternative to in-ground burial. It was completed in 2006. Photograph by Dennis Kleiman.

Niches in the columbarium. Interior design by Thomas Hauser. Photograph by Andrea Brizzi.

destroyed vistas and made maintenance costly, were removed. Green-Wood was certainly only too willing during World War II to spread the message contained in the September, 1942, letter from the United States War Production Board, General Salvage Program, addressed "To All Cemeteries":

A great many people have asked us if the metal from their cemetery plots would constitute a valuable contribution to the war effort.

The answer is, "Yes." Metal of this type is used in making the very highest grade of fighting equipment and is constantly needed for this purpose.

This is one of an estimated five to ten post cards of Green-Wood Cemetery which were published circa 1905.

Examples of an early cast iron hitching post and a path sign at Green-Wood Cemetery. Over the years, some of these signs have deteriorated and been replaced with new stamped signs. Green-Wood Cemetery has recently made arrangements to cast replacement signs in the old design.

Few lot owners, contacted by the cemetery in a plea to help the war effort, could say "no," and, with only a few exceptions, the metal fences have disappeared from Green-Wood's grounds.

Green-Wood Cemetery continues to evolve. Fountains, offering the soothing sound of splashing water, were installed in ponds during the nineteenth century, but were later removed; a fountain has recently been reinstalled in Valley Water. In the last decade, the cemetery has been removing some roads, paths, and a pond in order to sell those areas for gravesites. But four of Green-Wood's ponds remain. Burials continue at a rate of about 1,500 per year.

And, as popular tastes have changed, and many individuals have sought alternatives to in-ground burial, Green-Wood Cemetery has broadened

Tranquility Gardens, which opened in 2006, offers niches for the display of urns containing cremated bodies. Photograph by Andrea Brizzi.

Men of Progress, *painted by Christian Schussele in 1862, shows the great American inventors of the nineteenth century gathered together in this imaginary scene. Remarkably, four of these eighteen great men chose Green-Wood Cemetery as their final resting place: James Bogardus, second from the left, who developed the cast iron building front; Peter Cooper, sixth from the left (bending over), who built the first American railway locomotive; Samuel F.B. Morse, in the foreground to the right of center, with his patent model for his revolutionary telegraph device given center stage on the table, and Elias Howe, to the far right, who invented the sewing machine. Other individuals of note depicted here are Benjamin Franklin, the father of all American inventors (looking over the scene from the painting on the wall), Samuel Colt, and Charles Goodyear. Courtesy of the National Portrait Gallery, Smithsonian Institution.*

the range of its facilities. A marble and limestone crematory, built in 1954 and recently renovated, offers the increasingly-popular option of cremation; in some areas of the United States, cremation has become more popular than in-ground burial. Niches in the columbarium and the newly-opened Tranquility Gardens as well as crypts in the Hillside Mausoleum provide above-ground interments, an option previously limited to those who were wealthy enough to build their own tombs.

Yet, over the years, the essence of Green-Wood Cemetery has remained undisturbed. Many of its great monuments have weathered, but most have survived the ravages of time largely intact. Most of the original elegant cast iron road and path signs, and even several horse hitching posts, continue to adorn the cemetery. Many of the scenes of over one hundred years ago exist little-changed today.

Green-Wood Cemetery is still a remarkable place. It is an extraordinary arboretum, with thousands of varieties of shrubs and trees enriching 22 miles of roadways and 30 miles of paths. It is a bird sanctuary, with is current 478 acres (slightly smaller than Prospect Park and about one-half the size of Central Park) offering haven to permanent and migratory residents. In 1852, the aptly named Thomas Woodcock imported from England to Green-Wood Cemetery 48 skylarks, 24 woodlarks, 48 goldfinches, 24 English robins, 12 thrushes, and 12 blackbirds. Though the descendants of those birds may no longer be at Green-Wood, monk parrots indigenous to South America (escapees from a shipment through Kennedy Airport), as well as a host of other varieties of birds, now make it their home. Green-Wood, listed on the National Register of Historic Places in 1997, is a great repository of nineteenth century sculpture and architecture, offering a variety of styles in its vaults and mausoleums.

Green-Wood Cemetery, a city of almost 600,000, would inevitably have attracted some prominent men and women. But its virtues were particularly appealing for painters (ASHER B. DURAND, the leader of the Hudson River School, and GEORGE CATLIN, painter of American Indians), architects (JAMES RENWICK, JR., designer of St. Patrick's Cathedral and Grace Church, and WILLIAM ALCIPHRON BORING, responsible for the buildings on Ellis Island), soldiers of every American war (including sixteen Civil War generals for the Union and two for the Confederacy, as well as thirty-seven Union officers who were brevetted brigadier generals), and mayors (ten New York City mayors and twenty-two of the twenty-seven men who served as mayor of the City of Brooklyn).

Green-Wood has its share of suffragists (LOUISINE HAVEMEYER and HARRIET BURTON LAIDLAW), the famous (LEONARD BERNSTEIN, SAMUEL F.B. MORSE, PETER COOPER, HORACE GREELEY, HENRY WARD BEECHER) and the infamous ("BOSS" TWEED, diet doctor STEPHEN BERGER). Well-known names abound, including

Between 1850 and 1900, Green-Wood Cemetery was the final resting place of choice for America's politicians; no cemetery in the country during that period interred more of them. Overall, only Arlington National Cemetery in Virginia, with a total of 157 former Presidents, Vice Presidents, cabinet members, governors, and members of Congress, has more politicians within its borders than Green-Wood, where the total, by one count, is 110 (102 members of Congress, six governors, and two cabinet members).

By 1891, the year this photograph was published, the cemetery was filling up, as this scene near Henry Ward Beecher's grave shows.

Mining magnate MARCUS DALY (1841–1900) was born in Ireland, came to New York City at the age of eighteen, worked there, then went off to California to become a miner. After working in John Mackay's Virginia City mine, he was off to Montana, where he discovered one of the world's greatest concentrations of copper in 1882. Coincidentally, that was the same year that Thomas Edison illuminated New York City's Pearl Street with electric lights, creating a new market for copper as a conductor of electricity. Daly made his fortune in Butte, Montana, where he was known as "The Great Man Himself" and the "Copper King." Ultimately, his Anaconda Copper gained control of every mine in Butte. Butte produced one-quarter of all the copper being produced in the world; it also led the nation in suicide by dynamite. Its 50,000 residents had the highest per capita income in America and the highest rate of union membership. Daly personified the American dream; within twenty years of his arrival in this country as a penniless boy, Daly was a multimillionaire owning mines, banks, power plants, irrigation systems, and vast tracts of timber. He recruited miners, many of whom were Irish, to work for him, allowed them days off to watch his horses run at the race track near the mines, and gave out turkeys and wine to his workers on holidays. His mines worked around the clock, in three shifts, except on two days: Miners' Union Day and St. Patrick's Day. He founded Anaconda, Montana, just outside Butte, built a huge copper smelter there, and published its newspaper, the *Anaconda Standard*. Daly spent over half a million dollars on an unsuccessful campaign to make Anaconda the State capital. When he died, it was reported that his remains would be sent to Montana. But those plans were changed, and an eleborate tomb was built for him at Green-Wood Cemetery.

DELAFIELD, PITKIN, PRATT, LEFFERTS, and PIERREPONT, and household names such as COLGATE, SQUIBB, DURKEE, WESSON, LORILLARD, PFIZER, UNDERWOOD, F.A.O. SCHWARZ and STEINWAY.

The woman who jilted James Madison (KITTY FLOYD), the savant who amazed nineteenth century New York with his pronouncement that the whale was not a fish (SAMUEL LATHAM MITCHILL), the designer of the American flag (SAMUEL CHESTER REID), retailing's BROOKS BROTHERS, the "Father of Baseball" (HENRY CHADWICK), the man who made his fortune in the Anaconda copper mines of Butte, Montana ("Copper King" MARCUS DALY), the founder of the American Society for the Prevention of Cruelty to Animals (HENRY BERGH), the first black woman to be licensed as a doctor in New York State (SUSAN SMITH MCKINNEY-STEWARD), the owner of the Brooklyn Dodgers (CHARLES EBBETS), George Washington's favorite dentist (JOHN GREENWOOD), the man who helped feed black-out cake to Brooklyn (CHARLES EBINGER), the man who put the eraser on the pencil (EBERHARD FABER), the writer who penned the tongue-twister "Peter Piper picked a peck of pickled peppers" (JAMES KIRKE PAULDING), the businessman who built Pan American Airways into a billion dollar international power (JUAN TRIPPE), and printmakers CURRIER AND IVES, are all here. In Green-Wood are buried Theodore Roosevelt's

Springtime at Green-Wood Cemetery, looking across Valley Water. Photograph by Andrea Brizzi.

mother (MARTHA BULLOCK ROOSEVELT) and wife (ALICE HATHAWAY LEE ROOSEVELT), both of whom died tragically on the same day, and the man who would have been the first "President Clinton" had he carried Pennsylvania against James Madison in the election of 1812 (DE WITT CLINTON).

Entertainers (LOLA MONTEZ of Spider Dance fame, LAURA KEANE, who was the lead performer at Ford's Theatre when John Wilkes Booth assassinated President Abraham Lincoln, FRANK MORGAN, who gave us his immortal portrayal of the Wizard of Oz), inventors (ELIAS HOWE and the sewing machine, WALTER HUNT and the safety pin, JOHN THOMAS UNDERWOOD and the visible typewriter, ELMER SPERRY and the gyroscope), artists (LOUIS COMFORT TIFFANY, JOHN LA FARGE, and DUNCAN PHYFE), musicians (pianist and America's first matinee idol LOUIS MORREAU GOTTSCHALK, *Rock of Ages* composer THOMAS HASTINGS), and murder victims (HARVEY BURDELL, JAMES NOE, and EDWARD WHEELER HALL) are buried at Green-Wood Cemetery along with local, national, and international leaders of all descriptions.

Green-Wood's impact has been national. Along with its two American predecessors (Cambridge's Mount Auburn and Philadelphia's Laurel Hill), it provided the prototype for rural cemeteries in New Haven, Albany, Baltimore, and throughout the United States. As Andrew Jackson Downing wrote in 1849:

> Twenty years ago, nothing better than a common grave-yard, filled with high grass, and a chance sprinkling of weeds and thistles, was to be found in the Union. . . . At the present moment, there is scarcely a city of note in the whole country that has not its rural cemetery.

Becoming a public resort, Green-Wood Cemetery provided a model for the great popular parks created by Frederick Law Olmstead and Calvert Vaux, including Central Park and Prospect Park, which were to follow in the generation after its founding. Green-Wood also provided inspiration for the planned residential suburb in America.

Green-Wood Cemetery continues to be a place of beauty, a green oasis in urban Brooklyn. The words of Nehemiah Cleaveland, describing a visitor to Green-Wood Cemetery more than one hundred years ago, are equally applicable today:

> A short half-hour ago, he was in the midst of a discordant Babel; he was one of the hurrying, jostling crowd; he was encompassed by the whirl and fever of artificial life. Now he stands alone, in Nature's inner court—in her silent, solemn sanctuary. Her holiest influences are all around him, and his heart whispers, "It is good to be here!"

Furniture maker DUNCAN PHYFE. *Dictionary of American Portraits,* Dover Publications. Phyfe became the most prolific and most fashionable American cabinetmaker in the first quarter of the nineteenth century; the design and workmanship of its furniture were unsurpassed. He created master works in mahogany which gracefully combined English and French furniture styles. Chairs, sofas, and tables produced by him, often featuring lyres, crossed slats, outward sweeping curves, parallel rows of beading, and acanthus carving, were the best of his work. His pieces are so admired and have been so widely copied that the ultimate (though often incorrect) attribution for Federal mahogany furniture has long been "by Duncan Phyfe."

On the grounds of the Niblo Mausoleum.

CHAPTER TWO

The Early Years (1838~1860)

"JANE, MY WIFE"

JANE GRIFFITH (1816–1857) was not famous, but she was much loved by her husband Charles. On the morning of August 4, 1857, in a typical domestic scene of the time, she stood on the steps of their wisteria-covered brownstone at 109 West 13th Street in New York City, surrounded by a cast iron fence, with their dog at her side, and bade her husband good-bye. At the corner, the driver of the Sixth Avenue horse-trolley waited, and Charles soon boarded and was off to work. When he returned home at the end of the day, Charles found his wife dead, the victim of heart disease.

Detail of the monument to Jane Griffith, a marble gem still in fine condition, shows off sculptor Patrizio Piatti's exquisite work.

CHARLES GRIFFITH (1813–1882) hired PATRIZIO PIATTI (1824–1888), an Italian-trained sculptor and modeler who had relocated to New York City and who advertised that he "designed and executed to order" monuments, headstones, and mantel pieces "in the purest professional styles of the different ages of art," to create a lasting memorial to Jane. Piatti, after visiting the Griffiths' home to study it, created a marble masterpiece. Its location, in a hollow protected from the prevailing winds and storms coming off the harbor, has sheltered it from the severe weathering that has claimed many other monuments at Green-Wood.

Jane Griffith is shown as a housewife inside her domestic preserve, unsoiled by everyday affairs. Much of the original detailing of her monument, including the wisteria-covered row house, the cast iron fence, and

The elements have taken their toll on many monuments at Green-Wood. Often the extent of deterioration is a function of the material used. Cast zinc and granite have survived remarkably well. Marble, though a wonderful material to carve, deteriorates badly when exposed to the elements. And, marble at Green-Wood is most severely damaged when it faces toward New York Harbor, and the prevailing winds and storms that blow off it.

Notice the difference in the condition of these busts. That of Hiram Fogg, on the left, is in poor condition because it is shaded by a nearby tree; as a result, rainwater sits in the stone. The bust of his brother (at right), William Fogg, a prominent New York City merchant for whom the Fogg Museum at Harvard is named, is in much better condition because it is exposed to direct sunlight and therefore dries out much more quickly. William's bust has recently been confirmed by an expert to be the work of noted sculptor John Quincy Adams Ward.

the family dog, remain visible, though the details of Jane Griffith's face (copied by Piatti from a photograph) have weathered and disappeared. Charles Griffith is dressed in the working-dress of the period, a stovepipe hat and a swallowtail coat. Piatti's signature is just barely visible at the lower right of his masterpiece.

Charles Griffith continued to visit "Jane, My Wife" weekly at Green-Wood for the next twenty-five years, until his own death at the age of sixty-nine.

THE TRAGEDY OF THE FRENCH LADY, CHARLOTTE CANDA

CHARLES CANDA (1792–1866), who fought as an officer in Napoleon's army, emigrated to New York City in the early nineteenth century and opened a lady's school there. His only child, CHARLOTTE CANDA (1828–1845), was given the finest of educations, and was fluent in English, French, German, Spanish, and Italian.

On February 3, 1845, a party was given to celebrate Charlotte's seventeenth birthday. When the festivities ended, Charlotte and her father got in the family carriage and escorted one of her friends home. Arriving at the friend's home on Waverly Place in Manhattan, Charles accompanied the friend to her door, while Charlotte remained in the carriage as a storm raged. When Charles turned from the doorway, the carriage and Charlotte were gone.

Charles Canda did not know where his beloved daughter was. Racing home in a panic, he was unaware of the tragedy that had occurred. For as he had walked the friend to her door, the horses had bolted and raced toward Broadway. When they careened around the corner, Charlotte was thrown from the carriage and struck her head. Just as her father and mother, summoned to the scene, arrived to cradle her in their arms, she sighed her last breath and passed away.

The basic design of Charlotte's monument was sketched by her with the intention that it be used as a plan for a memorial to her recently-deceased aunt. After Charlotte's death, she was interred in New York City's Old St. Patrick's Cathedral on Prince and Mott Streets. Her father took her sketch and added the roses, flowers, birds, and wreaths that his daughter so loved. Her monument also includes fleurs de lis, lilies, acanthus leaves, down-turned torches, and a crucifix. The books, musical and drawing instruments that Charlotte was so fond of, and the parrots that were her constant companions, are also incorporated into it. Charlotte's effigy appears in the niche, showing her about to expire, with the heavens above waiting to receive her soul. She was interred at Green-Wood Cemetery on April 29, 1848.

The star above Charlotte's figure symbolizes immortal life. A butterfly with wings extended is emblematic of her liberated spirit. To commemorate Charlotte's age at the time of her death, 17 rose buds appear in a shield; the monument is 17 feet high and 17 feet deep.

Charlotte Canda's Monument, as it appeared in 1847, just after its completion. Note the monument at far right, in a separate plot surrounded by its own fence; it is that of her nobleman-fiance, who committed suicide in the Candas's house a year after her tragic death.

Charlotte Canda's personal copy of the Book Of Hours, *published by A. Giroux & Co. in Paris, France. Inside it is a note in French, apparently written by Charlotte, that (translated) reads: "Charlotte Canda had her first communion on the 10th of October, in St. Patrick's Cathedral, with Monseigneur Hughes. Guard this with reverence."*

This monument, with the exception of the angels (which were carved in Italy), was executed by JOHN FRAZEE (1790–1852) and Robert Launitz (1806–1870). The statue of Charlotte Canda was chiseled by Launitz, who also created monuments at Green-Wood to the New York City Volunteer Firemen, the Indian Princess Do-Hum-Me, and the Mad Poet McDonald Clarke, as well as the Pulaski Statue in Savannah, Georgia.

The Canda monument, built at great expense, is estimated to have cost

Though the Canda Monument has lost its elegant fence, and the pure white pebbles between that fence and the monument are long gone, its glory is still apparent.

On a stone in front of the main monument, together with Charlotte's name and the date and cause of her death, was carved a poem that reflected the resurrectionist attitude of the time. Though, after more than a century and one-half of exposure to the elements, the inscription can no longer be read, this circa 1870 photograph preserves it.

John Frazee trained as a stone cutter in New Jersey, then established a marble yard on Broadway in New York City, where he proudly declared that he was the first American-trained marble sculptor in America. His elaborate marble tablet and bust of John Wells, completed in 1824, survives in St. Paul's Chapel on Broadway. He was also an architect of the New York Custom House (now known as Federal Hall) on Wall Street.

Robert Launitz, a native of Russia, received a classical and military education, then studied sculpture in Rome. In 1828, he came to New York City, deaf and unable to speak English, and went to work in John Frazee's marble yard. He later became Frazee's partner, and helped to train sculptor THOMAS CRAWFORD.

The monument to Charles Albert Jarrett de la Marie, Charlotte Canda's fiancé, who was driven to suicide by grief over her death.

between $15,000 and $45,000 (about $450,000 to $1.3 million today). During the 1840's and 50's, it was the most popular cemetery monument in New York City, and perhaps the entire country; on any given Sunday a crowd gathered around it. The plot was immaculately kept, with white pebbles surrounding the monument and a spectacular cast iron fence, with its gates locked, enclosing it.

The Candas were Catholics and this monument is on land consecrated by the Catholic Church. Nearby, just beyond the border of their plot, is a monument bearing the coat of arms of Charles Albert Jarrett de la Marie, the young French nobleman who was Charlotte Canda's fiancé. A year after her tragic death young Charles committed suicide, shooting himself at the Canda's residence. Because of this suicide, he could not be buried on the consecrated ground where his beloved Charlotte lay. He reposes, however, as close to her as his suicide would allow.

INDIAN PRINCESS DO-HUM-ME

IN 1843, at the age of eighteen, DO-HUM-ME (1824–1843) came east with her father, a chief of the Sac tribe, who was representing his people at treaty negotiations. In Paterson, New Jersey, she met Cow-Hick-Kee, a member of another Indian delegation, and they soon married. The exotic couple continued on to New York City, quickly becoming the toast of the town. Nehemiah Cleaveland, an early Green-Wood Cemetery historian, wrote, "Gifts were showered upon them from all quarters, and the jewelry of Do-Hum-Me might have been coveted by many a fairer-hued bride."

As none other than showman P. T. Barnum recounts in his autobiography, he hired Do-Hum-Me and the other Sac Indians to perform war and wedding dances in his American Museum on the corner of Broadway and Ann Street in New York City. According to Barnum, Do-Hum-Me was "one of the beautiful squaws" and "a great favorite with many ladies." However, within weeks of her arrival in New York, Do-Hum-Me caught a cold on a stormy night, complications developed, and she was soon dead, just five weeks after the wedding. She died at Barnum's Museum, and Barnum described what followed:

The poor Indians were very sorrowful for many days, and desired to get back again to their western wilds. The father and the betrothed of Do-humme cooked various dishes of food and placed them upon the roof of the Museum, where they believed the spirit of their departed friend came daily for its supply; and these dishes were renewed every morning during the stay of the Indians at the Museum.

Green-Wood Cemetery, still in its early years and struggling to attract enough business to survive, was only too happy to offer one of its lots for the burial of the famous young woman. That she was an Indian, and therefore intriguing, only increased her promotional value. On March 15, 1843, Do-Hum-Me, wearing her wedding dress, was interred at Green-Wood Cemetery.

The marble monument to her was erected near Sylvan Water by her friends, including Barnum. It was carved by sculptor Robert Launitz.

The epitaph on the side of the monument to Do-Hum-Me reads:

> Thou art happy now for thou hast past
> the cold dark journey of the grave
> And in the land of light at last
> has joined the good, the fair, the brave.

Clearly Launitz's strength was not English spelling. A native of Russia, who was deaf and did not speak English, he carved in marble, for generations to see, his spelling of the Sac Indian "Cheif."

Robert Launitz's marble monument to Do-Hum-Me, in a hand-colored photograph, circa 1865. The wrought iron fence is no longer there. In 2006, the monument was adopted by a cemetery worker, who paid for its cleaning and joint work.

DE WITT CLINTON'S POST-BURIAL TRAVELS

NEW YORK's most revered man in the first half of the nineteenth century was DE WITT CLINTON (1769–1828). New Yorkers elected him United States Senator, governor, and mayor. If he had carried Pennsylvania in the election of 1812 as the peace candidate, Clinton would have been President of the United States. It was Clinton who was the prime visionary behind the momentous Erie Canal.

When Clinton died in 1828, he was interred in the Little Albany Cemetery. But by the 1850's, Green-Wood Cemetery was still struggling to survive, and was desperate for publicity. The acquisition of De Witt Clinton's remains, with the erection of a suitable monument, would be just the public relations bonanza that the cemetery needed. With the agreement of one of Clinton's descendants, the necessary arrangements for transferring his remains to Brooklyn were made. Henry Kirke Brown (1814–1886), the first American sculptor to cast in bronze in this country, and who is today best-known for his equestrian statue of George Washington which stands in Union Square Park, began work on his Clinton sculpture in 1850. Financed by public subscription, it was displayed in City Hall Park in New York City upon its completion in June, 1853. At a time when there was virtually no public sculpture in New York, its exhibition was front page news and caused a sensation.

There is a tension in Brown's Clinton statue, common to American

De Witt Clinton's Monument, shown in a recent photograph, was paid for by public subscription. Its placement at Green-Wood was big news in 1853 and brought the cemetery important publicity. In 1998, its cleaning and waxing was the Green-Wood Historic Fund's first restoration project.

sculpture of this era, between the dictates of artistic convention, that heroes had to be dressed as civic demigods of ancient civilizations, and the desire for historical accuracy. The solution here is a mix of the two: Clinton is wearing a Roman mantle and sandals, but is shown dressed above the waist in a suit appropriate to his era. Two bas reliefs of Clinton's greatest accomplishment, the Erie Canal, adorn the Richard Upjohn-designed base. One shows laborers and engineers at work, with pickax, spade, horse-drawn carts, and wheelbarrows, building the great 400-miles-long and four-feet-deep ditch. The other pictures a canal boat, laden with goods and immigrants, receiving cargo as American Indians sadly witness the westward march of a new civilization. Oak clusters adorn the base, symbolizing both strength and power. The detailing remains crisp and clear; the bronze of this monument has survived the elements remarkably well.

LOST AT SEA

IN THE EARLY 1840's, John Willis Griffiths told everyone in New York City who would listen that he could build a faster ship than any that had yet sailed the high seas. But his message fell on deaf ears until it was heard by WILLIAM HENRY ASPINWALL (1807–1875). Aspinwall ran one of the world's great trading houses. His ships made him money, and the faster they traveled, the more money he made.

Aspinwall felt that there was no harm in looking at Griffiths's plans. But when Aspinwall studied them, he had his doubts. Perhaps the six courses of sails could be reduced. Her shape might be modified to allow more room for cargo. Higher freeboards would keep waves off her decks. But Griffiths defended his design, and Aspinwall gave in, contracting for the world's first clipper ship.

As the ship took form at Smith & Dimon's East River shipyard, crowds began to gather to watch, and ridicule was heaped on Aspinwall and his partners. Many wags were sure that the ship's hull was backwards. Few thought that proceeding with this design, and investing more money in it, were worth the risk.

On January 22, 1845, with over one thousand spectators looking on, the *Rainbow* was launched. As soon as she hit the water, her grace was apparent. Her narrow forward body and stern, her long hollow hull (it was actually concave), and every inch of her and her 757 tons, were meant for speed. Built for the China trade, in which nails, wire, and tools, and virtually anything that could be found in a country store went to the East, and tea, silk, porcelain, and spices were brought back, she had dummy gun ports painted on her sides to scare off pirates who preyed on ships in the South China Sea.

The *Rainbow* left on her maiden voyage on February 1, 1845, bound for Hong Kong. That trip netted her owners more than twice the cost of her construction. She soon had very fast trips of eighty-four and eighty-six days from Hong Kong to New York to her credit.

This print, The First New York Clipper Rainbow, *shows her sailing off the southern tip of Manhattan; Castle Garden is the round structure at right. Courtesy of the Mariners' Museum, Newport News, Virginia.*

But the *Rainbow*'s triumphs were short-lived. On March 17, 1848, under the command of Captain William Hayes, who had agreed to take her on one last voyage before retiring, she set sail for Valparaiso and China. Months later, Robert Graham, a clerk at Aspinwall's firm, recorded in his diary:

Wed. Oct. 11: No news of Rainbow, 140 days out.

Mon. Nov. 9: By way of Baltimore, Kingston, and the Isthmus of Panama we have a letter from our Correspondents Alsop & Co. in Valparaiso dated Aug. 29th in which they mention that no tidings have yet been heard of the Rainbow. I am now afraid that this vessel is gone and that poor Capt. Hayes has really made his last trip, as he said he was going to.

Sat. Dec. 2: Nothing heard from the ill-favored Rainbow out about 200 days.

The *Rainbow*, Captain Hayes, and his crew, were never seen or heard from again. Speculation was that the *Rainbow*, only three years after her historic launching as the first clipper ship, foundered as she tried to navigate the dangerous waters off Cape Horn.

As Captain Hayes set sail on his final voyage, his wife undoubtedly had looked forward to the retirement years that they would spend together. Instead, broken-hearted, she ordered this stone memorial for placement at Green-Wood Cemetery. Few, happening upon this monument today, would know the story behind its inscription:

IN MEMORY OF MY HUSBAND WILLIAM H. HAYES. CAPTAIN OF THE CLIPPER SHIP RAINBOW. LOST IN 1848.

William Henry Aspinwall ran New York's largest trading house, built the Panama Railroad (joining the Atlantic and Pacific Oceans and substantially reducing travel time to the California gold fields), and dominated trade to South America and California. By 1855, Aspinwall's fortune was $4 million, the equivalent of about $100 million today.

Aspinwall also played an active role during the Civil War. He was a strong supporter of Lincoln and a founder and vice president of the Union League Club. When the garrison at Fort Sumter was besieged, Aspinwall offered to send ships, at his own expense, to privately restock it. After Major Robert Anderson surrendered the fort to Confederates, Anderson became a hero of Unionists, and Aspinwall hosted a New York dinner in his honor. Though Aspinwall supplied many of the ships of his Pacific Mail Line to the Union, and Howland & Aspinwall acted as government purchasing agent in England and Europe for arms, ammunition, and other equipment, Aspinwall refused all war profits, returning checks to the government for any payment in excess of costs. In 1863, he went to England as a secret Union emissary and convinced the British Government to seize the ships and ironclad rams which were being built there for the Confederacy. Aspinwall also donated worsted-wool jackets to New York's Seventh Regiment; those coats were thereafter known as "Aspinwalls."

There were fortunes to be made in the China trade, and merchant WILLIAM SHEPARD WET-MORE (1801–1862) took advantage of the opportunity. He moved to Canton, China, in 1829, where he created his own mercantile house, Wetmore and Company. Retiring, in 1847, with a vast fortune, Wetmore moved to Newport, Rhode Island. There, beginning in 1851, he had an ornate Victorian stone mansion, Chateau-Sur-Mer, built for him. Its construction marked the beginning of informal competition amongst Newport's summer residents to build more spectacularly and more lavishly than their neighbors. On thirty-five acres, it was landscaped with exotic trees, shrubs, and plants, which were an attraction in their own right. The mansion, of rough-cut Fall River granite, was furnished with "strange and interesting" Chinese lacquer furniture and porcelain.

In 1872, Richard Morris Hunt, the great American architect, remodeled Chateau-sur-Mer, adding the first French ballroom to a Newport mansion. It was purchased by The Preservation Society of Newport County in 1968, and is now open to the public.

William Shepard Wetmore's unusual memorial sits atop a hillock.

The monument to Captain William Hayes, who was lost at sea on what was supposed to be his last voyage before retirement.

Kindred Spirits *portrays the spiritual kinship of man and nature; nature here is benign and romantic. This was the very same view of nature that underlay the rural cemetery movement in which Green-Wood Cemetery played such an important role. Courtesy The New York Public Library, New York City, Astor, Lenox, and Tilden Foundations.*

As Jacksonian democracy took hold in the 1830's, Americans, who formerly had looked to Europe for their art, demanded their own domestic works. The Hudson River School of landscape painting, the first indigenous American school of painting, reached prominence in that era. Its first leader was Thomas Cole, but upon his death in 1848, ASHER B. DURAND (1796–1886) assumed Cole's mantle of leadership.

Kindred Spirits, finished in 1849, is the best-known painting of the Hudson River school. It was commissioned from Durand after Thomas Cole's death for presentation to William Cullen Bryant, the leader of New York's art circle who had delivered an eloquent eulogy at Cole's funeral. Cole is pictured, brush and sketchbook in hand, standing with Bryant, as they admire nature together. The Catskill Mountains scenery is bathed in a mellow light, and nature is pictured as benign, romantic, and unspoiled.

It is no surprise that Durand, as well as several other painters of the Hudson River School, including JOHN FREDERICK KENSETT (1818–1872) and the brothers WILLIAM (1823–1894) and JAMES HART (1828–1901), chose to be buried at Green-Wood Cemetery. Their paintings depict nature's abode as a holy place, a glorious place of God. And that was exactly the same way that Green-Wood was viewed by their contemporaries: as a moral place of nature, near the industrial city but unspoiled by it, where a sublime religious experience awaited. To understand the moral tone of this painting is to understand the ideas that shaped Green-Wood Cemetery. The saplings in the foreground of the painting symbolize nature's continual rebirth. Nature embodied a cycle of death and rebirth; Green-Wood, similarly, was a place of death and resurrection.

This painting was meant as a tribute to Thomas Cole, and Bryant is shown with his hat removed in respect. The broken tree in the foreground offers the same symbolism as the oft-seen cutoff column in the cemetery, denoting a life that has been ended in its prime (Cole died at the age of forty-seven), before reaching its full height. The bird flying off in the distance represents Cole's spirit, just released from his body, beginning its ascent to heaven.

William Cullen Bryant, in his poem *Green River*, expresses the sentiment behind both Durand's painting and Green-Wood Cemetery:

> I often come to this quiet place,
> To breathe the airs that ruffle the face,
> And gaze upon thee in silent dreams
> For in thy lonely and lovely stream
> An image of that calm life appears
> That won my heart in greener years.

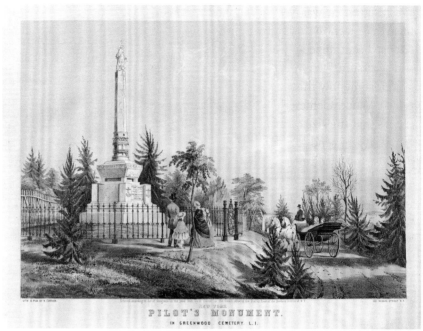

This print of the Pilot's Monument, dating from 1855, was published by NATHANIEL CURRIER. Green-Wood Historic Fund Collection.

THE PILOT'S MONUMENT

A detail of the Pilot's Monument, showing its marble storm-tossed waves.

ON FEBRUARY 14, 1846, harbor pilot THOMAS FREEBORN was doing his job. With a storm raging, it was his responsibility to safely guide the ship *John Minturn* into New York Harbor. But, despite Freeborn's best efforts, the beleaguered ship was driven relentlessly toward the New Jersey shore. Though the *Minturn* ran aground close to the beach, and within hailing distance of hundreds of would-be rescuers, Freeborn, and many members of the crew, could not be saved.

Freeborn's remains were initially interred at the Rutgers Street Burial Ground in New York City, but within months they were reinterred at Green-Wood Cemetery by his fellow pilots, who erected the Pilot's Monument to honor him and their profession.

Of marble, this monument features images associated with harbor pilots. Atop the sarcophagus at its base is a ship's capstan, with anchor cable coiled around it, and rising above is a mast whose truncated top symbolizes a life cut short. Atop the mast stands Hope, holding an anchor at her side. Across the front of the sarcophagus the doomed *John Minturn* struggles against the marble waves on its final voyage.

UP FROM ALABAMA

BORN IN VIRGINIA and educated in Georgia, DIXON HALL LEWIS (1802–1848) served as a states' rights United States Senator and Representative from Alabama from 1829 until his death. A power in

Washington, he was chairman of the Ways and Means Committee and lost the 1839 election for Speaker of the House by just four votes. Lewis opposed centralized government and was a strong advocate of nullification and secession.

Yet, somehow this powerful Southerner wound up in New York soil at Green-Wood Cemetery. There are two theories as to why this happened. One is that the size of the man made it inconvenient, after he died in New York City, to send him home. Lewis was a very large man, weighing 430 pounds, and furniture for his use had to be specially built. In the Congress and on railroads, two seats were needed to support his bulk. Shipping his substantial remains South would have been a daunting task. But the real reason Lewis is interred in a prominent place at Green-Wood is simple: he was so impressed by this place, and its beauty, that he decided that it was there that he wanted to be buried.

The monument to Dixon Hall Lewis at Green-Wood Cemetery describes him as "A Patriot and a Statesman noted for integrity, candor and truth."

THE WANDERING (THOUGH DECEASED) GOVERNOR

WILLIAM LIVINGSTON (1723–1790), after a full life, earned his right to a final resting place. As a boy, he lived with a missionary to the Mohawk Indians. Graduating at the head of his Yale College class, he took up law in New York City. But it was not until he moved to New Jersey that he performed yeoman work for his country, serving as a delegate to the Continental Congresses, brigadier general of New Jersey forces during the Revolutionary War, and as the first governor of that State. As governor, he refused to appoint to the position of postmaster a man who refused to accept Continental money. Livingston was a talented writer, famed for his poems and the biting satirical pieces he penned during the Revolutionary War. Tories had a special distaste for him, and many British efforts were unsuccessfully made to effect his capture. He also was a signer of the United States Constitution.

At the time of Livingston's death, he was serving his second term as New Jersey's governor; he was interred in the Presbyterian Church Burial Ground in Elizabethtown. But this was not to be his final resting place. In the winter of 1791, his remains were removed to the vault of his son BROCKHOLST LIVINGSTON (1757 –1823) (later a justice of the United States Supreme Court) in the Wall Street Church Burial Ground. But William Livingston's post-mortem journey was

William Livingston, the patriot who, after a few stops along the way, reached his final resting place.

This stone, marking the grave of 101-year-old Henry Gibson, was recently placed at Green-Wood Cemetery.

William Livingston is one of several Revolutionary War veterans who have been reinterred at Green-Wood Cemetery. His son, Brockholst, joined the Continental Army as a captain. Promoted to major, he served as an aide to Generals Schuyler and St. Clair, was at the siege of Fort Ticonderoga, and was on General Benedict Arnold's staff during the Saratoga campaign, witnessing General Burgoyne's surrender. In 1779, Brockholst Livingston left the service and went to Spain as secretary to his brother-in-law John Jay, the minister to that country. He was captured by the British as he attempted to return to New York City in 1782, and was imprisoned there. EBENEZER STEVENS (1751–1823), a native of Boston, was a member of Boston's Artillery Company and took part in the Boston Tea Party in 1773. Shortly thereafter, he moved to Rhode Island, where, when the war began, he raised three companies, was commissioned a lieutenant, and took part in the expedition against Quebec. Stevens later joined Henry Knox's artillery regiment, served as a captain before being brevetted a major, and commanded the Continental artillery at Ticonderoga and Yorktown. ASA HOLDEN and HENRY GIBSON (1751–1852) were also soldiers in the Revolutionary War.

still not over. On May 7, 1844, his remains (and those of Brockholst) were taken from their New York City vault, along with the remains of nine other members of his family, and were brought across the East River to Green-Wood Cemetery. There William Livingston has remained for over 150 years. It is now safe to assume that he has arrived at his "final resting place."

YOU CAN LOCK UP YOUR CHECK BOOK, BUT KEEPING IT LOCKED UP IS ANOTHER MATTER

As the Civil War was about to begin, Stephen Whitney (1776–1860), merchant, cotton speculator, and real estate investor, was one of the wealthiest men in America. In New York City, only John Jacob Astor had more to spend. But Stephen Whitney was anything but a spender. When he died in 1860, he left an estate estimated at $15 million (close to $400 million today). New York diarist George Templeton Strong felt that this estimate of Whitney's wealth was a bit exaggerated, "but he was close-fisted enough to have saved up thirty without doing the least good to himself or anyone else. His last act was characteristic and fitting. He locked up his checkbook and died."

Whitney, once gone, could no longer control his nest egg. His heirs, more profligate, had this elaborate and expensive tomb built. Known as Whitney Chapel, it has a desk and bench for a priest or devotee placed just inside the doorway. It sits atop Ocean Hill as a monument to Stephen Whitney, one of the richest Americans of his time.

The Whitney Tomb occupies a prominent spot atop Ocean Hill.

THE SINKING OF THE *ARCTIC*

Tension built in New York City early in October, 1854, when the steamer *Arctic*, one of the Collins Shipping Line's four crack transatlantic liners, was past due from England. Day by day anxiety increased

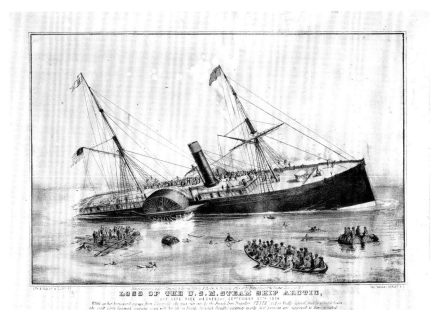

LOSS OF THE U.S.M. STEAM SHIP ARCTIC,
OFF CAPE RACE WEDNESDAY SEPTEMBER 27TH 1854

This print, Loss of the U.S.M. Steam Ship Arctic: Off Cape Race Wednesday September 27th 1854, *issued by* NATHANIEL CURRIER, *was based on a sketch made by a survivor. It was printed with this caption: "While on her homeward voyage from Liverpool, she was run into by the French iron propeller "VESTA" and so badly injured, that in about 5 hours she sank stern foremost, carrying down with her all on board; by which dreadful calamity nearly 300 persons are supposed to have perished." Courtesy of the Mariners' Museum, Newport News, Virginia.*

When the great ship *Titanic* went down in 1912, reporters harkened back to the sinking of the *Arctic* 58 years earlier. The similarities were chilling: the world's largest, fastest, and finest ocean liner, placing a premium on speed over safety on the run from England to New York, had suffered what appeared at first to be only a slight collision, then gone to the bottom within a few hours with the loss of most of its passengers for whom there were no lifeboats.

WYCKOFF VANDERHOEF, a Brooklyn native and resident, died on April 15, 1912, drowning when the *S.S. Titanic* sank.

until October 11, when word was finally received that on September 27, the *Arctic* had collided in dense fog with the French vessel *Vesta* off Newfoundland. Despite the efforts of the *Arctic's* crew to keep her afloat, her pumps were no match for the onrushing seawater, and she had steadily filled. When it became apparent that the battle was lost, her captain ordered four lifeboats lowered with women and children. But the crew and officers instead commandeered most of the seats and saved themselves. When, five hours after the collision, the *Arctic* went down, nearly all of her passengers went down with her. Sixty-one of the 153 officers and crewmen survived, but only 24 of 182 passengers escaped with their lives. Not a single one of those was a woman or child.

JAMES BROWN (1791–1877), one of the chief financial backers of the Collins Line, and the head of the famed Brown Brothers banking firm, lost his son William Benedict Brown (who had recently been promoted to a partner at Brown Brothers), William's wife Clara Moulton Brown, their infant daughter Grace, his daughter Maria, his daughter Grace, and her son Herbert. As George Templeton Strong wrote in his diary on October 12, 1854, "James Brown was hardly expected to live through yesterday, so crushed and shattered was he by the terrible news of his bereavement."

To honor those who went down with the *Arctic,* James Brown commissioned sculptor John Moffitt to design a monument. His work, of the finest Italian marble, stands at the center of the Brown family plot.

As a result of the *Arctic* disaster, reforms were instituted in ocean travel:

This photograph, circa 1875, of a detail of the Arctic Monument shows the stricken ship carved in marble; its mast and sails have since disappeared.

Close-up of the Arctic Monument today. Protected from the elements by a stone canopy, the ship has managed to retain much of its detailing.

The location of the Brown family plot, atop its own hillock in Green-Wood Cemetery, is testament to the wealth and power of that family. James Brown, the family patriarch, set up the New York City branch of Brown Brothers & Company in 1825. That firm became one of the most influential banking houses in the country (it is still in business today as Brown Brothers Harriman & Co., the nation's oldest and largest private bank), and James Brown was its most powerful member, taking a prominent role in virtually every major American financial matter that occurred during his lifetime.

There are many eminent individuals, including several other leading bankers and a top-flight architect, James Brown Lord, in this lot. But perhaps the most intriguing of the monuments that surround the *Arctic* Monument in the Brown Family plot are these to two individuals, husband and wife, who led obscure lives. At the front of the lot are the stones honoring two who were born into slavery in Virginia: CORNELIUS JOHNSON, "For upwards of 20 years a faithful colored servant in the family of James Brown," who died in 1859, "aged about 75 years," and MARY JOHNSON, who died at the age of 82 in 1879, "a faithful colored servant in the family of James Brown; who desire by this stone to commemorate her worth."

watertight compartments for passenger ships were mandated and sea lanes were instituted.

The winged sphere that memorializes Chester Jennings is an unusual nineteenth century resurrectionist symbol: the globe is the perfect form, or the soul, and the wings represent flight or ascension.

ANYONE FOR ROOM SERVICE?

CHESTER JENNINGS was always looking for a new way to drum up business at his City Hotel on Broadway just north of Trinity Church. Opening in the 18th century as the first hotel in New York City, it was for many years the largest and most conspicuous building there. The City Hotel catered to the rich and stylish of New York's artistic and literary circles, and in 1836 became the first hotel in America to offer its facilities to clubs for their regular meetings. Soon James Fenimore Cooper's famous Bread and Cheese Club and The Union Club were meeting there. Ever-aware of the latest trends, Jennings moved his dinner hour from noon to 3:00 p.m. to conform to the European fashion.

But certainly Chester Jennings's greatest accomplishment occurred in the 1840's when he introduced room service to New York. Jennings did this with a seemingly innocuous note at the bottom of his restaurant's menu, "Meals sent to Rooms to be charged extra." However, this apparently-harmless innovation was savagely criticized in New York's newspapers, flushed with Jacksonian egalitarian ideals, as "dangerous blue-blood habits," "a menace to the foundations of the Republic," and "a threat to democracy." But despite these criticisms Jennings persisted, and room service survived and prospered.

McDONALD CLARKE (1798–1842), a native of Bath, Maine, came to New York City in 1819, alone and penniless. Soon he was a familiar sight on Broadway, tall and thin, dressed in a blue frock coat and sporting a red silk handkerchief. He was eccentric, but his strange behavior was considered to be harmless, even amiable, by those who knew him. One writer recalled that Clarke "kept the town laughing while he sometimes was starving." Clarke often stood near St. Paul's Chapel, wearing a boot on one foot and a shoe on the other, his arms folded, his face turned towards the heavens.

Clarke attended fashionable Grace Church and eloped with actress Mary Brundage when her mother opposed their marriage. He was almost constantly penniless, however, and this doomed their marriage. Famed poet Fitz-Greene Hallock often helped Clarke through his difficult times.

In his many poems, Clarke celebrated the belles of Old New York and ridiculed snobbery and social injustice. His most famous couplet was, "Now twilight lets her curtain down, And pins it with a star." He also lectured in New York, to popular acclaim, on "Love and Matrimony."

On a March evening in 1842, Clarke was found on the street, destitute and incoherent, by a member of New York City's night watch, and was taken to the Asylum on Blackwell's Island. The next morning, he was found dead, apparently having drowned in water drunk from an open faucet in his cell.

Clarke's stone at Green-Wood, by noted sculptor Robert E. Launitz, bears a relief of him. These words were carved on it: "Poor McDonald Clarke—Let silence gaze, but curse not his grave." One of Clarke's verses, now so weathered as to be indecipherable, was cut into the marble:

> For what are earthly honors now?
> He never deemed them worth his care,
> And Death hath set upon his brow
> The wreath he was too proud to wear.

Nehemiah Cleaveland, the early historian of Green-Wood Cemetery, described the "Mad Poet of Broadway" in this colorful language:

> The poor inhabitant below was the possessor of talents which, had his mind and affections been better disciplined, might have won for him distinction. But his efforts were desultory and unequal. He became an unhappy wanderer—his own and others dupe—till at length reason tottered, and life sunk under the weight of disappointment.

WHISTLER'S FATHER

GEORGE WASHINGTON WHISTLER (1800–1849) was a well-respected railroad engineer. In fact, he was so revered that the men of his profession erected a brownstone monument to him at Green-Wood Cemetery. It is located just a few feet from the burial plot of his friend

This detail of the monument to the "Mad Poet of Broadway" displays his stone portrait. His poems are carved into the sides of his obelisk.

Some of the people interred at Green-Wood Cemetery have no monument. George Washington Whistler, who isn't even buried at Green-Wood, has this monument there in his honor.

Joseph Gardner Swift, the brother of Whistler's first wife, Mary Roberdeau Swift.

This monument, however, has created a good deal of confusion, for though Whistler's monument is here, he is not. Rather, George Washington Whistler is buried in Stonington, Connecticut, where he lived from 1837 to 1840.

His son, the painter James McNeil Whistler, is best known for his painting *Whistler's Mother*. George Washington Whistler was, of course, Whistler's Father.

NIBLO'S GARDENS

WILLIAM NIBLO (1789–1878) achieved great fame as the proprietor of Niblo's Garden, the fashionable theatre which he ran at Broadway and Prince Street from 1828 until around the time of the Civil War. It became *the place* to be entertained in New York City, with such featured attractions as the Ravel family acrobats, a vaudeville company, a dramatic season, a concert series, and a season of opera. Over the years the greats of the New York stage, including WILLIAM J. FLORENCE (1831–1891), Edwin Forrest, HENRY PLACIDE (1799–1870), Charles Kean, and MATILDA HERON (1830–1877) played there.

But William Niblo also had a less well-known garden. It was in front of his hillside mausoleum at Green-Wood Cemetery. There, while still very much alive, he regularly picnicked with friends. And, in order to add interest to those picnics, Niblo stocked Crescent Water, the pond just a few feet in front of his plot, with goldfish. Because Crescent Water was connected by underground pipes with the rest of Green-Wood's ponds, Niblo's goldfish were soon flourishing in every body of water in the cemetery.

William Niblo's hillside mausoleum, which dates from the 1850's, is surrounded by beautifully planted grounds. Niblo, who took such pride in Niblo's Garden, his theatre-garden, and made his fortune there, would be pleased to know that the gardens in front of his mausoleum are planted with flowering annuals every spring.

THE SEA CAPTAIN

FOR HALF A CENTURY, Captain JOHN CORREJA (1826–1910) brought his friends to Green-Wood Cemetery to picnic in his lot overlooking Cedar Dell. At times Correja could be seen sitting there by himself, absorbed in a book. In the late 1850's, Correja purchased Carrara marble in Italy, and brought it back on his ship. From that marble was carved the Sea Captain's Monument. The sextant, which was long a part of this monument but is now gone, was the same one that Correja used for years to guide his ship at sea.

THE FIREMEN'S MONUMENT

ON APRIL 2, 1848, when a fire broke out on Duane Street, the volunteer firemen of Southwark Engine Company No. 38 responded to the alarm. As they fought the fire, a wall collapsed, and two men, Engineer GEORGE KERR (1816–1848) and Assistant Foreman HENRY FARGIS, were killed. Deeply moved by these deaths, the volunteer firemen of New York City appointed a committee to erect a suitable memorial to their fallen fellows. That committee went to Green-Wood Cemetery, where its comptroller, JOSEPH A. PERRY, led them through the grounds in search of the best site available. They chose one on a rise overlooking New York Bay.

A marble monument, rich in fire-related symbolism, was sculpted by Robert E. Launitz (who, in 1866, almost twenty years later, was advertising his Monumental Works as the oldest such establishment in New York City, offering "Monuments of every class of the most Chaste and Original Designs, Statuary, Busts from Photographs, Mural Tablets, &c., &c., executed in the highest style of the Art"), and was proudly signed by him across its front. The central marble shaft, decorated with oak leaves symbolizing strength and endurance, stands almost 24 feet high, and is topped by a statue of a fireman saving a child. Adorning the fireman's hat is a wreath of oak leaves, the traditional reward given to a lifesaving hero. The coat of arms of New York City is carved on the base of the central shaft. Hydrants, hoses, speaking trumpets, hats, down-turned firemen's parade torches, hooks, ladders, and the leaves of water plants decorate the monument.

The Sea Captain's Monument has lost the sextant which John Correja used for years to guide his ships; the monument is shown in a recent photograph (top) and in one circa 1870 (bottom).

To the right of this central column is the marble monument to George Kerr, and to the left is a similar one to Henry Fargis. Both are also decorated with fire fighting items carved in stone: hats, trumpets, and down-turned parade torches (symbolizing that the line of descent continues despite death).

The committee responsible for this monument hoped that all firemen from New York City who had died in the line of duty and had already been buried elsewhere would be reinterred here. However, a search of New York's cemeteries was able to identify only two such men. When the families of those two insisted that their monuments be brought to Green-

The Firemen's Monument, in a nineteenth century print. Green-Wood Historic Fund Collection.

Detail of the front gate to the Firemen's Monument, from a photograph taken about 1870. The gate to this unique cast iron fence was supported by posts in the shape of fire hydrants, and chains attached the fire plugs to the posts. The gate was cast as hose-pipes, hook and ladder, parade torch, axe, trumpet, and "tormentor," tied together with a cast iron hose, and surrounded by a wreath of laurel. Crowning the gate was the inscription, "New York Fire Department, incorporated A.D. 1798," and atop that was a bell which rang when the gate was opened or closed.

The Brooklyn Fire Department, a separate entity from New York City's force until the consolidation of Brooklyn and New York in 1898, honored its fallen members with these marble monuments, erected within sight of each other.

Wood with their remains, the monument committee refused, and no reinterments occurred.

After the Firemen's Monument was erected, men of the Volunteer Fire Department who fell while discharging their duties were buried there. That tradition was short-lived, however, ending in 1865, only sixteen years later, when the volunteers were replaced by a force of full-time paid fire fighters.

This monument has changed substantially since its erection. Its open location, selected for its panoramic view, has exposed the marble to severe wind and rain, and much of its detailing has eroded. Mature trees now obscure the panoramic view of New York Harbor. Sadly, the marvelous cast iron fences, which did so much to unite these monuments and create a separate and special space for firemen, are gone.

These brownstone fire hydrants are topped by fire helmets adorned with a "6." This lot was purchased by none other than Boss Tweed, who led the Americus Six Fire Company; it was for the burial of members, but was hardly used.

Harry Howard was the model for the fire chief, standing center foreground with the fire horn under his arm, in The Life of a Fireman: The New Era, Steam and Muscle. *It was drawn by* CHARLES PARSONS. *Courtesy of the Museum of the City of New York.*

THE LIFE OF A FIREMAN

J UST ACROSS the road from Green-Wood Cemetery's Firemen's Monument is the plot of hero fireman HARRY HOWARD (1822–1896). An orphan, Howard worked his way up in New York City's Volunteer Fire Department, serving as runner, fireman, foreman, assistant engineer, and finally, in 1857, head of the department. As chief engineer, Howard introduced the permanent alert system that resulted in substantial reduction in fire insurance rates. Known as an extremely brave, dashing, and athletic fireman, he was the hero depicted in the famous Currier and Ives litho-

Harry Howard dedicated his monument to "My Foster Mother" who adopted and raised him after she was saved from a burning building. This photograph, taken around 1875, shows Howard's monument shortly after it was erected; the cast iron fence is no longer there.

graphic series *Life of a Fireman.* Howard, in his career as a fireman, is said to have personally saved one hundred lives, and was the hero of New York City; the only fireman in the city who was better known at that time was WILLIAM MARCY "BOSS" TWEED.

But Harry Howard's life also included its share of tragedy. Though engaged for many years, he never married; his intended's parents refused to accept an orphan as their son-in-law. Soon after Howard assumed leadership of the Volunteer Fire Department, and while he was still only in his mid-thirties, he was on his way to a fire on Grand Street when he was struck down by paralysis. Though he survived, he never fully recovered his strength. Twenty years later he was asked what part of his life as a fireman he looked back on with the most fondness. His reply was bitter: "Upon none of it. See this arm of mine [still paralyzed]. . . . That's what I got for being a fireman. What can compensate me for that? Nothing. And there was many a man who went to an early grave in Green-Wood on account of over-exertion as a fireman."

Howard was honored by having a fire company, Howard Engine Company No. 34, and Harry Howard Square, bounded by Canal, Walker, Baxter, and Mulberry Streets, named for him.

"GOOD-BYE BOYS, I DIE A TRUE AMERICAN"

WILLIAM POOLE (1821–1855), a butcher by profession, had other skills, too. He could throw a butcher knife through an inch of pine at twenty feet. Standing more than 6 feet tall and weighing over 200 pounds, Poole was a notorious street fighter, famed for his ferocity, who led the Native American (nativist, not Indian) gang in its ongoing conflicts with the Tammany gang. His nickname, "Bill the Butcher," was more related to his vicious fighting technique than to his profession.

On February 24, 1855, Poole lost his last fight. At the Stanwix Hall, a newly-opened barroom on Broadway near Prince Street in New York City, Poole was challenged by several Tammany bruisers. Putting $5 in gold on the bar, Poole wagered that he could take all of them in a fight. But before Poole could make his move, his rival, Lew Baker, shot Poole in the leg, abdomen, and through the heart. Despite these wounds, Poole somehow managed to struggle to his feet, grab a huge carving knife, scream that he was going to cut out Baker's heart, and take a few steps before he began to collapse. As Poole fell he flung the knife, and its blade quivered in the door jamb as Baker ran for his life.

Lew Baker set out for the Canary Islands, hoping to find safe haven there. GEORGE LAW (1806–1881), a wealthy leader of the Native American Party, loaned his clipper yacht *Grapeshot* to the authorities, who sailed in pursuit. Baker's desperate flight ended with his capture off the coast of Tenerife, and he was brought back in irons to stand trial. Three times he went to trial, but each time the jury hung, unable to reach a unanimous verdict, and Baker was finally released.

William ("Bill the Butcher") Poole.

This monument was installed by The Green-Wood Historic Fund in 2003 to mark the final resting place of William ("Bill the Butcher") Poole.

Poole, to the amazement of his doctors, clung to life for fourteen days. On March 9, 1855, Poole breathed his last words, "Good-bye boys, I die a true American," and gave up his final fight.

The Native Americans celebrated Poole as a hero. So many people crowded onto the roof of the house opposite Poole's to watch his funeral procession that the building collapsed, leaving four dead and many injured. More than 5,000 men, accompanied by six brass bands playing dirges, marched in his funeral procession from Christopher Street down crowd-lined Broadway to the Battery, then boarded ferries for Brooklyn, and marched on to Green-Wood Cemetery, At least one marcher was killed as rival gangs pelted the mourners with rocks and bricks, and the Seventh Regiment was called out to separate the rivals and restore order.

For weeks afterwards, Poole's funeral and his last words were the leading topics of conversation in New York. Plays were written in his honor, and those already being performed were rewritten so that at the final curtain the hero, draped in an American flag, could gasp "Good-bye boys, I die a true American" to thunderous applause. "Bill the Butcher" Poole lies in an underground vault at Green-Wood Cemetery, marked with a granite gravestone installed by The Green-Wood Historic Fund in 2003.

"THIS HUNTED, HAUNTED MAN"

In the summer of 1854, Harvey Burdell (1811–1857), a well-off New York City dentist and confirmed bachelor, met Emma Cunningham, a widow with five children, at the fashionable summer resort, Saratoga Springs. This meeting would profoundly change both their lives, for Emma Cunningham almost immediately began her nonstop efforts to marry Dr. Burdell and inherit his fortune. When she returned to New York City, she rented rooms in Dr. Burdell's house at 31 Bond Street for herself and her children, became manager of his premises, and set about pursuing her quarry.

However, despite Emma Cunningham's unrelenting efforts to win him over, Dr. Burdell refused to marry her, so she tried to convince him by having him arrested for slander and breach of promise to marry. Next, she staged a secret marriage in which her accomplice pretended to be Dr. Burdell. Though these strategies failed, there was no escape for Dr. Burdell. On January 30, 1857, he was found stabbed to death in his Bond Street home.

Sensational newspaper coverage reported every detail of the grisly murder as thousands of spectators gathered to gawk at the scene of the crime. Authorities held an inquest there, and the witnesses testified while seated in the late Dr. Burdell's dentist's chair. One "expert" proposed that the deceased's eyes be examined, theorizing that the last thing seen by him, the face of the murderer, would still be on them. After some debate, the authorities rejected that idea.

On February 4, 1857, Dr. Burdell's funeral procession set out from his Bond Street home for Grace Church on Broadway. While services were

An artist's sketch of Dr. Burdell in his casket.

held there, crowds gathered, and soon Broadway was blocked from Union Square to Bond Street. After the formalities at the church were completed, a path was cleared through the crowd, and the hearse, followed by fifty carriages, proceeded down Broadway, between the throngs, all the way to the Hamilton Avenue Ferry. The funeral procession then made its way by ferry to Brooklyn, and the journey was completed by carriage up the slope to Green-Wood Cemetery.

The murderous attack on Dr. Burdell, in a contemporary woodcut.

The snow lay deep at the cemetery. Though many curious strangers were there, few of Dr. Burdell's relatives made the trip, and no memorial speech was made at his graveside as he was laid to rest.

Emma Cunningham was soon arrested for Dr. Burdell's murder. She sat through her trial in the black mourning clothes of a widow, often with her veil obscuring her face. District Attorney A. Oakey Hall (later New York City's mayor during the Tweed Ring's reign), opened to the all-male jury by describing the crime as one "perpetrated to a great extent with the ignorance of human nature which, compared with men of the world, women at all times . . . have possessed. . . ." He reminded the jury of murderesses in history, and spoke of Dr. Burdell as "this hunted, haunted man by this fiend in woman's shape." For two days the prosecutor presented testimony, aided by a wooden model of 31 Bond Street and four paintings, one of each side of the murder room. But no witness had seen or heard the murder, and the prosecution was without evidence or passion.

The defense brought out testimony that, the day after the murder, Emma Cunningham had no wounds. It called a professor of surgery from the New York College of Medicine, who had dressed a corpse in clothing and then had two students stab it. The professor concluded that only a person of great strength could have caused the wounds that took Dr. Burdell's life. Mrs. Cunningham's doctor told the jury that she suffered from inflammatory rheumatism in her shoulders, and her strength was "very much diminished."

Emma Cunningham, on trial for murder, wore mourning clothes in order to win the jury's sympathy.

The judge instructed the jury that it was not to let its sympathy for the fair sex interfere with its deliberations:

> Above all, gentlemen, you must not forget that although you are sitting upon the life of one who belongs to that sex which instinctively appeals to you for your protection and support and sympathy, and which forms the tenderest ties and associations of life, and is always so promptly and willingly rendered, you are to shut your eyes and steel your hearts to these considerations.

The judge also pointed out to the jury that no bloody clothes were found in the house.

After deliberating for only thirty-five minutes, the jury returned a verdict of not guilty. Emma Cunningham, as the verdict was pronounced, collapsed into the arms of her daughter.

Even with Dr. Burdell dead and buried, Emma Cunningham was not through scheming to gain Dr. Burdell's fortune. Nothing if not persistent, she threw herself into a new plan, pretending to be pregnant and insisting that she was carrying Dr. Burdell's baby. Enlisting a doctor to supply a newborn baby at the appropriate moment, she waited until her "term" was complete. Unbeknownst to Emma Cunningham, however, this doctor had gone to the authorities and was cooperating with them. He arranged to borrow a baby from Bellevue Hospital, and when that baby was handed to Emma Cunningham, the police burst into her room and arrested her again.

But once more Emma Cunningham demonstrated her resiliency. She fought the charges, and ultimately they were dropped. Disappearing from public view, she lived out her life without Dr. Burdell's fortune which she had so coveted and for which she had schemed so long and hard.

The baby used to entrap her became famous as "Baby Anderson," a featured attraction at P. T. Barnum's American Museum.

For years after Dr. Burdell's death, the only monument adorning his grave at Green-Wood Cemetery was a plain wooden board, on which was simply written, "Harvey Burdell, M.D." In 2007, Dr. Burdell (and Emma Cunningham) finally were given granite gravemarkers.

FROM THE POTTER'S FIELD

You didn't have to be wealthy to be buried at Green-Wood Cemetery. It helped, though, particularly if you wanted a prime location, or if you wanted to have a plot for you and your family. But public lots were available, where single graves could be purchased at relatively modest prices. And, if you had good friends or comrades, they might even pay for your final resting place at Green-Wood Cemetery.

George W. Struthers (1817–1848), according to the inscription on his marble monument, was "among the first to enroll his name amid the First Regiment New York Volunteers" when the Mexican War began in 1846. After taking part in "several of the hardest fought battles in the Mexican Campaign," Struthers returned to New York "enfeebled by disease

Barnum ran this advertisement for "Baby Anderson:"

THE BOGUS BURDELL BABY is now to be seen at this Museum, having arrived from Bellevue Hospital and with its real mother, Mrs. Anderson, been placed at this establishment to gratify, for A FEW DAYS ONLY, the public curiosity. This is the genuine BORROWED BABY, which was the valuable instrument, through which District Attorney A. Oakey Hall, Esq., and Dr. Uhl, exposed the stupendous Bond Street fraud and which was pronounced by Mrs. Cunningham to have the "exact nose and chin" of the late DR. BURDELL . . . NO EXTRA CHARGE for admittance to the Museum, notwithstanding this additional attraction.

The marble monument to George Struthers, Mexican War soldier. Note the eagle, the laurel wreath, the backpack marked "U.S.," and the cap, all of which refer to Struthers's gallant service to his country.

Detail of the exquisite carving of the George Struthers Monument.

contracted in the service of his Country." Struthers's rapidly failing health required his hospitalization and quickly claimed his life.

When no one claimed his remains, Struthers was buried in New York City's Potter's Field. But, when the men of the Harrington Guard learned of this ignominious end, they had Struthers's body brought to Green-Wood Cemetery, and had this monument built in his honor. There he was interred on August 31, 1853.

ONE SPRIGHTLY WOMAN

OF THE over half a million individuals interred at Green-Wood Cemetery, the one who lived the longest was SARA W. KAIMS (1737–1854), who lived to the age of 117 years, three months, and sixteen days. However, what made her long life even more remarkable was that, according to Green-Wood Cemetery's 1867 directory, she "gave birth to twenty-two children and retained her sprightliness to the last." Sprightliness at the age of 117 is no easy task.

THE AMERICA'S CUP

THERE WAS NEVER really any question what profession GEORGE STEERS (1820–1856) would choose. His father, Henry, was a successful British shipbuilder who immigrated to America in 1819. George was born the next year in Washington, D.C., and grew up in his father's shipyard at the foot of East 10th Street in New York City. At the age of ten he built his first boat, a scow, and at sixteen he built the sloop *Martin Van Buren*. His first large ship, the sloop *Manhattan*, was built when he was nineteen, and many other ships soon followed. From boatyards on the East River, George Steers launched such notable ships as the ocean steamer *Adriatic* for the famed Collins line, the schooner *Gimcrack* (upon which the New York Yacht Club was founded) and the steam frigate *Niagara* (which laid the first transatlantic cable).

But George Steers gained his greatest fame as a builder of racing yachts. His most famous craft was *America*, the legendary boat which he designed and built for six members of the New York Yacht Club in 1851. Soon after she was completed, *America* sailed off to challenge for the Queen's Cup at the annual Royal Yacht Club Regatta off Cowes, England.

On August 22, 1851, at 10:00 a.m., the starting gun sounded, and fifteen schooners and cutters began their race. Though the upstart "low black schooner" *America* got off poorly, within half an hour she managed to work her way through the spectator fleet and into second place, then fell back to fifth. When the wind picked up, and white caps began to appear, *America* made her move, dramatically pulling away from the competition and stretching her lead to seven and one-half miles.

When *America* crossed the finish line in triumph, the English spectators were "as mute as oysters." But Queen Victoria, who had watched the race,

George Steers, the young man who designed America. Dictionary of American Portraits, *Dover Publications.*

was more hospitable. She came aboard *America* with her husband and the Prince of Wales and gave one guinea to each crew member as prize money. Rebuking the Royal Yacht Club for its inhospitable behavior, she feted *America*'s crew and builders at her estate, and had a duplicate of the Queen's Cup made and presented to the victors. That silver trophy was known thereafter as the America's Cup.

The schooner yacht America, *with a low freeboard, sharp bow, wide beam amidships, and simple pilot boat sail plan, became a symbol of Yankee ingenuity and success.* America *is pictured in this print, winning the Club Cup off Cowes on August 12, 1851.*

America had triumphed in the most famous yacht race ever held. Daniel Webster, when he heard of her victory, rejoiced with his countrymen: "Like Jupiter among the gods, *America* is first and there is no second!" George Templeton Strong, the New York diarist, was taken aback by the extent of the public rejoicing:

> Newspapers crowing over the victory.... Quite creditable to Yankee shipbuilding, certainly, but not worth the intolerable, vainglorious vaporings that make every newspaper I take up now ridiculous. One would think yachtbuilding were the end of man's existence on earth.

America's dominance was so clear that yacht design was revolutionized on both sides of the Atlantic.

But tragically, within five years of his great triumph, George Steers, only thirty-seven years old, was thrown from his carriage by a runaway horse near his home in Great Neck, Long Island, and fatally injured. His ship *America*, however, lived on, sailing through incarnations as a transporter of secret agents, Confederate blockade runner, Union warship, Naval Academy training vessel, and yacht of Benjamin Franklin Butler (former Civil War general and governor of Massachusetts). Her end came in 1945, when she was scrapped.

Detail of the marble monument to George Steers.

John Greenwood, George Washington's favorite dentist. Dictionary of American Portraits, *Dover Publications.*

J OHN GREENWOOD (1760–1819) had little formal education, and at an early age apprenticed to a cabinet-maker, then served as a fife boy during the Revolutionary War. He was at the Battle of Bunker Hill, scouted for Benedict Arnold's expedition to Canada, and took part in the campaign around Trenton. Later, Greenwood became a privateersman, made some money, and studied dentistry.

By 1785, John Greenwood had established a dental practice in New York City. Greenwood is credited with originating the foot drill, spiral springs to hold plates of artificial teeth in the mouth, and the use of porcelain for false teeth.

John Greenwood's monument. He died almost twenty years before Green-Wood Cemetery was founded, and was later reinterred there.

Dr. Greenwood's most famous patient was George Washington. In 1795 Greenwood made a set of false teeth for Washington out of gold, ivory, and perhaps some human teeth, but definitely not out of wood. Part of this set is believed to have been carved by Charles Wilson Peale, who also painted several portraits of Washington. Washington, pleased with Greenwood's work, used him as his dentist for the rest of his life. Two sets of teeth made by Dr. Greenwood for the Father of Our Country survive to this day.

A TONGUE-TWISTER

I T WAS JAMES KIRKE PAULDING (1778–1860), a prominent writer who made a name for himself by championing American art and parlayed his nationalist reputation into appointment as Secretary of the Navy during the Martin Van Buren administration, who in his novel *Koningsmarke* (1823) coined the tongue-twister "Peter Piper picked a peck of pickled peppers."

BUSINESS ACUMEN (OR LACK THEREOF)

W ALTER HUNT (1796–1859) was quite an inventor. Over the years he created a flax-spinning machine, a machine to make boxes out of wood pulp, an icebreaker boat, a fountain pen, a self-closing inkwell, and suction shoes for walking on ceilings (though not the ones used by Fred Astaire or Lionel Richie).

But Hunt was not much of a businessman. In the early 1830's he created the first sewing machine. Concerned, however, that it would economically ruin the nation's seamstresses, he decided not to patent it. In 1854, he

James Kirke Paulding created America's best known tongue-twister.

changed his mind and sought a patent, only to be turned down; ELIAS HOWE had patented his own sewing machine eight years earlier.

One day in 1849, finding himself with no money to pay back a $15 debt, Hunt spent three hours twisting and bending a piece of wire. Hunt promptly sold the rights to this simple invention, the safety pin, for $100 and settled his debt, then watched as manufacturers earned millions from his innovation. Hunt never earned another cent from that brainstorm.

HE WASN'T JUST DOT AND DASH

TODAY SAMUEL F. B. MORSE (1791–1872) is remembered for his great invention, the telegraph, which revolutionized human communication by allowing messages to be transmitted faster than a messenger could travel. Yet, there was a great deal more that this extraordinary man accomplished during his lifetime. He learned photography from its inventor, France's Louis Daguerre, then introduced that process to the United States. Even earlier, Morse was a very prominent painter. He studied at the Royal Academy in London, England, and had artistic (if not financial) success as a portraitist and painter of historical scenes. By 1826, Morse was New York City's most eminent portraitist, and was so respected in artistic circles that he was elected the first president of the newly-created National Academy of Design. Painter Thomas Cole, the first leader of the Hudson River School, described Morse as the "keystone of the arch" of American

Samuel F.B. Morse poses, in this engraving made shortly before his death, with a few of his international medals and his great invention, the telegraph.

painting. But beginning in the early 1830's, Morse painted less and less as his duties at the National Academy (he held its presidency for twenty years) and his interest in science increased.

At the time *The Muse—Susan Walker Morse* was painted, Morse was in crisis about his artistic career, lamenting the sacrifices he had made to pursue his muse and the only limited success he had achieved. Just after Morse completed this painting,

The Muse—Susan Walker Morse, *depicts Samuel Morse's daughter. He painted this masterpiece during 1836 and 1837; it was described by the* New York Mirror *as "the most perfect full-length portrait that we remember to have seen from an American artist." Courtesy of The Metropolitan Museum of Art.*

This unusual three-sided monument stands in a place of honor, atop its own hill, overlooking Crescent Water, memorializing Samuel F.B. Morse and his brothers. Morse's parents had eleven children, but only three of them, Samuel, Richard, and Sidney, survived infancy. Photograph by Andrea Brizzi.

his tribute to the arts picturing his sixteen-year-old daughter in an idealized Neoclassical setting, Morse learned that the commission to paint in the Capitol Rotunda in Washington, D.C., which he had so ardently sought, had gone to someone else.

Morse thereafter lost all enthusiasm for painting. He increasingly devoted his energies to perfecting the telegraph, and in 1838 demonstrated his invention to President Van Buren, Van Buren's Cabinet, and members of Congress. Science, rather than art, occupied him thereafter.

CITY HALL

As NEW YORK CITY grew at the beginning of the nineteenth century, its need for a new City Hall was apparent. The city fathers held a design competition, and JOHN McCOMB, JR. (1763–1853) and Joseph Mangin submitted the winning entry. They split the prize of $350, and McComb was appointed superintendent of construction.

City Hall, in a photograph dating circa 1917. Its appearance has changed little over the years.

John McComb, Jr., in this painting by SAMUEL LOVETT WALDO, holds the plans for his triumph, City Hall, which appears behind him. Fittingly, this painting now hangs in that building. Courtesy of the Art Commission of the City of New York.

As construction proceeded, McComb was directed to cut costs $15,000 by not using the marble he had planned for the entire facade of the building. Instead, he was told that because the city was only developed to the south, few would see the north side anyway, and cheaper red sandstone would suffice there.

City Hall was completed in 1812. Within a generation, the city considered, but finally rejected, proposals to sell it. Years later, on October 13, 1858, City Hall was put up at auction to satisfy a judgment against the city. The winning bid, made by Mayor Daniel Tiemann's clerk, was $50,000. Tiemann then sold City Hall back to New York City.

When City Hall was later damaged by fire, that damage went unrepaired for years. By the 1890's, City Hall, left to its own devices by an indifferent government, was considered "an offense to the sight of the community and a menace to the health" of the city. The mayor proposed that a new City Hall be built, and that this old relic be moved stone-by-stone and reerected on either Central Park West as a new home for the New-York Historical Society or at 42nd Street and Fifth Avenue to house the new public library. But ultimately these suggestions were rejected, and City Hall remains in its rightful place.

In the 1950's, City Hall underwent much-needed restoration, with its badly-deteriorated marble replaced by Alabama limestone, and with granite substituted for its brownstone facade on the north side. It has recently undergone further restoration, and continues in its role as the center of New York City government.

DRESSING THE POLICE UP IN UNIFORMS

Early New York City police uniforms.

BORN INTO a prosperous New York City merchant family, JAMES WATSON GERARD (1794–1874) long had a sense of civic responsibility. During the War of 1812, he joined The Iron Greys to defend New York Harbor against possible British attack. The most successful trial lawyer of his time, Gerard tried more cases and lost fewer than any of his contemporaries. In the vanguard of social reform, Gerard served for many years as a member of the Society for the Prevention of Pauperism, and was the chief founder of New York's House of Refuge for Juvenile Delinquents in 1825, the first shelter exclusively for juveniles in America. During the last twenty years of his life, Gerard was active in public education, serving the New York City school system as trustee and inspector. He was several times offered the position of commissioner of the Board of Education, but always declined, feeling he could do more for schoolchildren as school inspector.

But Gerard's greatest feat was more prosaic. In the early 1840's, at a time when there were no uniformed police anywhere in America, he launched a one-man campaign to have New York City's "rattle watch" shed its motley collection of rags, dignified by only a small metal shield, and to outfit the men in uniforms. Gerard traveled to London to observe its bobbies. Upon his return, he had his tailor make up a costume of blue coat with brass buttons, added a helmet and club, and wore his outfit to Mrs. Coventry Waddell's fancy dress ball on Fifth Avenue in fashionable Murray Hill to dramatize his idea.

This sculpture dresses up James Gerard's mausoleum.

Soon thereafter, Mayor JAMES HARPER and the Common Council adopted Gerard's idea for New York City's 200-officer force. Its officers were outfitted with long blue cloth coats decorated with brass buttons, and with the letters M.P. (Municipal Police) on their stand-up collars. However, these uniforms evoked little but derision, and the officers were scornfully referred to as "Mayor's Pups." The men themselves were none too happy with their new garb: American citizens, born free and equal, should not have to walk the streets dressed in the livery of servants. Given these objections, the experiment in police uniforms was soon abandoned, and New York City's finest did not appear in uniform again for another ten years.

The Chauncey Tomb is impressive, even though Confederates had nothing to do with building it.

In this detail of an 1852 cartoon, Lola Montez blows a good-bye kiss to her royal male admirers as she forsakes Europe for America.

This granite gravestone was installed in the 1990's, courtesy of Bruce Seymour, author of Lola Montez, A Life, *to replace the badly-worn original marble.*

A NICE STORY, BUT . . .

FOR YEARS the story has been told that the impressive Chauncey family tomb, constructed of Tuckahoe marble, was made from stones quarried by Confederate prisoners of war while they were being held at Sing Sing Prison. It's a nice story, but it isn't true. An 1858 print of Green-Wood Cemetery shows the Chauncey tomb already there. Of course, there were no Confederate prisoners of war anywhere in 1858; the Civil War didn't begin until 1861.

THE LEGENDARY LOLA MONTEZ

BORN IN 1824 as Maria Delores Eliza Rosanna Gilbert in Limerick, Ireland, she was raised in Scotland and educated in Bath and Paris. At the age of fifteen, in order to avoid an arranged marriage with sixty-year-old Sir Abraham Lumley of India's Supreme Court, she eloped with Lieutenant James of the British Army, and accompanied him when he went to serve in India. A year later, after leaving her husband, she performed in Paris, billed as "Spanish Dancer LOLA MONTEZ," and attracted attention throughout Europe for her beauty and eccentricities. Her affairs with Czar Nicholas I, Franz Liszt, Honoré de Balzac, and Alexandre Dumas were legendary. Dumas said of her, "In her was mind and heart enough for a dozen kings."

Leaving Paris for Munich, she performed in ballet and pantomime. King Ludwig of Bavaria took her as his mistress, built a palace for her, gave her an annuity, anointed her Baroness of Rosenthal and Countess of Landsfeldt, and made her his chief political adviser until armed revolt against her power and influence forced his abdication in 1848.

Returning to England, Lola Montez married another British Officer, only to be prosecuted for bigamy by her first officer/husband, now-Captain James. She fled to Spain, and in 1851, came to New York City. There, and on the stages of Boston, Philadelphia, New Orleans, San Francisco, and Australia, she performed her notorious Spider Dance for overwhelmingly-male audiences (most women considered her to be the embodiment of immorality), spinning wildly as she pretended to shake spiders from her petticoats. In New York, she was the companion of Walt Whitman, William Dean Howells, and Commodore Vanderbilt.

One account described her this way: "She was a brunette of the Spanish type, with dark blue eyes and long lashes. To her personal charms she added an arch and vivacious manner, and fluent conversation, in four languages." Her unique personality, defiance of convention, flair for publicity, cosmopolitan background, and great beauty, made her a sensation from the cities of the East to the mining camps of California.

In 1856, Lola Montez, toning things down, toured America and Europe, delivering lectures on "Women, Love, and Spiritualism." This venture, however, did not go well, and she returned to New York discouraged. Turning to religion, she devoted her last years to helping "outcast women," and died in poverty.

Lola Montez was one of the great personalities of her time, and *The New York Times* began her January, 1861 obituary with this: "There are few readers of the newspaper literature of the day who are not familiar with the name of that eccentric, brilliant, impulsive woman, known as Lola Montez."

Her friends erected a simple marble slab in her memory. It had only two words on it: "Eliza Gilbert," an abbreviated version of her given name, and told nothing of the fame and fortune of the woman it honors.

Several years ago, officials at Green-Wood Cemetery were approached by a museum which wanted this memorial for its collection, and offered to place a reproduction in its stead at Green-Wood. That never happened, and the original monument remains in its rightful place.

This photograph by daguerrotypists Southworth and Hawes, taken in 1851, shows Lola Montez, the international celebrity, soon after her arrival in America. Gift of Edward Southworth Hawes in memory of his father, Josiah Johnson Hawes. Photograph © 2008 Museum of Fine Arts, Boston.

Southworth and Hawes, in another image apparently made during the same sitting, captured Lola Montez's independent, nonconformist side: she poses in a way no "lady" would ever pose—holding a cigarette. But Lola Montez was not concerned about whether she appeared to be a "lady"; her concern was being treated as an equal. The Metropolitan Museum of Art, Gift of I.N. Phelps Stokes, Edward S. Hawes, Alice Mary Hawes, and Marion Augusta Hawes, 1937 (37.14.41). Photograph, all rights reserved, The Metropolitan Museum of Art.

Brooklyn Borough Hall (right foreground) and the Brooklyn Courthouse (center background), in a 1910 post card. Gamaliel King was the architect of both buildings. It was under the Romanesque dome of the Courthouse, which was built in 1861, that the famous trial of Henry Ward Beecher for "improper conduct" was held. The courthouse was torn down in the 1960's for the construction of Brooklyn Law School.

BROOKLYN'S CITY (NOW BOROUGH) HALL

A CONTEMPORARY described GAMALIEL KING (1795–1875) as a man with "a good deal of cleverness, great industry, and a touch of genius." King started off in Brooklyn as a grocer, learned carpentry, then became a builder, and later an architect. His best-known work was Brooklyn's City Hall.

In 1835, King entered the newly-created City of Brooklyn's design competition for its City Hall. Though his plans finished second, his influence resulted in him being named superintendent and resident architect for construction of the winning entry. However, the Panic of 1837 forced Brooklyn to postpone construction.

When, in 1845, the funds necessary to proceed with construction became available and a second competition was held, King submitted a Greek Revival entry which was remarkably similar to his competitor's winning plans of ten years earlier. This time, however, King's pilfered entry finished second, but on a revote the next day his submission was selected, and his courthouse was built according to those plans between 1846 and 1848. It survives today, in downtown Brooklyn, as Borough Hall.

BROOKLYN'S SLAVE AUCTION

HENRY WARD BEECHER (1813–1887), pastor of Brooklyn's Plymouth Church, was a national leader in the fight against slavery. Though many members of his congregation and citizens throughout Brooklyn supported his efforts, some did not. His outspoken advocacy of abolition resulted in threats against his life and constant rumors that a mob would put the torch to his church.

But Beecher was not intimidated, and looked for new ways to dramatize the horrors of slavery. It occurred to him that there could be no more dramatic lesson about the outrage of slavery than a slave sale from his pulpit. So Beecher scheduled his first slave auction at Plymouth Church for June 1, 1856.

Excited crowds began to gather in Brooklyn Heights hours in advance of the scheduled event, and the streets around the church were jammed

A Man of Many Moods.

Henry Ward Beecher was one of the most famous Americans of his time. This illustration, from a nineteenth century biography, shows his "many moods."

Crowds gathered when Beecher spoke. This illustration shows the inside of Plymouth Church, packed as usual to hear "The Great Divine." Many of its congregants chose Green-Wood Cemetery as their final resting place.

with people and carriages. As the church filled, thousands who had hoped to get inside were turned away.

Beecher, appearing in front of the congregation, gave a brief scriptural introduction. He then announced that a young Negro woman had been sold by her own father, and was headed South into slavery. But she could still be saved:

> She was bought by a slave trader for twelve hundred dollars, and he has offered to give you the opportunity of purchasing her freedom. She has given her word of honor to return to Richmond if the money be not raised, and slave though she be called, she is a woman who will keep her word. Now Sarah, come up here, so that all may see you.

Sarah came up onto the pulpit, and sat in a chair at Beecher's side. The bidding was about to begin, and Beecher, ever a master of theatrics, assumed the role of slave auctioneer:

> Look at this remarkable commodity—human flesh and blood like ourselves! You see the white blood of her father in her regular features and high, thoughtful brow. Who bids? You will have to pay extra for that white blood, because it is supposed to give intelligence. Stand up, Sarah! Now look at her trim figure and her wavy hair! How much do you bid for them? She is sound of wind and limb—I'll warrant her! Who bids? Her feet and hands—hold them out, Sarah—are small and finely formed. What do you bid for her? She is a Christian woman—I mean a praying nigger—and that makes her more valuable, because it insures her docility and obedience to your wishes. "Servants, obey your masters," you know. Well, she believes in that doctrine. How much for her?—Will you allow this praying woman to be sent back to Richmond to meet the fate for which her father sold her. If not, who bids?

Beecher had done his job well, whipping the congregation to a fever pitch. For the next half-hour, cash was stuffed into contribution boxes and congregants removed their rings, bracelets, and watches, passing them forward. Above the excitement, Beecher's voice rang out: "In the name of Christ, men and women, how much do you bid?" A gentleman rose to his feet, announcing that any shortfall would be made up by several members. The congregation exploded with cheers.

Sarah's freedom was purchased and she went to live in a small house in Peekskill which had been purchased for her. Beecher later staged several other slave auctions at Plymouth Church, but it is unlikely that any had the emotional impact of this first one.

NEGRO LIFE IN THE SOUTH—OLD KENTUCKY HOME

EASTMAN JOHNSON (1824–1906) was one of the great American portrait and genre painters of the nineteenth century. Born in Maine, his given first name was Jonathan, but he was always known by his middle name, Eastman. At the age of sixteen, he went to Boston to work in a lithography shop. Soon thereafter, he started his art career, doing crayon portraits

Painter Eastman Johnson in a photograph circa 1890.

Negro Life in the South—Old Kentucky Home, *Eastman Johnson's controversial painting. Courtesy of the New-York Historical Society.*

of many of the distinguished men of Cambridge, Massachusetts, Newport, Rhode Island, and Boston. In Washington, D.C., he set up his easel in a Senate committee room, and drew portraits of the country's leaders.

Travelling to Europe in 1849, Johnson studied in Dusseldorf with Emanuel Leutze, whom he assisted with his landmark work, *Washington Crossing the Delaware*, then spent the next four years refining his technique in The Hague. Johnson's work was so impressive that he was offered a position as painter to the Dutch court; though flattered, he declined.

In 1858, Eastman Johnson set up his studio in New York City, where he would work for the rest of his life, and in that year he painted *Old Kentucky Home*. Other paintings of this period, including *Husking Bee* and *Cranberry Pickers*, brought him fame, and he was elected to the National Academy of Design in 1860. Johnson is best-known for his sentimental scenes of everyday life and his portraits of the prominent men of the time, including depictions of prosperous New York families in domestic scenes. He was one of the most famous and fashionable American painters of his time; at the height of his career his fee was an astounding $10,000 (equal to about $200,000 today) per painting.

Negro Life in the South—Old Kentucky Home is widely considered to be Eastman Johnson's masterpiece. Completed in 1859, it was meant to be a scene in the South, but in fact was painted in Johnson's father's Washington, D.C., backyard. Family servants served as many of the models; the woman pictured at the far right is Mary Johnson, the painter's sister. When this canvas was exhibited at the National Academy of Design, it was called *Negro Life in the South*, but by 1867 it was widely known as *Old Kentucky*

Home, a name adopted from the title of the then-popular song by Stephen Foster. It sold in that year for $6000, a large sum for that time. Contemporary critics considered this painting to be one of the best genre paintings ever done by an American artist, and it is today Johnson's most famous work.

Completed as the country was about to plunge into civil war, this picture generated tremendous controversy. Advocates of slavery applauded it, noting that its peaceful scene, with well-fed, well-dressed, and contented slaves, indicated that the system they cherished would survive. However, abolitionists interpreted this painting quite differently. As one abolitionist commented, "How fitly do the dilapidated and decaying negro quarters typify the approaching destruction of the 'System' that they serve to illustrate . . . this dilapidation, unheeded and unchecked, tells us that the end is near."

Remarkably few monuments at Green-Wood Cemetery, even those to its most famous individuals, contain even a suggestion of that person's accomplishments. Eastman Johnson's monument, however, is an exception (though an understated one) to that rule. It identifies him as "artist," while curiously leaving no separation, or punctuation, between his name and his profession. After noting his dates and places of birth and death, it fittingly observes, "HIS WORKS ARE HIS MONUMENT."

Eastman Johnson's memorial at Green-Wood Cemetery is one of the few monuments there which identify the deceased's profession.

Veterans' Day Ceremonies, 1997, the 14th Brooklyn.

CHAPTER THREE

The Civil War Era
(1861–1865)

FACING SOUTH IN PRAYER

JOHN YATES BEALL (1833–1865) was born in Walnut Grove, Virginia, into a wealthy Shenandoah Valley plantation family. Educated at the University of Virginia, where he studied law, he joined Botts Greys at the time of John Brown's raid on Harper's Ferry, and remained with that unit when it became a brigade of the Confederate States' Army of Northern Virginia at the outbreak of the Civil War. Commissioned a captain in the Second Virginia Infantry, he fought under Generals Turner Ashby and Stonewall Jackson before he was forced to leave the army after a shot broke three of his ribs.

After a long recovery, Beall volunteered for the Confederate Navy, and was commissioned an Acting Master. Though suffering from tuberculosis, he led his men on commando raids across Chesapeake Bay, attacking Union ships and lighthouses. In late 1863, after some success, including the capture of the schooner *Alliance* and four other ships, the "notorious" Beall and his men were captured by Union forces. Despite the fact that they were all enlisted in the Confederate Navy, they were placed in irons, and plans were made to try them as pirates. In response, Confederate President Jefferson Davis ordered an equal number of Union prisoners, both officers and sailors, placed in irons, and threatened reprisals if anything happened to Beall and his men. After a standoff, Beall and most of his men were freed in a May, 1864, prisoner exchange. Beall fought briefly near Richmond, then made his way, with a few of his raiders, to Canada on "special service."

By the fall of 1864, Beall was ready to proceed with his new plans. On September 19, dressed as a civilian, he boarded the unarmed steamer *Philo Parsons* on Lake Erie, putting into motion his overly-ambitious plan to capture the Union war-vessel *Michigan* and to free 3,000 Confederate officers who were being held as prisoners of war on Johnson's Island in Sandusky Bay. As the *Philo Parsons* proceeded toward Detroit, making its scheduled stops, Beall's associates gradually came on board. At the appointed time, armed with revolvers and axes, they seized the boat from its crew. Chasing after another steamer, the *Island Queen*, they captured her, took what they could, and scuttled her. But Beall's scheme fell apart when a Confederate agent he was relying on for help was captured, and Beall's men, confronted by the U.S. gunboat *Michigan*, decided that the plan could not succeed and refused to go on. Union forces were rushed to the area, but Beall managed to escape back to Canada.

John Yates Beall, Confederate infantryman, Naval officer, and saboteur, was executed only weeks before the end of the Civil War. Courtesy of the Virginia Historical Society, Richmond, Virginia.

This marble carving of Civil War hero Lieutenant Henry Hidden was created by sculptor Karl Müller, who signed it on the bottom. Hidden is shown in the same pose as those on page 67. Green-Wood Historic Fund Collection.

Within a few months John Beall launched what would be his last mission. In December, 1864, he crossed into New York State with nine other Confederate agents, hoping to carry out their plan to free seven Confederate generals by derailing the train on which they were being moved outside of Buffalo. But this plan also failed and things went awry when a Niagara City police officer spotted Beall and his companions as they waited at the Buffalo railroad depot for a train to take them back across the Canadian border to safety, thought they looked like escaped prisoners of war, and arrested them.

Beall, identifying himself as "Baker," was brought in chains to New York City's Police Headquarters on Mulberry Street. Placed in lineups, he was viewed by witnesses to the recently-failed Confederate plot to burn New York City and split the Union. Though no witness picked Beall out, his detention continued. He wrote in his leather-bound notebook, lamenting his fate:

> The Christmas of '64 I spent in a New York prison! Had I, 4 years ago, stood in New York, and proclaimed myself a citizen of Virginia, I would have been welcomed; now I am immured because I am a Virginian . . . What misery I have seen during these four years, murder, lust, hate, rapine, devastation, war! What hardships suffered, what privations endured! May God grant that I may not see the like again! Nay, that my country may not! Oh, far rather would I welcome death, *cine* as he might! Far rather would I meet him than go through four more such years.

The investigating detective soon convinced the jailer guarding "Baker" to try to get a confession from him. Selling Beall a *Book of Common Prayer* for $1, the turnkey won the prisoner's confidence. Beall, whose own fortune was estimated at $1 million, offered $1000 in gold for help in escaping. On December 31, Beall recorded in his diary:

> This year is gone. . . . To-day I complete my twenty-ninth year. What have I done to make this world any wiser or better? . . . Will I see the year 1865 go out; or will I pass away from this world of sin, shame and suffering?

Two nights later, Beall's cell was searched and he was transferred to Fort Lafayette in New York Harbor, where he was accused of spying and charged with "violation of the laws of war."

At trial, the clerk and one of the owners of the *Philo Parsons* testified that Beall had seized their ship. The turnkey at Police Headquarters, who had never mailed Beall's letters that urgently asked Confederate authorities to send certificates attesting that he was acting under Confederate authority and orders, told of Beall's bribe offer. And the Confederate agent who was arrested with Beall implicated him in the plot to derail the train near Buffalo. Beall argued that he was an officer in the Confederate service, but he was found guilty and sentenced to hang. As he awaited execution, he spent $2000 of his fortune to buy clothing and luxuries for his fellow Confederate prisoners held at Fort Lafayette.

Great efforts were made to have Beall's death sentence commuted. Confederate General Roger Pryor (a fellow prisoner at Fort Lafayette), Senator Thaddeus Stevens of Pennsylvania and Governor John Andrew of Massachusetts, all appealed for mercy. A petition, urging that Beall's life be spared, was signed by six Senators, eighty-five members of the House of Representatives, the Librarian of Congress, and other citizens, and was presented to President Lincoln. Beall, scheduled to hang on February 18, won a seven-day postponement, and his mother visited to say her good-byes. But Lincoln refused to intervene, leaving it to General John A. Dix to decide whether or not a pardon would be issued. Dix, feeling that only the President could spare Beall, refused to act to save the condemned man.

A gallows was borrowed for the execution from the Tombs, New York City's prison, and was reassembled on Governor's Island in New York Harbor. On February 25, 1865, just six weeks before Robert E. Lee surrendered his army at Appomattox Court House, John Yates Beall, facing South in prayer as a black hood was pulled over his head, was hanged. The *New York World* wrote of Beall's last moments: "Let those of us who must die for the right side do so as well as he who died for the wrong side." Lincoln was not without regrets: "The case of Beall on the Lakes, there had to be an example . . . I had to stand firm . . . I can't get the distress out of my mind yet."

Several months after Beall's execution a "weird and lurid story" was circulated by an intimate friend of his that John Wilkes Booth had met with President Lincoln at midnight to appeal to him, and that Lincoln, moved to tears, had promised a pardon, but that Secretary Seward had overruled Lincoln. This rejection, so the story went, had impelled Booth, in revenge, to hatch his assassination plot.

Beall was buried at Green-Wood Cemetery, where the cemetery's records listed his cause of death as "strangulation," in a lot purchased by his family. In 1869, his family reclaimed his remains and took them South, selling the plot where he had been buried back to the cemetery.

HIS LAST GALLANT CHARGE

Colonel George W. Taylor, Third New Jersey Volunteers, gave this account of Lieutenant Henry Hidden's last action three miles east of Bull Run in Virginia:

> I had under my orders of the First New York Cavalry 16 men and one corporal, under First Lieutenant Hidden. Just before leaving the railroad I ordered this officer to advance in the open fields and reconnoiter, and if the force was not greatly superior to his own he might charge them. He went off at a brisk trot, nor did he check his horses until he charged into the midst of their pickets, the enemy being greatly superior in numbers, and having the advantage of cover of pines. He lost his life in the gallant charge, but drove the enemy into rapid retreat, leaving arms and many knapsacks and blankets. Thirteen prisoners were taken, with a lieutenant and noncommissioned officer. They proved to be the First Maryland Regiment.

Detail of the monument to Lieutenant Henry B. Hidden, who sacrificed his life for his country. This bronze is signed "K. Müller." Karl Müller, who worked for the Union Porcelain Company for years, also designed the monument to "Soda Fountain King" John Matthews at Green-Wood. Lieutenant Hidden's bronze recently was cleaned and restored by The Green-Wood Historic Fund.

This photograph of Lieutenant Hidden was undoubtedly the one used as the reference for his Green-Wood Cemetery monument. Courtesy of Massachusetts Commandery Military Order of the Loyal Legion and the U.S. Army Military History Institute (hereafter referred to as U.S.A.M.H.I.).

Colonel Abraham Vosburgh barely had time to get his elaborate uniform dirty before succumbing to disease. Courtesy of U.S.A.M.H.I.

The monument to Colonel Vosburgh, with its cast iron fence, circa 1870. Note that the posts of the fence were cast as bayoneted rifles. This was a very popular tourist attraction; a path was worn just outside the fence by the thousands who came to pay their respects.

Colonel Fowler's monument.

According to the March 9, 1862, official report of Brigadier General Philip Kearny, "A cavalry charge, unrivalled in brilliancy, headed by Lieutenant Hidden, Lincoln Horse, broke, captured, and annihilated [the enemy's pickets], but was paid for with his life. [Lieutenant Stewart], late of West Point, and many foot-men are in our hands."

Captain J. K. Stearns reported: "I here learned of the glorious death of Lieutenant Hidden, of my company. He was a splendid officer and a courteous gentleman, whose loss is regretted by all who knew him, but by none more than myself."

Dated 1863, the inscription on this bronze relief tells the story this way: Lieutenant HENRY B. HIDDEN. Born in New York. Killed at Sangster's Station Virginia March 9th 1862 At the Age of Twenty-Three Years In a Gallant and Successful charge with 14 Dragoons upon 150 Rebel Infantry. "He illustrated the cavalry service and opened for it a new era."

The quoted inscription is also from General Kearny. Kearny, one of the best known and most respected soldiers of his time, was killed just a few months after Hidden's death, at Chantilly, Virginia, when he accidentally rode into enemy lines, was called upon to surrender, and tried to fight his way out.

PRO PATRIA

ON APRIL 22, 1861, Colonel ABRAHAM S. VOSBURGH (1825–1861) marched at the head of the 71st New York State National Guard as it hurried off to Washington, D.C. It was one of the first regiments to respond to Abraham Lincoln's desperate plea for armed units to defend the nation's capital against Confederate attack. Vosburgh, however, was soon dead of consumption, an early casualty of the Civil War.

President Abraham Lincoln laid a laurel wreath on Vosburgh's body, and the colonel was returned to Brooklyn and interred at Green-Wood Cemetery. The members of the 71st Regiment erected a monument to Vosburgh, topped by an eagle and bearing the inscription "Pro Patria" (For Country). Surrounded by a spectacular cast iron fence, with posts shaped as bayoneted rifles, its gate was adorned with a cast iron Union cap, belt, and sword. This site became, in the ensuing years, one of the leading attractions in the cemetery.

For many years after Colonel Vosburgh's death, surviving members of the 71st Regiment fired three salutes on Decoration Day over the grave of their leader.

DISASTER AT THE CRATER

JUST A FEW FEET from Green-Wood Cemetery's marker for section 76, a small, unobtrusive granite stone stands alone, marking the final resting place of General EDWARD FERRERO (1831–1899). That stone gives no clue of the tragedy that befell so many men as a result of the inaction of this man.

Edward Ferrero was born in Spain to Italian parents, and came to this country as an infant. Italian political refugees, including Garibaldi, often came to his home to visit his father. Edward began his career as a dance instructor at his father's fashionable school, later owned a hotel and ballroom near West Point, and taught dancing to the cadets at the nearby U.S. Military Academy. His *The Art of Dancing, Historically Illustrated* was published in 1859.

At the outbreak of the Civil War, Ferrero was a lieutenant colonel in New York's 11th Regiment. He raised the 51st New York Regiment, the Shepard Rifles, in 1861, and commanded a brigade against Roanoke Island. Later in the war, he commanded brigades at Second Bull Run, Antietam, and South Mountain, and served in Pope's Virginia Campaign. For his service at South Mountain and Antietam, Ferrero was rewarded with a promotion to brigadier general in 1862. He served at Fredericksburg, Vicksburg, Knoxville, Cincinnati, and Bean's Station, and was brevetted a major general in 1864.

During the last campaign of the war, General Ulysses S. Grant, recently appointed General in Chief of the Armies of the United States, directed the strategy of the armies under Generals George Meade and Benjamin Butler in an effort to capture General Robert E. Lee's Army of Northern Virginia and the Confederate capital of Richmond. In a series of bloody battles through Virginia at The Wilderness, Spotsylvania Court House, and Cold Harbor, Grant and Meade moved their troops relentlessly southward. On June 15, 1864, they attacked Petersburg, the lifeline to Richmond. If Petersburg fell, then the Confederate capital could not be held for more than a few days. But four days of combat failed to create a break in the Confederate defenses, and Grant began to dig in.

Ferrero had organized the "colored division" of General Ambrose Burnside's 9th Corps, despite ridicule from other officers who scorned his black, ex-slave troops as "Ferrero's Minstrels" and "Dixie Cut-ups." Ferrero believed that his troops, given a chance, would acquit themselves well in combat. But it was during this siege outside Petersburg that disaster struck.

As the siege dragged on, with Grant stymied by heavily dug-in Confederate troops, a plan was hatched by the men of the 48th Pennsylvania Volunteer Infantry, who had been coal miners before the war, to tunnel underneath the Confederate lines, detonate a massive explosion, storm through the breach splitting Lee's army, and end the war. After Grant approved this gamble, despite his belief that the digging would turn out to be little more than "a means of keeping the men occupied," the Pennsylvanians, scorned by the army engineers, worked for a month digging their 500 foot-long tunnel with only the most primitive of tools, including picks, shovels, and empty cracker boxes to carry dirt. Their tunnel would become the longest military mine built up to that time.

Another famed unit which went off to fight for the Union early on was Brooklyn's "Fighting Fourteenth" Regiment of the New York State Militia. The 14th was outfitted by the City of Brooklyn in colorful Chasseur-style uniforms of baggy red pants, short dark blue jacket with false red vest, red and blue cap, and white leggings. It was recruited in Brooklyn, where E D W A R D B R U S H F O W L E R (1837–1896) enrolled on April 18, 1861, to serve three years; he was mustered in the next day as one of its three lieutenant colonels. It was a fighting unit; during its three years of service, it took part in 21 engagements. The first of these was on July 21, 1861, at First Bull Run, when the 14th charged four times into Confederate artillery and musket fire. For their ferocity in battle, the 14th's men were labelled the "Red Legged Devils" by Stonewall Jackson and his men. Fowler was wounded in action in August, 1862, and was appointed the 14th's colonel in October, 1862. He led his men at Gettysburg and continued at their head until June 14, 1864, when they completed their service. In all, the 14th had 5 officers and 83 enlisted men killed in action, 3 officers and 61 enlisted men wounded in action, 74 enlisted men lost to disease and other causes, and 17 enlisted men who died "in the hands of the enemy." Its most severe losses occurred at the Battles of First Bull Run, Sulpher Springs, Gettysburg, and Spotsylvania Court House. Fowler was brevetted brigadier general on March 13, 1865. The name of the 14th Brooklyn is proudly kept alive today by a reenactment unit. *Photograph courtesy of U.S.A.M.H.I.*

General Edward Ferrero, who drank while his men died. Courtesy of U.S.A.M.H.I.

General Edward Ferrero's gravestone.

In the meantime, Ferrero's troops, the freshest men available, trained to spearhead the assault. Though the Confederates suspected that a mine was being dug, and started countermines in an effort to locate and destroy it, they did not dig deeply enough, and the Union mine remained undetected.

However, on the day before the detonation and attack were to begin, Meade, with Grant's agreement, lacking faith in the abilities of Ferrero's black troops and fearing criticism that he had treated the black troops as cannon fodder by ordering them to lead the charge, ordered Burnside to lead off with white troops. Though Burnside had championed the mine and had insisted that Ferrero's men should lead the attack, he was overruled, and was forced to order Brigadier General James H. Ledlie's fought-out white soldiers to be in the vanguard when the troops stormed through the expected gap in the Confederate line.

On July 30, 1864, at dawn, Union forces successfully detonated six tons of powder, and the entire 18th South Carolina Regiment, Pegram's Battery, and about half of the 23rd South Carolina Regiment that had been assigned to defend the Pegram's Salient section of the Confederate trenches, were blown into the sky. A *New York Times* correspondent described the scene in the Crater just after the massive explosion: "bodies of dead rebels crushed and mangled out of all semblance to humanity, writhing forms partly buried, arms protruding here and legs struggling there—a very hell of horror and torture."

With 45,000 Union troops massed for action against a line manned by only 1,800 Confederates, the four divisions of Burnside's Ninth Corps, Ledlie's in front and Ferrero's now last, moved against the shattered Confederate line. But their efforts ended in disaster. Without supervision from either Ledlie or Ferrero, who sat in a bombproof shelter oblivious to the developments around the Crater and passed a bottle of rum back and forth, their troops lacked leadership and direction. Failing to push the attack by rushing around the huge crater (170 feet long, 60 feet wide, and 30 feet deep) left by the explosion and splitting Lee's army, the Union men moved forward slowly.

The Confederates, some dead, some stunned, and some panicked, fired virtually no shots for twenty minutes to half an hour after the detonation. But the hesitation of the Union troops gave the rebels crucial time to regain their senses, bring up reinforcements, and organize a counterattack. When the Confederates finally reformed and opened fire, the Union men fell back in disarray into the Crater, trying to escape the withering crossfire volleys finally coming from the Confederates on their left and right. Rebels stood on the rim of the Crater, shooting down on the trapped Union men. Other Southern forces brought two Cohorn mortars within close range and lobbed shells into the troops massed in the Crater. Sharpshooters from Georgia, Virginia, and Alabama brigades picked off anyone who tried to escape. As one Union officer recalled, "The men were dropping thick and fast, most of them shot through the head. Every man that was shot rolled down the steep sides to the bottom, and in places they were piled up three and four deep." Bayonetted muskets, which had been abandoned on the field earlier, were picked up by the Confederates and flung, like javelins, into the pit. Heavy canister fire from a Confederate battery swept Union soldiers who somehow had managed to scramble to the crest of the Crater.

Finally, a white flag went up in the Crater, and 1101 Union men, with eleven regimental flags, surrendered. Black troops and their white officers, engaged for the first time against the Army of Northern Virginia, were met with particular brutality; many were shot even after they gave up. As Union men were escorted to the rear by their Confederate captors, some were killed by Union artillery. In all, 5640 Union troopers were killed, wounded, or missing in action. General Grant lamented the lost opportunity:

> Such opportunity for carrying fortifications I have never seen before and do not expect again to have . . . I am constrained to believe that had instructions been promptly obeyed, Petersburg would have been carried with all the artillery and a large number of prisoners without loss of 300 men.

A contemporary woodcut, the Explosion of the Mine Before Petersburg. *This explosion formed the Crater.*

A court of inquiry was convened to investigate the debacle, and found that Ferrero, Ledlie, and their commander, General Ambrose Burnside, were primarily responsible for the failure of the attack. The court criticized Ferrero for "not going forward with [his troops] to the attack" and for "being in a bombproof habitually, where he could not see the operation of his troops [and] did not know the position of two brigades of his division." Somehow, however, Ferrero avoided punishment for his dereliction of duty. General Grant later submitted a statement to the Congressional Committee on the Conduct of the War, stating that he believed in hindsight that, had the black troops been allowed to lead the attack, things would have gone better.

With the failure at the Crater, the war was prolonged for eight months. It would not be until late March, 1865, that Grant was able to mount his

In all, there are 16 Union and 2 Confederate generals buried at Green-Wood Cemetery, as well as 37 Union officers who were brevetted brigadier generals. A brevet is "a commission conferring upon an officer a grade in the army additional to and higher than that which, at the time it is bestowed, he holds by virtue of his commission in a particular corps of the legally established military organization." With a brevet, the officer is eligible for assignment to duty with the new rank; in the absence of such assignment by the President, it has no effect on the officer's pay, benefits, or seniority.

A total of 1366 Civil War Union officers received a brevet for brigadier general. Some of those appointments were controversial. Colonel WILLIAM GURNEY (1821–1879) was brevetted brigadier general of volunteers in May, 1865, for gallantry in action. That honor for Gurney did not sit well with Colonel Henry M. Hoyt of the 52nd Pennsylvania Infantry, who in his application for a brevet wrote that he should receive one "because a Brevet Brig. Gen. has been conferred upon Col. Gurney, 127th N.Y. Volunteers who was the sole cause of our disaster at Fort Johnson, 3 July 1864." And, not surprisingly, some mistakes were made in awarding brevets. EDWARD WALTER WEST (1836–1916) served in several regiments during the Civil War as a private, first lieutenant, acting aid-de-camp, sergeant, and second lieutenant. Though he was breveted colonel and brigadier general on the recommendations of Generals Casey and Heintzelman, supposedly for his service as lieutenant colonel of the 33rd New Jersey, and those brevets were confirmed by the Senate, someone in the War Department discovered that West had declined that appointment, and the Department refused to issue his brevet commissions.

final push through Petersburg, resulting within weeks in the evacuation of Richmond and Lee's surrender at Appomattox.

After the war, Ferrero returned to New York, and for the next three decades he managed several large ballrooms there, including one in Tammany Hall, until shortly before his death.

The Drummer Boy Monument. The Monumental Bronze Company made memorials of both Union and Confederate soldiers. Its catalog, issued around 1882, offered a generic soldier for $450 (just over $8000 in today's money); for an additional $150 (the equivalent of about $3000 now) a likeness of a specific war hero would be sculpted from a photograph. Though the company claimed that it sold thousands of zinc soldiers, it is more likely that the correct number is in the hundreds.

Two examples of the various "white bronze" monuments at Green-Wood Cemetery.

Only one firm, the Monumental Bronze Company of Bridgeport, Connecticut, manufactured "white bronze" cemetery monuments. These were actually of pure zinc, and were made from the mid-1870's until World War I. Sales appear to have reached their peak around 1888, and tapered off thereafter.

A full time artist working at the company's headquarters in Bridgeport created wax models of the monument. A plaster cast of the wax model was then made, followed by a second plaster cast that was cut into sections to assure the sharp detailing of the sand casts and the cast zinc. After the zinc was cast and hardened, the zinc pieces were assembled and then fused together by molten zinc being poured into the joints. This apparently novel technique of assembly made the pieces virtually inseparable.

All monuments were made to order, and could be done in any custom design. They were sold throughout the country and in Canada; subsidiaries in Detroit, Chicago, Des Moines, New Orleans, and Ontario marketed them. But they never were considered artistic and never became popular. It is the rare cemetery that has more than one or two white bronze monuments. Marble and granite monument dealers, trying to protect their own business, refused to sell white bronze pieces, leaving their sale to struggling agents who worked on commission. Moreover, some cemetery officials mistakenly believed that zinc, like iron, had to be frequently painted in order to be maintained, and banned its use.

By and large, these zinc memorials imitated granite and marble monuments in their design; their primary advantages were that they were maintenance-free, more durable than marble (detailing on zinc monuments is just as sharp today as it was the day they were made), and cheaper than granite. The protective coating, which was brushed onto the zinc after it was sandblasted at the foundry, has become a characteristic gray-blue zinc carbonate with exposure to the elements (except in the Salt Lake City area, where it turned white).

The greatest problem with white bronze monuments has been the removal by vandals of the name tablets that were attached to them with ornamental, unslotted screws. A legend has arisen that these hollow zinc monuments were used by bootleggers to hide their liquor.

The Monumental Bronze Company remained in business until 1939, mostly making car and radio parts in its last years of business, but casting an occasional tablet in order to allow the names of recently deceased individuals to be added to existing monuments.

LITTLE DRUMMER BOY

O N APRIL 22, 1861, when the first Brooklyn troops marched off to the Civil War, twelve-year-old drummer boy CLARENCE MAC-KENZIE (1848–1861) beat the march cadence for the Thirteenth Regiment. Less than two months later, young Clarence was dead, killed in his tent in Annapolis, Maryland, by a bullet fired by a soldier who was drilling in preparation for battle. Young Clarence was Brooklyn's first casualty of the Civil War. His casket, draped with an American flag and followed by a detachment of soldiers from the Thirteenth Regiment marching to muffled drums, was brought to Green-Wood Cemetery, where he was interred.

For years Clarence Mackenzie lay buried on the Hill of Graves in a public lot, with his only memorial a wooden board on which was written "Little Drummer Boy." In 1878, Effie Brower, in her book on Green-Wood Cemetery, wrote: "There has been some effort made to build a monument for him, but so much time has gone by it may be forgotten, and his memorial lives only in the hearts of those who bore the heat and the fire of those darker days of our land." Fortunately, Clarence Mackenzie was not forgotten, and soon after these words were written his remains were moved to a spacious plot, at the top of the Soldiers' Lot, which Green-Wood had donated for the burial of Civil War veterans. This great monument, cast in zinc by the Monumental Bronze Company of Bridgeport, Connecticut, was erected there to honor him.

GLORY

A S THE CIVIL WAR began, no black volunteers were allowed to join the armed forces fighting to save the Union; it was widely thought that allowing them to fight would send the wrong message—that this was a war of abolition. By 1862, however, escaped slaves were making themselves useful to Union forces as laborers, cooks, and orderlies. And, with increasing Confederate success in battle, Lincoln and his fellow Republicans became convinced that they could spare no resource, including using ex-slaves as soldiers, in their efforts to crush the South. Further, European public opinion could be rallied to the Union cause if the war was seen as being fought over the moral issue of the abolition of slavery.

During the summer of 1862, Congress confiscated the property of the Confederacy, including slaves. As 1863 began, Lincoln issued his Emancipation Proclamation, which freed slaves in the Confederacy and stated that blacks would be "received into the armed forces of the United States." Against this background, Massachusetts's 54th Regiment was formed that spring, with white officers with strong abolitionist credentials put in command. Greeley's *New York Tribune*, sympathetic but concerned, voiced the thoughts of the North at these developments: "Loyal whites generally become willing that they should fight, but the great majority have no faith that they will do so. Many hope they will prove cowards and sneaks—

General George Crockett Strong, shown here in a woodcut from Harper's Weekly, *was mortally wounded as he led his brigade, including the black troops of the 54th Massachusetts Regiment, in the attack on Fort Wagner.*

In 1853, Vermont native GEORGE CROCKETT STRONG (1832–1863) graduated from the United States Military Academy, then served as an ordnance officer at several posts. At the outbreak of the Civil War, Strong was Chief of Ordnance to General Irvin McDowell, and later was General George McClellan's Assistant Ordnance Chief. He was then assigned to the staff of Major General Benjamin F. Butler, whom he served as adjutant general and then chief of staff. Strong's performance as a field commander in Louisiana resulted in his promotion to brigadier general in 1862.

The resurrectionist beliefs depicted at Green-Wood Cemetery were also expressed by many of the men who fought in the Civil War. One Pennsylvania soldier wrote that "religion is what makes brave soldiers." Another soldier wrote to his sister, "If it is his will that I should sacrifice my life for my country then the Lord Jesus will receive my spirit. Pray that I may be a faithful soldier of the cross and of my country." A private with the 33rd Mississippi penned this to his wife: "Christians make the best soldiers as they would not fear the consequences after death as others would." Describing death as "the destruction of a gross, material body," an Illinois cavalryman expressed his belief that "a soldier's death is not a fate to be avoided, but rather almost to be gloried in." And a Massachusetts private found strength in his belief in resurrection: "our cause is just I am willing to risk my life in its defence, believing that if I shall fall . . . it is but going home to my savior whom I love."

The June 18, 1863, attack of the 54th Massachusetts Regiment on Fort Wagner is depicted in this 1890 chromolithograph. Though the attack is pictured in daytime, it actually took place at night.

Detail of the monument to General George C. Strong, the twenty-nine-year-old who commanded the attack that is depicted in the movie Glory. *Strong's monument features marble eagles and cannon. The maker made a mistake here; the cannon should be down-turned to symbolize death. This monument was criticized more than a century ago by Nehemiah Cleaveland, in his guide to Green-Wood Cemetery, for its poor construction and materials. Several carved eagles have fallen off it and the marble has aged badly.*

others greatly fear it." Though black regiments had been formed as early as the fall of 1862, and had fought at Vicksburg during May and June, 1863, they had received little publicity, and doubts remained.

It was in July, 1863, that the paths of Massachusetts's 54th (Colored) Infantry and George Crockett Strong fatally crossed. Colonel Robert Gould Shaw, the white officer who commanded the 54th, was anxious to give his men a chance to prove that black men would fight. The attack on Fort Wagner, the huge Confederate earthen works on Morris Island, South Carolina, which protected the mouth of Charleston Harbor, was to be led by Strong, who had a reputation as a brilliant young officer. Strong, at Shaw's request, asked that the 54th, composed mostly of well-educated free blacks from throughout the North, be transferred to his brigade so that it could spearhead the assault. Division commander Major General Truman Seymour was only too glad to oblige, telling another officer, "Well, I guess we will let Strong lead and put those damned niggers from Massachusetts in the advance; we may as well get rid of them one way as another."

In the early morning hours of July 10, 1863, Strong led his brigade in boats from Folly Island across a narrow channel to Morris Island. But Strong, in his eagerness to lead his men into combat, prematurely jumped into the water as he approached the shore, and almost drowned. After struggling ashore, Strong led the charge, quickly routing the Confederate defenders who were scattered along the beach. One hundred and fifty rebels, a dozen artillery pieces, and five regimental flags were quickly captured. On the next day, Strong's men attacked the 1700-man garrison which was dug in behind Fort Wagner's thirty-foot-high sand parapets. However, they were driven back with substantial losses.

It was not until a week later that Strong's final attack on Fort Wagner, which would be memorialized more than a century later in the movie *Glory*, was launched. After a thunderous artillery barrage by Union ships and land batteries shelled the fort on July 18, Strong's brigade, with the 54th Massachusetts leading, moved forward as the sun was setting. As the six hundred men of the 54th moved down the beach to position themselves for their assault, the question of whether black troops would fight was still unanswered in the public mind.

Captain Luis Emilio, in his history of the 54th Massachusetts, described the scene:

> Presently, General Strong, mounted upon a spirited gray horse, in full uniform, with a yellow handkerchief bound around his neck, rode in front of the Fifty-Fourth, accompanied by two aids and two order-lies. He addressed the men; and his words, as given by an officer of the regiment, were: "Boys, I am a Massachusetts man, and I know you will fight for the honor of that State. I am sorry you must go into the fight tired and hungry, but the men in the fort are tired and hungry too. . . . Don't fire a musket on the way up, but go in and bayonet them at their guns." Calling out to the color-bearer, he said, "If this man should fall, who will lift the flag and carry on?" Colonel Shaw, standing near, took a cigar from his lips, and said quietly, "I will." The men loudly responded to Colonel Shaw's pledge, while General Strong rode away to give the signal for advancing.

The troops fixed bayonets, shook hands with their comrades, and exchanged slips of paper with the addresses of next of kin to be notified if they did not return, while their leader, Colonel Shaw, affectionately told them that this was their chance to "prove themselves as men." Shaw, who had had a premonition that he was about to die, challenged his men to "take the fort or die there."

With the ocean on one side and a swamp on the other, the men moved several hundred yards up the narrow beach directly toward Fort Wagner, and got within two hundred yards before intense fire from cannister and grape shot opened up on them. Braving buried land mines, sharpened palmetto stakes, and a water-filled moat, Shaw led his men to the top of the wall, where, illuminated by flashes from cannon, he waved his sword over his head and screamed, "Forward, 54th," then pitched forward with a wound through his heart. Five more regiments from Strong's brigade charged the moat, but were driven back with heavy losses.

In the attack on Fort Wagner, the 54th Massachusetts lost nearly 50% of its men, killed or missing, including its colonel, lieutenant colonel, and seven most senior captains. The next morning, Confederate grave diggers buried 800 Union men, including Shaw, in a mass grave in front of the fort. But a message had been sent. The *Atlantic Monthly* wrote, "Through the cannon smoke of that dark night the manhood of the colored race shines before many eyes that would not see." The *New York Tribune*, after quoting General Strong that "the Fifty-Fourth did well and nobly; only the fall of Colonel Shaw prevented them entering the fort . . . they moved up as

Types From the March, *Edwin Forbes's drawings of faces of Civil War soldiers.*

EDWIN FORBES (1839–1895) is best remembered today for his Civil War illustrations. Born in New York City, he studied painting with Arthur Fitzwilliam Tait. When the Civil War began, Forbes enlisted in the Army of the Potomac. However, as the war dragged on, he left Union service to become a staff artist/reporter for *Frank Leslie's Illustrated Newspaper*. Forbes's sketches of camp life and battlefield action appeared as woodblock prints in that weekly from 1862 to 1864. These prints were particularly important in reporting the Civil War because they allowed the mass production and publication of war illustrations in newspapers and magazines before the technology necessary to mass produce photographs had been developed.

Forbes's sketches, later made into copperplate etchings, were published in 1876 as *Life Studies of the Great Army*, and were awarded a medal at the Centennial Exposition. General William Tecumseh Sherman purchased the original prints and decorated his office in the War Department in Washington, D.C., with them.

In 1891, Forbes published a second volume devoted to the Civil War, *Thirty Years After*. Included in that volume was this sketch of *Types From the March*. It captures the faces of several Civil War soldiers, giving us some idea of what the men buried in Green-Wood Cemetery's Soldiers' Lot looked like.

In the Soldiers' Lot, monuments to men who died (top to bottom) at Bristoe Station, Shiloh ("A Mother's Offering to Her Country"), and Antietam Creek (a German immigrant).

gallantly as any troops could, and with their enthusiasm they deserved a better fate," enthused, "It made Fort Wagner such a name to the colored race as Bunker Hill had been for ninety years to the white Yankees." The *Boston Commonwealth* quoted a white Union soldier near Fort Wagner as saying, "We don't know any black men here, they're all soldiers." Before the war was over, 179,000 black soldiers and 10,000 sailors would fight for the Union.

General Strong was wounded in the thigh in the attack of July 18, and was sent back to New York City for treatment. Any wound at the time was dangerous; one of every seven soldiers wounded in combat during the Civil War died from his wounds, compared to a rate of one in fifty during the Korean War and one in four hundred in Vietnam. Strong contracted tetanus as he traveled home, and died on July 30. On the day after his death, the United States Senate confirmed his nomination as major general.

Less than two months after the attack on Fort Wagner, the Confederates, pounded by Union ships and shore batteries, and haunted by the stench of rotting corpses, abandoned Fort Wagner. Since then, the Atlantic Ocean has reclaimed the spit of land upon which Strong, Shaw, and the men of the 54th Massachusetts charged.

THE SOLDIERS' LOT

Green-Wood Cemetery, in a patriotic gesture during the Civil War, created the Soldiers' Lot for free veterans' burials. As an entry in the cemetery's record books reads, several of its lots were "appropriated for the interment of all the soldiers of New York State who fell in battle, or died from sickness incurred while in duty during the war."

Several German immigrants who fell serving their adopted country are buried in the Soldiers' Lot. Men who fell at the Battles of Bristoe Station (Virginia), the Wilderness (Virginia), Antietam (Maryland), Gettysburg (Pennsylvania), and Shiloh (Tennessee) are also buried there.

NEW YORK'S DRAFT RIOTS OF 1863

Opposition to a military draft existed in New York City long before the Vietnam War. In 1863, as Civil War casualties and desertions mounted, and as the Confederacy neared its "high tide," the federal government enacted the Union's first conscription law. At the time, New York City was a hotbed of anti-Union and pro-Southern sentiment. Many workers, particularly Irish and German immigrants, were fervently anti-black, anti-abolitionist, anti-Republican, and anti-draft, and the Conscription Act ignited this sentiment. On July 4, in New York City, Governor John Seymour, in one of the most inflammatory speeches ever given by a public official, shouted to a crowd that had gathered to voice its opposition to the draft, "Remember this! Remember this! The bloody, treasonable and revolutionary doctrine of public necessity can be proclaimed by a mob as well as a government."

A woodcut of looting and arson during New York City's 1863 Draft Riots: the police charge rioters outside the New York Tribune *Building in this* Harper's Weekly *woodcut.*

It was not long before the mob issued its own proclamation. On July 13, 1863, the second day scheduled for the lottery drawing of Ninth District draftees, a demonstration against the Conscription Act began in New York City. The crowd, estimated at from 5,000 to 15,000 men and women, soon turned violent, quickly turning its energies to armed insurrection, with the city, its institutions, and its citizens coming under attack for five long days. Stores were looted, disabled war veterans from the Invalid Corps who intervened were killed, the chief of police was beaten unconscious, and police precincts and armories were attacked. Black boardinghouses, a black church, and the Colored Orphan Asylum on Fifth Avenue were torched.

Henry Jarvis Raymond (1820–1869) founded *The New York Times*, edited its first issue on September 18, 1851, and remained its editor-in-chief until his death. It debuted as the *New-York Daily Times*, with a price of one cent, printed in the morning and evening of each weekday, with a weekly Saturday morning edition; no Sunday *Times* was published until April 21, 1861. The paper reflected Raymond's personality, emphasizing reason over passion and impartiality over partisanship. Raymond was also active in politics, serving as speaker of the New York State Assembly, lieutenant governor, a founder of the Republican Party and the author of its original statement of principles, chairman of the Republican National Committee during Lincoln's Administration, and a Congressman from 1865 to 1867. He was also Abraham Lincoln's and Andrew Johnson's close friend.

During the Civil War, Raymond was a strong voice for quelling the rebellion at any cost, restoring the Union, establishing the supremacy of the Constitution, and supporting President Abraham Lincoln. When others expressed discouragement, Raymond sought to rally public opinion for the Union. But on August 22, 1864, when it appeared that Lincoln stood no chance of defeating George McClellan in the upcoming election, Raymond wrote to his friend, the President, "The Tide is setting strongly against us." The next day Lincoln, with the same foreboding, wrote:

This morning, as for some days past, it seems exceedingly probable that this administration will not be reelected. Then it will be my duty to cooperate with the President-elect as to save the Union between election and the inauguration, as he will have secured his election on such ground that he cannot possibly save it afterwards.

But the tide turned when General William Tecumseh Sherman wired on September 3, "Atlanta is ours, and fairly won." Admiral David Farragut soon occupied Mobile Bay, and Lincoln, buoyed by these military victories, was reelected.

The only book Raymond ever wrote was a biography of Lincoln.

Henry Raymond, founder and editor of The New York Times *and a power in the Republican Party.*

Eighteen blacks were lynched; a crippled black coachman was strung up as the mob chanted "Hurrah for Jeff Davis," then set his corpse on fire.

New York City policemen, armed with wooden truncheons, fought pitched battles, taking on armed mobs that outnumbered them 50 and 100 to 1. Almost every member of the police force was wounded during the riots; three policemen and almost 200 of the soldiers who had been called back from the war front to regain control of the city were killed.

The homes of abolitionists and Republicans became prime targets of the mobs. On July 14, at about noon, two men on horseback, shouting and waving swords, led a mob against the home of abolitionists ABIGAIL HOPPER GIBBONS (1801–1893) and her husband JAMES S. GIBBONS (1810–1892) (a cousin of Horace Greeley) near Eighth Avenue and 29th Street. The Gibbons's two daughters fled to a neighbor's house as men with pickaxes stormed in and destroyed what they could. Other rioters joined in, looting and smashing what remained, only to be driven off twice by soldiers and police, and to return a third time to set the house on fire. Neighbors, concerned that the fire might spread to their houses, extinguished the flames.

Further south, near City Hall, a mob singing "We'll hang old Greeley to a sour apple tree, and send him straight to hell!" chased newspaper editor HORACE GREELEY (1811–1872) from his offices at the *New York Tribune* and set fire to the building. Greeley was saved when he ran into a Park Row restaurant and was hidden by a waiter under a tablecloth. The *Tribune*'s offices were spared when police reinforcements arrived, routed the mob, and extinguished the fire. Over the next three days the offices of the *Tribune* were attacked three more times. At the nearby offices of *The New York Times*, founder and editor HENRY RAYMOND, armed with the latest in armament, three rapid fire Gatling guns that he had borrowed from the military, kept the mob at bay.

GEORGE BLUNT (1802–1878), who headed a prominent nautical publishing house, found a black man hanging from the lamppost in front of his house. On the man's chest was a note, apparently meant for Blunt: "We will be back for you tomorrow." Blunt made his way to several newspaper offices, and asked that they print his invitation to the rioters to come visit him at home, where he would be waiting with a Colt revolving rifle and two revolvers. Though his invitation was widely circulated, no rioters took him up on his offer.

Not until July 17—after lynchings of blacks, sackings of their houses and those of their sympathizers, pitched battles, and the loss of many lives—did five Union Army regiments, called back from the front right after turning back the Confederate invasion of the North at Gettysburg, restore order to New York City.

Estimates of the dead from these riots range from just over one hundred to more than one thousand. According to Green-Wood Cemetery's records, four individuals buried there died during these riots. WILLIAM ELDER, a native of Ireland and thirty-seven-year-old resident of West

12th Street in New York City, was "killed in a riot" on July 13. The next day, twenty-four-year-old THOMAS GIBSON, also a native of Ireland, was "shot in a riot" and died at Bellevue Hospital. Elder and Gibson may well have been rioters. Two children, five-year-old ELIZABETH MARSHALL and ten-year-old CHARLES FISBECK, died on July 14, 1863, in New York City of gun shot wounds, apparently casualties of the Draft Riots.

A CONFEDERATE GENERAL'S SECRET BURIAL

ROBERT SELDEN GARNETT (1819–1861), a native of Virginia, graduated from the United States Military Academy at West Point in 1841, taught tactics there, served in various Army posts thereafter, including aide-de-camp to General Zachary Taylor, and distinguished himself during the Mexican War at the Battles of Monterrey and Buena Vista. From 1852 to 1854, he was Commandant of the Corps of Cadets and instructor in infantry tactics at West Point. He then served on the West Coast, where he designed the seal of the new State of California.

In 1854, Garnett married MARIANNA NEILSON (1832–1858) of New York City, then served in the Northwest before going off to Europe in 1858 on sick leave. When word reached him in 1861 that the Civil War had started, he resigned his commission and returned to his native Virginia, where he served as adjutant general organizing Confederate troops. In June, 1861, he was commissioned a brigadier general of the Confederate Army, and given command of forces in the western section of that State. However, that section of Virginia was pro-Union, and Garnett had little local support, lacked cavalry and guns, and was short on supplies. With 4,500 men "in a most miserable condition as to arms, clothing, equipment, and discipline," Garnett dug in to hold the mountain passes that ran from the Shenandoah Valley to Wheeling and Parkersburg.

But on July 13, 1861, Garnett's forces were routed at the Battle of Carricks Ford by a body of Union troops six times their size, and Garnett was mortally wounded as he led his rear guard in covering the retreat across the Cheat River. Confederate General Edward Porter Alexander, who had been a cadet at West Point when Garnett was its superintendent, described Garnett's death in his memoirs:

> . . . his whole aspect was to me military discipline idealized & personified. And indeed his death illustrated it as perfectly as it could be done. His men behind some breastworks seemed a little restless under a heavy fire being poured at them to which Gen. Garnett did not wish to reply. He remarked to one of his staff, "The men need a little example," & he got out in front of the breastwork & walked calmly & slowly back and forth in the rain of bullets till one struck him down killing him almost instantly.

For this Garnett gained the distinction of being the first general on either side to fall in battle during the Civil War.

After Garnett was mortally wounded, his body fell into the hands of

Robert Selden Garnett, the first general killed in the Civil War. Courtesy of U.S.A.M.H.I.

Detail from the Garnett obelisk. These inscriptions hint at General Garnett's secret burial: the left side of the monument bears his wife's name and life dates, the right side those of his infant son, and the front, on which one would expect to find his name, bears only the inscription, "TO MY WIFE AND CHILD."

Confederate General Robert Selden Garnett was interred secretly at Green-Wood Cemetery in 1865. His grave has been unmarked until this gravestone, obtained from the Veterans Administration by Green-Wood's Civil War Project, was installed in 2008.

Robert Garnett's cousin, Confederate General Richard Brooke Garnett, came out of an ambulance on the morning of July 3, 1863, at the Battle of Gettysburg, to lead his brigade in Pickett's Charge. Too sick to walk, he rode a horse at the head of his Virginians, and made it to the Union lines on Cemetery Ridge, where he disappeared. His body was never recovered, though his sword was found years later in a Baltimore shop.

Union forces. General McClellan had it returned to Garnett's family, and he was buried in Baltimore. It was not until after the Civil War, in August, 1865, that his body was exhumed and reinterred secretly, because of fear of repercussions from strong anti-Southern feelings, at Green-Wood Cemetery in his family's plot. No entry of his interment was made in the cemetery's ledgers, and no notation of his death was carved into the Garnett family obelisk. It was not until 1959 that his presence at Green-Wood became public knowledge.

IS THAT A *NEW YORK TIMES* CORRESPONDENT BEHIND THAT STUMP?

A NATIVE of Scotland, WILLIAM SWINTON (1833–1892) was educated at Toronto's Knox College and at Amherst College, then became a Presbyterian minister. However, he soon turned to teaching. Scholarly and frail, he taught history and the classics to young ladies at Brooklyn's Mt. Washington College Institute, and wrote literary reviews for *The New York Times*. By 1862, Swinton was off to the front lines to cover the Civil War for that newspaper, and to record history for posterity.

Swinton had a deep understanding of strategy and tactics. His analyses of the war, published in the *Army and Navy Journal* in 1863 and 1864, were considered first rate by many military men. But Swinton's blunt criticisms of generals, often issued under the pen name "Occident," soon made him very unpopular with the authorities. After Swinton wrote critically of General Ambrose Burnside, Burnside was so enraged that he wanted Swinton shot; restraining himself, he had Swinton arrested, threatened with a court-martial, and expelled from the army camps.

The Times then enlisted the help of Congressman Elihu B. Washburne of Illinois, who had been instrumental in restarting Ulysses S. Grant's career early in the war, to introduce Swinton to Grant. Somehow, however, Washburne neglected to mention that Swinton was a newspaperman; instead, he told Grant, who by then was commander of all Union armies, that Swinton was an historian studying the operations of the Army of the Potomac. On the night of May 5, 1864, during the Wilderness campaign, Swinton's scheme to ingratiate himself with Grant collapsed. When Grant and General George Meade (commander of the Army of the Potomac) left their campfire and staff officers behind to confer privately in the shadows, an alert aide saw something moving near them, circled around, and found Swinton crouched behind a stump eavesdropping. For Swinton's efforts, he was stripped of his credentials as a correspondent and forbidden to remain with the army.

Nevertheless, as the war wound down, Swinton, drawing upon his extensive personal experience and many contacts, was well-positioned to write its history. As he noted in his preface to *Campaigns of the Army of the Potomac* (1866),

While the Army of the Potomac was yet in the field, there were many who, believing that I would in time make the fitter record of the doings and sufferings of that army than was possible in the brief chronicles which it was my duty to prepare for the press, began even then to furnish me with oral and written information.

When the war ended, Swinton traveled through the South, interviewing the military and civil leaders of the Confederacy. Relying on those interviews and his own knowledge, he wrote the draft of his war history, then submitted it to many generals, including Confederates Robert E. Lee and Joseph E. Johnston and Union Generals George C. Meade, Joseph Hooker, and Winfield Scott Hancock, for their review. But no copy of his manuscript was sent to Grant; their feud was not forgotten, and Swinton colored his account to deny Grant the credit he deserved.

Swinton shocked many Northerners with the dispassionate tone of that book, published at a time when passions from the war still ran very high. Many Unionists objected to his use of the term "Confederates," rather than the more widely used "rebel." Swinton authored several other Civil War books, including *The Times Review of McClellan; His Military Career Reviewed and Exposed* (1864), *The Twelve Decisive Battles of the War* (1867), and *History of the New York Seventh Regiment During the War of the Rebellion* (1870).

Swinton taught at the University of California from 1869 until 1874, then had great success writing school textbooks. His grave at Green-Wood Cemetery is unmarked.

KILLED BY A COMRADE IN ARMS

Edgar A. Kimball (1822–1863) trained as a printer and was the proprietor and editor of the *Age*, a liberal Democratic newspaper published in Woodstock, Vermont. In 1847, he was appointed captain of infantry in the United States Army, and served with distinction during the

Lieutenant Colonel Edgar Addison Kimball, who survived combat in the Mexican and Civil Wars only to be shot down by a fellow Union officer. Courtesy of U.S.A.M.H.I.

This woodcut, from a sketch by EDWIN FORBES, depicts the Battle of Antietam, September 17, 1862. It shows Kimball and his men, fighting on the Union left under General Burnside, in their successful attack on a Confederate battery.

Mexican War at Contreras and Churubusco. Kimball was the first soldier over the walls of Chapultepec and received Mexican General Bravo's surrender. For Kimball's service during that conflict he was brevetted major. Returning from the war, he resumed his career as a journalist in New York City.

When the Civil War began, Kimball was commissioned a major in the Ninth New York Volunteers, also known as Hawkins' Zoaves. After his unit overran the enemy's works during the Battle of Roanoke Island, North Carolina, he was promoted to lieutenant colonel and given command of a regiment.

Kimball survived the Battles of Antietam and Fredericksburg, only to be killed on April 12, 1863, by Union Colonel Michael Corcoran while camped near Suffolk, Virginia. One account was that Corcoran was trying to pass through the lines on urgent business, only to be stopped by a drunken Kimball, who demanded the countersign. When Corcoran refused to give it, Kimball made a movement that Corcoran interpreted as threatening, and Corcoran shot him. Another version was that Corcoran and Kimball were rivals, and Corcoran either mistook, or pretended to mistake, Kimball for an assassin.

But by all accounts Kimball was a hero, and when his body was returned to New York City, it lay in state in the Governor's Room of City Hall, as crowds stood on line to file past and pay their respects. His rosewood coffin, studded with nails and adorned with six massive silver handles, was draped with an American flag. Wreaths and bouquets were everywhere; one read "WE MOURN," another "OUR LOSS." Kimball's sword, belt, and cap were displayed nearby.

As Colonel Kimball's coffin began its journey to Green-Wood Cemetery, elements of four regiments formed up, and a twenty-one gun salute was fired in City Hall Park. The procession moved north to Bond Street, then south on Broadway to South Ferry, passing flag-draped buildings decorated to honor the fallen soldier. Kimball's remains were placed in Green-Wood Cemetery's Receiving Vault, and his burial at the cemetery was delayed until the Ninth New York Volunteers returned to New York City from the front.

On one side of the monument to Lieutenant Colonel Edgar Addison Kimball are listed the battles he fought in during the Mexican War (Contreras, Churubusco, Molino Del Rey, Chapultepec, and Carita De Belen) and on the opposite side the names of his Civil War battles (Roanoke, Camden, South Mountain, Antietam, and Fredericksburg) are carved.

BASEBALL'S FIRST STAR

IN THE LATE 1850's, Brooklyn was the hotbed of baseball. As the *Brooklyn Daily Eagle* observed, "Nowhere has the National game of Baseball taken a firmer hold than in Brooklyn and nowhere are there better ball players." But when a local boy, JAMES CREIGHTON (1841–1862), made his baseball debut in 1858 with the Brooklyn Niagaras, no one could

Jim Creighton, baseball's first star. Courtesy of the National Baseball Hall of Fame and Museum, Inc., Cooperstown, New York.

have known that he would soon become the first great baseball star.

At the time, baseball was still in its infancy, and the rules of the game barred pitchers from snapping their wrists when delivering a pitch to the plate. After all, a pitcher was supposed to make it easy for the batter to hit his pitches. Creighton would have none of that, and soon developed his "wrist throw," a low underhand delivery in which he snapped his wrist to throw his "speedballs," according to one observer, "as swift as [if] sent from a cannon," while also putting a spin on the ball. And, Creighton mixed in a few of his "dew drops," slow pitches which kept hitters off stride and made hitting against him even more difficult. Though some criticized this new style of pitching as illegal and unsportsmanlike, none could argue with Creighton's success as he won game after game.

Soon a bidding war broke out for James Creighton's services, with the top Brooklyn teams making their offers. Creighton signed with the Brooklyn Excelsiors in 1860, and led that team on baseball's first big barnstorming tour. As the Excelsiors played their way across upstate New York, Canada, Pennsylvania, Delaware, and Maryland, opposing pitchers began to copy Creighton's delivery. Baseball clubs were formed in the tour's wake and were often called the "Creightons" in his honor.

Jim Creighton was also a great hitter; he is said to have gone through an entire season without making an out. But ultimately his hitting killed him. On October 14, 1862, Creighton batted against the Unions of Morrisania. As he swung, he heard an unusual sound, and thought that his belt had "snapped." After circling the bases with a home run, he collapsed; his mighty swing had ruptured his bladder. Four days later Jim Creighton, baseball's first star, only twenty-one years old, died at his father's home at 307 Henry Street.

The Creighton Monument, as it appears today. Creighton's friends had this monument erected in his honor. Across its marble face are carved a pair of crossed bats, a base, a score book, and a scroll with "Excelsior" on it. Down-turned bats decorate its corners, but the marble baseball which topped the monument is long gone.

THE GOTHIC REVIVAL MAIN GATES

As GREEN-WOOD CEMETERY flourished in the late 1850's and the early 1860's, its trustees looked for ways to enhance its appearance. They decided that Green-Wood needed an appropriately-imposing entrance gate, and hired Richard Upjohn and Son to design it.

Upjohn was also an important supporter of Green-Wood Cemetery in its early years. When a public meeting was held in the 1840's to build enthusiasm for the fledgling cemetery, in the hopes of insuring its survival, Upjohn rose to speak in its support. By the time Upjohn was given the commission to draft the plans for the main gates, he had already designed the Receiving Vault and several cottages and shelters at Green-Wood Cemetery.

Upjohn, who was the architect of many important churches, including Brooklyn's Grace Church, reserved the Gothic Revival style, which he considered to be the best, for Episcopal churches; for other sects he built in Romanesque style. For Green-Wood's gates Upjohn chose Gothic Revival because of its upward, heavenly thrust (as would Cass Gilbert for the Woolworth Building half a century later).

In 1966, Green-Wood Cemetery's main gates were designated a New York City landmark. They are the only part of the cemetery which has that designation. In 2006, Green-Wood Cemetery was designated a National Historic Landmark by the Secretary of the Interior, only the fourth American cemetery to be so honored.

Richard Upjohn (1802–1878) was one of the most prominent architects in America. Born in England, he came to the United States in 1829, and went to work as a draftsman. Upjohn soon declared himself an architect, and began designing Greek Revival villas and Gothic Revival churches. It is Upjohn who is credited with introducing the Gothic Revival style to America. His greatest work is New York City's Trinity Church, completed in 1846 and still standing on Broadway at the head of Wall Street. A leader of his fledgling profession, Upjohn helped to found the American Institute of Architects and served as its president from 1857 to 1876.

Though Richard Upjohn had substantial ties to Green-Wood Cemetery, he ultimately chose to be buried elsewhere. However, his son, RICHARD MICHELL UPJOHN (1828–1903), who was born in England, trained as an architect by his father, and collaborated with him on Green-Wood Cemetery's main entrance gate, is interred there. He also worked with his father during the 1860's and 1870's on many churches; his own most famous work was the State Capitol in Hartford, Connecticut. A long-time resident of Brooklyn, he was president of the New York chapter of the American Institute of Architects and was a founder of the Long Island Historical Society.

The Main Gates were recently restored. Their flanking offices and reception areas, with their fine slate roofs, are still in use today.

The Gothic Revival style of architecture was, for historical reasons, associated with the birth of democracy, knights struggling for the Magna Carta, and the superiority of medieval Christianity. For nineteenth century Americans, this style was linked to the Christian contemplative life, and was particularly appropriate for the entrance to a rural cemetery, a sanctuary from the urban corruptions of the time.

Typical of Gothic Revival structures, these gates, built 1861–1863, have both symmetrical and asymmetrical features. The central towers and gates are balanced, but the flanking office wings are of different sizes and shapes. Pointed arches, battlements, steep slate roofs, towers, clustered columns, openwork gables, trefoils and quatrefoils, iron bannerettes, and foliated ornaments, are some of the Gothic Revival elements decorating these gates.

One architectural historian has called Green-Wood's main gates "the culmination of the Gothic Revival in New York." They rise 106 feet at their central spire and 90 feet on the two flanking tops. Resurrection is their theme, and the religious reliefs that adorn them, carved in Nova Scotia yellow sandstone by English-born sculptor John M. Moffitt, reflect this emphasis on rebirth in their titles: *Come Forth*, *The Dead Shall Be Raised*, *I Am the Resurrection and the Life*, and *Weep Not*. Still higher up on the gates are reliefs of Faith, Hope, Memory, and Love.

The gates are of red sandstone quarried in Belleville, New Jersey. This is the building material that Upjohn introduced to New York City in the 1840's, using it for Trinity Church. Popularly known as brownstone, it dominated New York City's and Brooklyn's streets for the rest of the century.

Brownstone has a tendency to flake (either because of fissures sustained while being blasted from the quarry or from being laid improperly with its grain exposed), and the gates have suffered that fate. Well-intentioned but poorly-thought-out efforts to "repair" the stone by coating it with a stucco have led to water retention and further deterioration, and, in 1995, this material was removed from the brownstone. A bell tops the gates, and that bell still sounds, as it has for over a century, to announce the arrival of the next funeral procession.

THE MOST MAGNIFICENT SOLDIER

Fitz-John Porter (1822–1901) was decorated for gallantry during the Mexican War, then taught cavalry drill and tactics at West Point. When the Civil War began, Porter went off to join the fight, and soon made a name for himself. He was described by John Hay, assistant private secretary to President Lincoln, as "the most magnificent soldier in the Army of the Potomac," and as "one of the best soldiers in all the Federal army" by an adversary, Confederate General Edward Porter Alexander. Like many of the officers who had served under their beloved General George McClellan, Porter, commander of the Fifth Corps, despised General John Pope, who had succeeded the timid "Mac." Porter, however, had the poor judgment to say so openly. After Second Bull Run, Pope charged Porter with disloyalty, disobedience, and misconduct in the face of the enemy for his refusal to attack as ordered. Porter, relieved of his command, was found guilty at a controversial court martial presided over by anti-McClellan officers. Most historians have concluded that Porter was a talented and dedicated officer whose offense was indiscretion in expressing his disdain for General Pope.

Cashiered from the Army and barred from holding any United States governmental position, Porter spent the ensuing years trying to clear his name. President Grant, convinced that the matter was a political hot potato, refused to reopen it. It was not until a rehearing before a board of officers in 1878, at which statements from Confederate Generals Lee,

Born in England in 1837, John M. Moffitt apprenticed at the age of fifteen to a London sculptor, and after completing his service came to New York City. One of his first commissions there, in the early 1860's, was for the figures for the main gates at Green-Wood Cemetery. With places of business on Hudson Street and West 14th Street, Moffitt advertised himself in New York City's 1871 directory as a sculptor and builder of "Vaults, Tombs, Monuments, Altars, Fonts & Tablets" whose "principal works" at Green-Wood Cemetery included the "Entrance Gateway," the Arctic Monument, the Steinway Vault, the Gordon Burnham Monument, the Thomas Read Monument, the Thomas C. Durant Vault, and the monument to Mrs. Alfred W. Craven. Moffitt also sculpted *The Four Ages of Man* for Green-Wood's Fort Hamilton Parkway entrance (also known as the Eastern Entrance). Many of the altars for the principal churches of New York City were Moffitt's work. He also executed the memorial reredos for the Packer Memorial Church in Mauch Chunk, Pennsylvania, designed the Soldiers' Monument for East Rock Park in New Haven, Connecticut, and the drum for the Yorktown Revolutionary Monument (erected in 1881). Moffitt died in London in 1887.

One wonders which "fight" is being referred to in Porter's epitaph: the Civil War, the effort to clear his name, or his life in general. Note the misspelling of Porter's first name, leaving out the hyphen.

General Fitz-John Porter assumes the Napoleonic pose which was so popular with Civil War officers. Courtesy of U.S.A.M.H.I.

Youth, *the first of the* Four Ages of Man *that adorn the nineteenth century visitors' lounge at Green-Wood Cemetery's Fort Hamilton Avenue entrance.*

Professor Thaddeus Lowe's observation balloon Intrepid *holds an observer aloft, allowing him to reconnoiter the enemy at Fair Oaks. This was the same balloon that carried General Porter on his unscheduled advance on Richmond.*

During the Civil War, as Union troops were stalled outside Richmond, General Fitz-John Porter went up in the observation balloon *Intrepid,* which was tethered 100 feet in the air, to check on the deployment of Confederate troops. However, as Porter settled in, the *Intrepid's* anchoring rope broke, and he drifted several miles behind Confederate lines before he was able to bring the balloon down. Union troops raced out and rescued Porter before the Confederates could capture him. It was later said that Fitz-John Porter advanced on Richmond in his balloon faster than any Union

Bronze bust of General Thomas Sweeny by James Kelly. Sweeny often was wounded in battle, but was never deterred. Green-Wood Historic Fund Collection. Gift of Benjamin Pietrobono.

Longstreet ("If you had attacked, we would surely have destroyed your army"), and other Confederate officers established that Porter was confronted by a much larger force in his front and chose to wait in a strong defensive position to be attacked rather than foolishly take the offensive against superior numbers, that Porter was exonerated. The board of officers concluded that

> Porter's faithful, subordinate, and intelligent conduct that afternoon saved the Union Army from the defeat which otherwise would have resulted. . . . We believe not one among all the gallant soldiers on that bloody field was less deserving of such condemnation than he.

Again, however, politics intruded, and it was not until 1886 that Porter was finally restored to the rank of colonel, without back pay.

After the War, Porter declined an offer from the Khedive to command the Egyptian army. He served instead in the post-war years as New York City's Commissioner of Public Works, Police Commissioner, and Fire Commissioner, and died in 1901.

NOT WOUNDED, FOR A CHANGE

G ENERAL THOMAS SWEENY (1820–1892) lost his right arm to a bullet during the Mexican War. This, however, did not prevent him from becoming as daring a leader as there was on either side during the Civil War. Sweeny, throwing caution to the wind, persisted in leading his men into battle, and was wounded nearly every time he did so. General Ulysses S. Grant, aware of Sweeny's reputation, saw him unscathed after one battle and could not resist: "How is it, Sweeny,

Thomas Sweeny's Monument.

that you have not been hit? There must be some mistake. This fight will hardly count unless you can show another wound."

The action that Sweeny saw during the Civil War, however, was apparently not enough for him. Mustered out of federal service in August, 1865, he was elected Secretary of War of the Irish Republic by the Fenian Congress. In an effort to bring pressure on the British to free Ireland, he led a force of Irish-Americans north to capture Canada. The invasion was a fiasco, and for his efforts he was arrested, but soon released, by United States officials.

A PROFILE IN COURAGE

I N EARLY 1861, in an effort to appease Southern secessionists and preserve the Union, Congress approved a version of the Thirteenth Amendment to the Constitution that protected slavery in the States against any future interference by the federal government. However, before the States could ratify that amendment, the Civil War broke out, and that proposal was shelved.

By 1864, great changes had occurred in the United States, and a very different Thirteenth Amendment was then being considered by Congress. This amendment, if enacted, would outlaw slavery. JOHN BROOKS HENDERSON (1826–1913), United States Senator from Missouri, was convinced that the Thirteenth Amendment only could become law if it was sponsored in the Senate by a border-state senator. He decided that he would be that Senator, even though he was convinced that this sponsorship would be so unpopular back in Missouri that it would destroy his political career. Ultimately, Henderson's strategy for passage of the Thirteenth Amendment paid off with its enactment into law. But, sadly, his judgment concerning the consequences of his action also was proven correct: though he ran for governor in 1872, and for Senator the next year, he was defeated in both elections and his political career was over.

John Brooks Henderson, U.S. Senator from Missouri, who sponsored the Thirteenth Amendment to end slavery even though he believed that his sponsorship would doom him politically. His wife, MARY FOOTE HENDERSON (1842–1931), a native New Yorker who was president of the Missouri Suffrage Association (1876), organized the St. Louis School of Design (1876) and the Woman's Exchange (1879), and wrote Practical Cooking and Dinner-Giving *(1876), is beside him in her family's tomb.* Dictionary of American Portraits, *Dover Publications.*

HERE A GENERAL, THERE A GENERAL . . .

HENRY WAGER HALLECK (1815–1872), who served as General-in-Chief of all Union Armies during the Civil War, was by all accounts a man of great intellect; his nickname, "Old Brains," recognized this. However, Halleck was also an unsuccessful military leader because of his excessive caution and aloofness. Though his *Elements of Military Arts and Sciences* (1846) became the authoritative manual for officers during the Civil War on the art of war, Halleck had a poor grasp of field tactics and rarely ventured into combat. His brusque personality earned him more enemies than friends; President Abraham Lincoln said of him, "I am Halleck's friend because he has no others."

Interestingly, of the eighteen Civil War generals buried at Green-Wood Cemetery, four are buried within a few feet of each other. Halleck married ELIZABETH HAMILTON (1831–1884), the granddaughter of Alexander Hamilton, in 1855. General GEORGE WASHINGTON CULLUM (1809–1892) is interred in the same plot. Early in the Civil War, Cullum was commissioned brigadier general of volunteers, and served as chief of staff to General Halleck when the latter was General-in-Chief of the armies. Cullum also directed engineering operations on the western rivers and was chief of engineers during the siege of Corinth. He served on the U.S. Sanitary Commission and was the superintendent of the U.S. Military Academy from 1864 to 1866. In 1865, Cullum was brevetted major general. After Cullum retired from active service in 1874, he married Henry Halleck's widow; she is interred between her two husbands, Halleck and Cullum.

Elizabeth Hamilton's brother, GENERAL SCHUYLER HAMILTON (1822–1903), left his farm when the Civil War began and volunteered as a private in the famed Seventh New York, soon becoming military secretary to General Winfield Scott, who was the General-in-Chief. When Scott retired, Hamilton, with the rank of colonel, was assigned as assistant chief

General-in-Chief Henry Wager Halleck. Green-Wood Historic Fund Collection.

Photograph of General George Washington Cullum, by Matthew Brady. Green-Wood Historic Fund Collection.

General Schuyler Hamilton. Courtesy of U.S.A.M.H.I.

Confederate General Nathaniel Harrison Harris, a native of Mississippi, had ties to New York; members of his family lived on Washington Square, in New York City. Courtesy of U.S.A.M.H.I.

of staff to General Halleck, his brother-in-law. Hamilton was commissioned brigadier general in November of 1861, and given command of the Department of St. Louis. He commanded his division so well that he was promoted to major general in 1862, but was forced to resign when stricken by malaria. Hamilton is interred just two lots from his sister and Generals Halleck and Cullum.

And, just a few feet away from the final resting place of these three generals, perhaps to balance things a bit, is Confederate General NATHANIEL HARRISON HARRIS (1834–1900), a native of Vicksburg, Mississippi, who was known as a hard-hitting combat officer. Harris fought at Seven Days, Second Bull Run, and Antietam, led his regiment at Chancellorsville (where they took part in Stonewall Jackson's flank attack) and Gettysburg, took command of Mahone's Division late in the war, and surrendered it at Appomattox.

Elizabeth Schuyler Hamilton reposes between her husbands, General Halleck and General Cullum.

ATOP THE UNITED STATES CAPITOL, THE STATUE OF *FREEDOM*

WHEN HE was commissioned in 1855 to create the statue of *Freedom* for the United States Capitol's dome, THOMAS CRAWFORD (1813–1857) already had a substantial reputation as a sculptor, and had designed the sculptural grouping for the east pediment of the United States Senate wing. Working in his Rome studio on what he called *Freedom Triumphant in War and Peace*, the expatriate New Yorker completed a full-size plaster model of his work shortly before dying from a tumor behind his eye.

The next year, Crawford's model was shipped from Italy aboard a leaking ship that eventually was condemned, and it was a year before the model's five sections finally arrived safely in Washington, D.C. The colossal statue was cast in bronze from 1860 to 1862 by Clark Mills at a foundry on the outskirts of that city. Ironically, this cast of *Freedom* was produced by slave labor. It weighed over seven tons, was 19'6" tall, and stood atop a pedestal of almost the same height. Erected in sections, the final piece of the head and shoulders was placed atop the Capitol on December 2, 1863, and a crowd looked on as Crawford's work was honored at noon that day by the firing of thirty-five guns, a salute answered by cannon volleys from the twelve forts protecting Washington from Confederate attack during the then-raging Civil War.

The statue of *Freedom* completed the Capitol's modern silhouette. President Lincoln had insisted that this work continue while the war raged;

completion was intended to symbolize the Union's ability to proceed with its business despite the strain of war.

Freedom is portrayed as a mythical Roman female with long flowing hair under a star-encircled helmet. Crawford had originally intended to top his female figure with a liberty cap. However, at the suggestion of Secretary of War (and soon-to-be Confederate President) Jefferson Davis, who pointed out that the cap that Crawford had designed was of the style worn by ancient Roman slaves who had been freed, and would thus be a provocation to the South, Crawford changed the headgear to a feathered helmet. The crest of eagle's head, talon, and feathers are references to Indian dress. *Freedom* wears a tunic secured by a brooch inscribed "U.S." and a toga decorated with balls and fringe. Her right hand is on the hilt of a sheathed sword, ready but restrained, and her left hand holds a laurel wreath of victory and a striped shield of the United States. Crawford, concerned that the symbolism of his great work be fully understood by the People, described it this way:

> I have said the statue represents "armed Liberty." She rests upon the shield of our country, the triumph of which is made apparent by the wreath held in the same hand which grasps the shield; in her right hand she holds the sheathed sword, to show the fight is over for the present, but ready for use whenever required. The stars upon her brow indicate her heavenly origin; her position upon the globe represents her protection of the *American* world—the justice of whose cause is made apparent by the emblems supporting it.

On May 9, 1993, the statue of *Freedom* was removed by helicopter from its perch atop the Capitol for repair. After extensive restoration it was airlifted back to its place of honor on October 23, 1993.

A bust of Thomas Crawford, sculpted by Tommaso Gagliardi in 1871, is in the Capitol. Crawford, to whom this tribute is paid for his contributions to the decoration of the Capitol, is the only sculptor so honored.

Sculptor Thomas Crawford, who designed the statue of Freedom *which adorns the Capitol, was one of America's most important early sculptors; he died at the height of his career.* Dictionary of American Portraits, *Dover Publications.*

Thomas Crawford's Freedom *is shown, in this rare photograph from 1863, being placed atop the Capitol dome.*

Freedom, *standing atop the United States Capitol since the Civil War, has long enjoyed a spectacular view of Washington, D.C.*

[89]

I

N 1848, LAURA KEENE (1826–1873) made her stage debut at the Lyceum Theatre in London, and quickly became a popular comedic performer. She made her first appearance on an American stage in 1852, and within a few years became the first woman in America to manage a substantial theatre. From 1855 until 1864, she managed Laura Keene's, the Metropolitan and Olympic Theatres in New York City, doing virtually everything that had to be done to run a theatre, from painting scenery to writing scripts to playing the female lead. Known as "The Duchess" for her firm management, Laura Keene made important contributions to the theatre, making the matinee performance a regular theatre feature and introducing the long run for a hit show.

Keene was also the first producer of *Our American Cousin* in America, and it became a hit and her most famous production. On Good Friday, April 14, 1865, she was starring in that show at Ford's Theatre in Washington, D.C., and was making plans to celebrate her one thousandth performance, when word came that President Abraham Lincoln would be attending the performance that night. That fateful night, Lincoln was assassinated by John Wilkes Booth. It was Laura Keene who recognized fellow-actor Booth as he limped across the stage after the shooting, who announced to the audience that the President had been shot and urged it to remain calm, who brought water to the wounded Lincoln, and who held his head in her lap as he lay mortally wounded. After the dying President was carried across the street to the Petersen House, Keene sat in the front room there with the hysterical Mary Todd Lincoln, trying to calm her.

Laura Keene, the theatrical pioneer who was thrust into the middle of historic events at Ford's Theatre on April 14, 1865.

Actor DAVID CHRISTIAN ANDERSON (1824–1894) toured as far away as Australia with Laura Keene and Edwin Booth, the dean of American actors. Anderson's stone at Green-Wood Cemetery, paid for by Booth, uses theatre imagery to honor him.

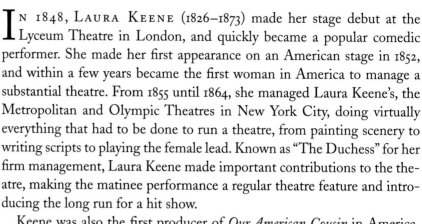

The playbill for Ford's Theatre, April 14, 1865, the night President Abraham Lincoln was assassinated by John Wilkes Booth. Note that the largest type on the playbill was reserved for Laura Keene's name; she was a "big name star." The small print below her name described her as "The Distinguished Manageress, Authoress, and Actress." The April 14 performance was a benefit which was to be the last of that run.

Laura Keene's Green-Wood Cemetery monument.

On April 14, 1861, Fort Sumter was surrendered to rebel forces. The next day, President Abraham Lincoln called for troops to hurry to Washington, D.C., to defend the nation's capital. Colonel Lefferts immediately reported to New York State's governor that the famed Seventh Regiment was "ready to march forthwith." The following afternoon the Seventh paraded down Broadway, on its way south, to wild cheers. That scene, as the regiment passed Prince Street, is depicted in this Thomas Nast painting. On the balcony of the Ball, Black & Co. building at left stands Major Robert Anderson, who less than a week earlier had surrendered Fort Sumter to Confederate forces. Colonel Lefferts is at the far left of the officers marching at the head of the regiment. The Seventh was one of the first units to arrive in Washington, D.C., and helped to protect it from Confederate attack. *The Departure of the Seventh Regiment to the War, April 19, 1861.* Courtesy of The Seventh Regiment Fund, Inc., New York City.

AT THE HEAD OF THE SEVENTH REGIMENT

MARSHALL LEFFERTS (1821–1876) began his part-time military career as a private in New York's famed Seventh Regiment, a unit composed of the wealthy and social elite of New York City. He was soon elected lieutenant colonel, and was in command when the Seventh marched down Broadway, the first regiment to leave New York City for duty at the outbreak of the Civil War.

On April 14, 1861, Fort Sumter, after a Confederate barrage, surrendered. The next day, President Abraham Lincoln issued a call for 75,000 militia men to enter national service for ninety days and to come to Washington to defend it. When the 6th Massachusetts Regiment, the first fully-equipped unit to respond, entered Baltimore on April 19, it was attacked by Southern sympathizers. Four soldiers and twelve citizens were killed. To prevent further reinforcements, Baltimore's mayor and chief of police ordered the destruction of railroad bridges and telegraph lines. Washington was cut off, and rumors spread that Virginia regiments and Maryland men were closing in. Washington civilians were formed into companies, public buildings were sandbagged, and the Treasury was made ready for a

Colonel Marshall Lefferts, leader of the Seventh Regiment. Lefferts also helped to survey the City of Brooklyn (Marshall Street, just south of the Brooklyn Navy Yard, was named for him) and Green-Wood Cemetery, and served as president of several telegraph companies. Green-Wood Historic Fund Collection.

General Abram Duryée. Green-Wood Historic Fund Collection.

ABRAM DURYÉE (1815–1890) was another well-known amateur soldier who started his military career with New York's Seventh Regiment and made a name for himself during the Civil War. Beginning his military career as a member of the State Militia in 1833, he had risen to colonel of the nationally-famous Seventh Regiment by 1849. In the ensuing decade he was called out with the Seventh to quell a series of New York City riots. At the outset of the Civil War, in less than one week, he raised the Fifth New York Volunteers, popularly known as "Duryée's Zouaves," a regiment of 940 men. Duryée led the advance toward Big Bethel and afterwards was commissioned brigadier general, with command of 13,000 troops in Baltimore. He took part in the Battle of Cedar Mountain and led his troops in successful efforts to delay overwhelming Confederate forces at Gaines' Mill and Second Bull Run, where he was twice wounded. He commanded a division at Antietam, and though his men fought gallantly there, they were shot to pieces in the Cornfield, with Duryée suffering three wounds. After he took a thirty-day leave of absence in order to regain his health, he returned to find that his command had been split up, and he had been passed over for promotion. His protests proved futile, and he resigned. The 165th and 4th Regiments of the New York National Guard also bore his name. After the war, Duryée was brevetted major general of volunteers. He was appointed Police Commissioner of New York City in 1873, and served in that position for many years.

FITZ JAMES O'BRIEN (1828–1862), an Irish immigrant writer/brawler who was a leader of New York City's bohemian circle in the years before the Civil War, enlisted as a private in the famed Seventh Regiment when Lincoln issued his first call for troops. O'Brien wrote about the change for many of the men from their society life at home to the life of a soldier:

We are here. . . . Dandies, who were the pride of club windows, were not above brown paper parcels. . . . Delmonico, calm and serene, superintended sandwiches. . . . Fellows who would at Delmonico's have sent back a turban de volaille aux truffes because the truffes were tough, here cheerfully took their places in file between decks, tin plates and tin cups in hand, in order to get an insufficient piece of beef and a vision of coffee.

Efforts were made to soften the impact of military life on the men; always traveling first class, the Seventh went off to war with 1,000 velvet-carpeted footstools from Tiffany & Co. But those efforts were unavailing: the footstools somehow got waylaid in shipment, and the men of the Seventh never received them.

In 1862, O'Brien was wounded in the shoulder during a skirmish. Tetanus set in and he died. H. L. Mencken claimed that O'Brien was the only significant artist killed during the Civil War.

final defense. Lincoln looked north: "Why don't they come?" When he visited wounded troops of the 6th Massachusetts on April 24, the President was desperate: "I don't believe there is any North. The Seventh Regiment is a myth. Rhode Island is not known in our geography any longer. You are the only Northern realities." But, the next day the Seventh arrived, followed by other militia units, and Washington was safe.

With the title of general, Lefferts served as military governor of the Frederick, Maryland, district. He also commanded the Seventh when it was ordered, along with other regiments, to restore order to New York City during the Draft Riots of July, 1863.

After the war, Lefferts was chosen commandant of the Veteran Corps of the Seventh Regiment. On July 3, 1876, he set out by train for Philadelphia, intending to march at the head of his men in the great military procession planned for the one hundredth anniversary of the Declaration of Independence. He was not well, however, and died on the train ride.

MEDAL OF HONOR

ON MAY 15, 1864, at Resaca, Georgia, while commanding a brigade, Captain PAUL AMBROSE OLIVER (1830–1912) of Company D, 12th New York Infantry, "assisted in preventing a disaster caused by Union troops firing into each other." That other brigade was commanded by Benjamin Harrison, and when Harrison was elected President, Oliver was awarded the Congressional Medal of Honor for his heroism.

Later in the Civil War, Oliver was ordered to the headquarters of the Union Army by General U. S. Grant, and he rendered "invaluable and highly meritorious" service at Appomattox, where he took part in the paroling of the Confederate Army of Northern Virginia. He was brevetted brigadier general in May 1865.

After the war, Oliver established a gunpowder factory in Wilkes-Barre,

Pennsylvania, and introduced many improvements of his own invention to the manufacture of explosives. He is widely credited with inventing dynamite and black powder, though this is controversial because others made the same discoveries at about the same time.

Oliver is one of thirteen Medal of Honor recipients buried at Green-Wood; eleven won their awards for acts of heroism during the Civil War, one during the Spanish-American War, and one during the Boxer Rebellion.

Paul Ambrose Oliver, Congressional Medal of Honor winner who may have invented dynamite and black powder. Courtesy Wyoming Historical and Geological Society and Dictionary of American Portraits, *Dover Publications.*

The most prominent of the other Medal of Honor winners at Green-Wood Cemetery is BENJAMIN FRANKLIN TRACY (1830–1915). In 1862, as the Civil War heated up, he recruited New York State's 109th and 137th Regiments, becoming colonel of the former. Tracy led a regiment at the Wilderness, seizing the colors and spearheading four charges on the Confederate works, and at Spottsylvania, where exhaustion forced him to surrender command. His gallantry at the Wilderness earned him the Congressional Medal of Honor. In September, 1864, he was appointed colonel of the 127th U.S. Colored Troops. Soon thereafter, he assumed command of the prison camp at Elmira, New York, where 10,000 Confederates were held. He was brevetted brigadier general of Volunteers in March, 1865.

After the war, Tracy practiced law, was appointed United States Attorney for the Eastern District of New York, and served as a judge of the New York State Court of Appeals from 1881 to 1883.

In 1889, Tracy was appointed Secretary of the Navy by President Harrison, and became known as "The Father of the Fighting Navy;" virtually every important ship that took part in the Spanish-American War, including the first great battleships, were built while he was Secretary.

Tracy chaired the commission that, in 1896, drafted the charter for Greater New York, and ran unsuccessfully as the Republican candidate for mayor of New York City. His funeral was attended by thousands.

The memorial to Benjamin Franklin Tracy.

YOUR PRISON CELL IS RIGHT THIS WAY . . .

Two *Brooklyn Eagle* newspapermen, JOSEPH HOWARD, JR. (1833–1908) and FRANCIS MALLISON (1833–1877), were convinced that they had a can't-miss scheme to get rich during the Civil War. Any fool knew that every time President Lincoln ordered a new draft of Union recruits, the price of gold skyrocketed. Howard's and Mallison's plan was simple: buy gold, then create a bogus report that Lincoln had issued a new call for troops, have the New York newspapers publish the "news," and watch their investment take off.

There was only one problem with their scheme: it didn't work. In May, 1864, as planned, they circulated to New York City's newspapers their phony Presidential proclamation, announcing a draft of 400,000 men and

Benjamin Franklin Tracy, Medal of Honor winner and Secretary of the Navy.

Joseph Howard, Jr., in a photograph taken in the 1890's, long after his Civil War escapade.

calling for a day of fasting, over the bogus signatures of Abraham Lincoln and Secretary of State William H. Seward. The *World* and the *Journal of Commerce* rushed out extras announcing the new draft. A huge crowd gathered outside the newspaper offices, demanding that the proclamation be rescinded. Every available policeman was rushed to the scene, and the garrison on Governor's Island was called to arms.

But the night editor of *The Times* was suspicious, believing that he would recognize the handwriting in such an important Associated Press announcement. Checking further, he discovered that, mysteriously, the *Herald* had never received a copy of this proclamation, that it had not arrived in an Associated Press envelope, and the delivery boy who brought it had left at once. An inquiry to the Associated Press confirmed his suspicions: "The 'Proclamation' is false as hell and not promulgated through this office. The handwriting is not familiar." Extra editions were rushed out again, this time announcing that the proclamation was a hoax. The Associated Press offered a reward for the conviction of the individual behind the hoax.

President Lincoln angrily ordered Major General John Dix, Commander of the New York Department, to close down the two newspapers that had printed the phony proclamation and to imprison their owners. Dix, believing that these editors had been duped, ordered their newspapers closed, but did not arrest them.

But arrests did follow. Howard, who had been predicting that the price of gold was about to soar, was arrested by the police and soon confessed. He and his cohort, Mallison, were imprisoned in Fort Lafayette, the notorious island fortress in New York Harbor where Confederate prisoners of war, Peace Democrats, bounty jumpers, blockade runners, and spies were held.

Mallison, on the strength of a plea from his ill mother, was soon pardoned by Lincoln. But, when Howard's friends appealed for his release, President Lincoln is said to have replied, "Be quiet, it will blow over." It did blow over, and Howard was released after fourteen weeks of confinement. Lincoln, never one to bear a grudge, soon appointed Howard official recorder at military headquarters of the Department of the East.

MARCHING THROUGH GEORGIA, THEN ON TO BROOKLYN

HENRY WARNER SLOCUM (1827–1894), soldier, Union general, and politician, was born in Delphi, New York, graduated from the United States Military Academy in 1852, and saw action during the Seminole War. Resigning from the Army to practice law in Syracuse, New York, he served as county treasurer, State legislator, and colonel and artillery instructor in the State militia.

When the Civil War began, Slocum was appointed colonel of the 27th New York Infantry, and was severely wounded at First Bull Run. In 1861, he was commissioned brigadier general of volunteers, and was promoted to major general the next year. Slocum fought at Second Bull Run, South Mountain, Antietam, and Chancellorsville, and commanded the extreme right flank of the Union Army (the point of the fishhook on Culp's Hill) at Gettysburg. When his XII Corps was ordered to join General Joseph Hooker's Army of the Tennessee, Slocum, who had been angry at Hooker since Chancellorsville, offered his resignation. However, it was refused, and Slocum was given the command of the District of Vicksburg. In 1864, Slocum took command of the Army of Georgia and joined Sherman for the March to the Sea. It was Slocum's men who were the first Union troops to enter Atlanta.

After the war, Slocum returned to Brooklyn, where he practiced law and was active in civic affairs. Three times elected to Congress (1868, 1870, 1882), he also served as the president of the Brooklyn Board of City Works and was a member of the Gettysburg Monument Commission. Slocum

Henry Slocum in his Civil War uniform. Courtesy of U.S.A.M.H.I.

Hancock at Gettysburg, oil on canvas by THURE DE THULSTRUP (1848–1930), 1886, Courtesy of The Seventh Regiment Fund, Inc., New York City. Born in Stockholm, Sweden, into a military family (his father was Swedish Minister of War from 1850 to 1861), Thulstrup graduated from the National Military Academy there. In 1870, he went to Paris, was commissioned an officer in the French Foreign Legion, served in Algeria, and fought against Germany in 1871. After studying drawing in Paris, he immigrated to Canada in the early 1870's, worked there and in New England as a topographical engineer, then settled in New York City, where he painted scenes from American battles.

This painting shows General Winfield Scott Hancock rallying the II Corps to turn back Pickett's Charge at Gettysburg. It was one of several paintings which Thulstrup created for a print series that was published by Louis Prang. Typical of Thulstrup's work, it contains a multitude of figures and extraordinary detail.

Thulstrup also worked as an illustrator for the *New York Daily Graphic*, *Harper's Weekly* (under the aegis of cartoonist Thomas Nast), and *Frank Leslie's Illustrated Weekly Newspaper*. After Thulstrup's wife died in 1915, his eyesight began to fail, and he lived out the last nine years of his life at the Episcopal Home for Old Men and Aged Couples.

Henry Slocum was badly wounded at First Bull Run; this memorial honors William Moir Smith, who died in Richmond, Virginia, from wounds he received during that battle.

Caspar Trepp finally has a stone marking his grave.

was also a member of the board of trustees of the Brooklyn Bridge and pushed to make it toll-free. He took an active role in the defense of General FITZ-JOHN PORTER, delivering a speech in Congress in 1884 urging Porter's exoneration twenty years after he had been found guilty at a court martial. Slocum also served as president of the Coney Island and Brooklyn Railroad Company and the Brooklyn Club, and was a founder of the Soldiers' Home in Bath, New York.

THE ULTIMATE SACRIFICE

BORN IN SWITZERLAND, CASPAR TREPP (1829–1863) received military training and served as an officer in the British Foreign Legion from 1848 to 1857 before settling in New York City. When the Civil War began, Trepp volunteered for service, helped to organize two regiments of Berdan's Sharpshooters, and was commissioned captain of Company A, First United States Sharpshooters, on August 20, 1861.

Hiram Berdan organized the U.S. Sharpshooters, 1st and 2nd Regiments, from experienced marksmen. They were armed with the best weapon available, the .52 caliber breech-loading Sharps rifle, and it was often equipped with a telescopic sight. With camouflage in mind, the men were dressed in green kepis and uniform blouses, with blue pants (later changed to green) and canvas or leather leggings. By the end of 1864, the Sharpshooters had been so decimated that they were consolidated into a single regiment; by early 1865, they were dispersed to other units.

Trepp spent two years in the field, often skirmishing, and took part in the Battles of Second Bull Run, Chancellorsville, and Gettysburg. During his service, he was promoted to major and then lieutenant colonel. On November 30, 1863, at Mine Run, Virginia, Trepp was shot through the head and killed by a Confederate sniper. He was buried in a crude coffin on the battlefield in front of his entire regiment, later reinterred on a farm at Brandy Station, and finally brought back to New York at his wife's request. Trepp's brigade commander described him as "an officer of the highest merit and one whose military knowledge and achievements have long been the admiration of all who knew him."

Forty-nine days after Trepp's death, his wife Harriet died of typhoid fever, and the Trepps' orphaned children, ages six, four, and two, were eventually separated.

Caspar Trepp lay in an unmarked grave at Green-Wood Cemetery for more than a century. In 1988, through the efforts of a reenactment unit, Berdan's Sharpshooters, Company B, First Regiment U.S. Sharpshooters, and Congressman Charles Schumer, a stone was placed to mark his grave.

THE NEWS THAT KILLED HIM

DR. VALENTINE MOTT (1785–1865) was the greatest surgeon of his time. Yet his medical training was of no help to him when he received the shock of his life.

On the morning of April 15, 1865, as was his habit, Dr. Mott sent for his barber. When the barber arrived, he asked Mott if he had heard the terrible news. Dr. Mott said he had not, and was then told that President Lincoln had been mortally wounded the night before at a theatre in Washington. Dr. Mott immediately turned pale, began violently trembling, and staggered into his bedroom, where he shared the shocking news with his wife. Unable to speak further, he sagged into a chair, barely able to sit. Acute pains coursed through his back, and all energy drained from him. He was helped to bed, grew weaker day by day, and died on April 26. His cause of death was listed as "mortification."

A contemporary woodcut of Dr. Mott, as he reports the shocking news of Lincoln's assassination to his wife just before he is stricken.

MURDER . . . AND SPIRITS

IN JULY, 1842, the country's attention turned to John Anderson's tobacco store when Mary Cecilia Rogers, the "Beautiful Seegar Girl" who worked there, disappeared. Three days later, her bruised body was found floating in the Hudson River. Though the murder of Mary Rogers was never solved, it had important ramifications. Her death was the first murder investigation to be sensationalized by New York's tabloid newspapers and to be covered on an ongoing basis by them. Two laws were enacted in 1845, as a direct result of Mary Rogers's death: the Police Reform Act, which modernized New York City's Police Department, and the New York State law that made abortion a crime (rumors that Mary Rogers had had an abortion were rampant). Her story became the basis for Edgar Allan Poe's *The Mystery of Marie Roget*, his sequel to *The Murders in the Rue Morgue*.

Valentine Mott's impressive hillside mausoleum is protected by an elaborate cast iron gate.

Tobacconist JOHN ANDERSON (1812–1881) met Mary Rogers in 1837, when Mary and her mother came to New York City and boarded in his house for a year. Anderson hired Mary, in 1838, to work in his thriving Broadway tobacco shop, which was centrally located near City Hall and specialized in "fine cut" chewing tobacco glossily packaged as "Anderson's Solace Tobacco." Young and comely, she was there to attract male customers; it was, according to an account of the time, a "recently adopted practice of hiring pretty girls as clerks in cigar stores for the purpose of attracting 'men about town'." With Mary working at Anderson's shop, it became a gathering place for New York's young sports.

When Mary's body was discovered, Anderson became one of the prime suspects in her killing, and was arrested, held briefly, and interrogated. Of the several suspects who were arrested and questioned, only Anderson made a statement to the police which never appeared in the press; both his arrest and his statement were hushed up by influential Tammany politicians who intervened on his behalf. Nevertheless, Anderson's arrest prevented him, a powerful and respected merchant, from later being nominated by Tammany Hall for mayor of New York City. Anderson supplied Poe with information for *The Mystery of Marie Roget*; some have speculated that he did so in order to deflect attention from himself.

After Anderson's death in 1881, his daughter, hoping to claim an estate

This engraving, probably made years after her death, shows Mary Rogers's body floating in the Hudson River.

The was the view from John Anderson's tomb, circa 1890, with Green-Wood Cemetery's main gates to the left, and New York's ship-filled harbor in the distance.

John Anderson's Greek Revival tomb, in the form of a Greek temple, was built in the early 1860's. Greek Revival architecture, sometimes referred to as "columnar," was particularly popular in America in the 1830's and 1840's. It conjured up America's role as the successor to ancient Greece as the bastion of democratic ideals, and was associated with the latest social movements. This architectural style is particularly appropriate for Anderson's tomb, for he used his great wealth to support a variety of progressive causes, including that of his close friend, the Italian patriot Garibaldi. During the Civil War, when Jersey City lacked funds to put its troops in the field, Anderson sent $60,000 (almost $1.4 million today) to its mayor so that it could do so. In 1873, when renowned Professor Louis Agassiz was denied funding by the Massachusetts Legislature for a school to instruct teachers in natural history, Anderson gave him $50,000 for that purpose. Greek Revival features of this tomb include its fluted columns, Ionic capitals, pilasters, pedimented gable, heavy cornices with unadorned friezes, and horizontal transoms. The four statuettes, two in front and two in back, are of the evangelists, Matthew, Mark, Luke, and John, and are signed by their sculptor, John M. Moffitt.

that included the land under the Plaza Hotel, contested his will, claiming that he was insane when he signed it. Though the suit was ultimately settled, the testimony at trial revealed some strange goings on.

The daughter's attorney, in an effort to prove Anderson's incapacity, focused on Anderson's obsession with Mary Rogers. Testimony indicated that Anderson was a believer in Spiritualism, and that he was regularly visited by Mary Rogers's ghost, with whom he spoke. According to former State Senator Abner Mattoon, Anderson said Mary "appeared to him in the spirit from time to time," and that Anderson had many, *very* many, unhappy days and nights in regard to her." Other testimony had Anderson relying on Mary Rogers's spirit for stock market tips.

Nor were Anderson's strange thoughts limited to Mary. He believed that his house was haunted and held seances with the ghost of his friend Garibaldi (whom Anderson had supported financially in his battle to unify Italy, and to whom Anderson had paid a stipend until his death). One witness swore that when Anderson was his house guest, Anderson woke him up to ask if they could remain together until sunrise; "things were after him." Another time this witness had seen Anderson run out of his house only partially clothed. Anderson told him that his dead son Willie also roamed his house. Later, another witness, called to defend Anderson's sanity, testified that Anderson did indeed say his house was haunted, but "by people who want money."

Anderson also believed that people were trying to kill him. He offered a friend $100,000 to prevent the conspiracy against him. Anderson kept a wary eye on his cook, making sure she did not put pins in his food.

Few, if any, tombs in Green-Wood Cemetery have a better location than John Anderson's. From its portico, not far from the main gates, spectacular views of New York Harbor and the Manhattan skyline unfold in the distance. But perhaps best of all for John Anderson's purposes, its commanding position offers him fair warning when any spirits, including Mary Rogers's, may try to approach.

CHRISTY'S MINSTRELS

Growing up in New Orleans, Edwin P. Christy (1815–1862) saw blacks entertaining in that city's Congo Square section. In 1842, drawing upon these observations, he organized the Christy's Minstrels, and altered the way in which minstrel shows were presented, introducing the use of white musicians wearing "black face" make-up while they performed jig dancing and magic acts. Performing as E. P. Christy, he was the interlocutor who stood in the middle of the line of performers and carried on conversations with the end men. He also wrote some songs and purchased others from prominent writers, including *Old Folks at Home* from Stephen Foster. His troupe toured the West and South, met with great success in New York and London, and became the world's most famous blackface group.

His fame was so great that other troupes began to call themselves the "Christy Minstrels," and E.P. was forced to buy warning advertisements and to bring lawsuits to prevent this use of his name. However, despite his efforts, minstrel troupes touring Europe were generically referred to as "Christy Minstrels."

In 1854, after the departure of key player George Christy, and in ill health, E.P. retired with his fortune. On May 21, 1862, while "temporarily insane," he jumped to his death from the second-story window of his New York City residence.

Thomas Dartmouth Rice (1806–1860), the "Father of American Minstrelsy," began his career in blackfaced minstrelsy in 1832, and soon became a sensation, playing to packed houses throughout the East. When he premiered in London, the press agreed that his performance was the theatrical novelty of the year. Enjoying extended engagements in England, he was the first blackface performer to gain international renown. His hit songs, such as *Jump Jim Crow* and *Virginia Mummy*, to which he shuffle-danced in the character of "Daddy" Rice, were hummed and whistled throughout America and Europe. In tribute to Rice, men wore "Jim Crow" hats and smoked "Jim Crow" pipes; his figure, carved in wood, appeared in front of many shops. Rice's tremendous success, along with that of Edwin Christy and others, made black-faced minstrelsy the most popular form of American entertainment between 1840 and 1880. However, Rice spent freely, drank some, and squandered his fortune. His career ended abruptly when he was paralyzed by a stroke; no longer able to dance, his last stage role, ironically, was that of Uncle Tom, which he played for only two nights before falling asleep on stage and getting himself fired. Rice died in poverty, and his burial at Green-Wood Cemetery, in what is now an unmarked grave, was paid for by public contributions. All of New York's minstrels, except Edwin Christy, financed what became one of the city's largest theatrical funerals; Christy, a notorious tightwad, refused to contribute. *Dictionary of American Portraits*, Dover Publications.

Edwin P. Christy, the founder of the famous Christy's Minstrels, in an 1848 lithograph designed and drawn by Napoleon Sarony.

Along Grape Avenue.

CHAPTER FOUR

The Post-Civil War Period
(1866-1875)

THE SOLDIERS' MONUMENT

ERECTED IN 1869, Green-Wood Cemetery's Soldiers' Monument honors the 148,000 New York men who fought "in aid of the war for the preservation of the Union and the Constitution." It gives voice to two themes: the sacrifice of the Republic's citizen-soldiers, and the unity, stability, and prosperity with which the nation hoped to emerge from the Civil War. The Soldiers' Monument's subject is typical for public, monumental sculpture: uncontroversial myths of civic community.

Because construction of the Soldiers' Monument began only four years after the end of the Civil War, it is an historical oddity. Monuments to that war, particularly those on a large scale, were more typically erected much later, in the 1880's and 1890's, when the pain and anguish from the hostilities were beginning to fade, replaced by the rosy glow of nostalgia. The monument was dedicated in 1876.

Interestingly, the molds for the four life-size soldiers who surround the central shaft, representing the four branches of army service, were used more than once. In 1866, New York City erected a Civil War monument at Calvary Cemetery in Queens. Monument maker John G. Draddy, working at Calvary from a design created by James Godwin Batterson (who also designed the obelisk to General Worth on Fifth Avenue and Broadway and monuments at the battlefields of Antietam and Gettysburg), grouped the same four military figures around a granite obelisk. The central column at Green-Wood is capped; the obelisk at Calvary is topped by the figure of Peace. The figures at Green-Wood, cast from the bronze of captured Confederate cannons, are surrounded by two graceful concentric granite curbs; the plot at Calvary is surrounded by a low and boxy iron fence.

In 1991, the casts of the four battle scenes depicted in relief on the sides of the central monument, which had been stolen many years earlier, were refabricated, based on photographic records, and were replaced. From 2001 to 2002, the four Civil War soldiers were recast in bronze and the objects that they had held, but had long ago had disappeared--ax, musket, rammer, and sword—were remade.

PRECIOUS GEORGIE AND OTHER CHILDREN

INFANT DEATH was widespread in the nineteenth century. THEODORE CUYLER (1822–1909), the longtime pastor of Brooklyn's Lafayette Avenue Presbyterian Church, and a national figure in both the temperance and abolitionist movements, was not spared this tragedy. GEORGE SIDNEY CUYLER, described on his monument as "one of the twin sons of

Green-Wood Cemetery's Soldier's Monument commemorates the New Yorkers who served during the Civil War. This photograph, circa 1875, shows three of the soldiers holding their accouterments.

The Civil War Soldiers' Monument was rededicated in 2002 with reproduction bronzes.

Detail of one of the bronze Civil War Soldiers, cast by the Modern Art Foundry in 2002.

Precious Georgie's marble cameo has been protected from the elements by glass, and is still in pristine condition more than a century after its placement at Green-Wood Cemetery. It is signed by noted sculptor Charles Calverley.

Theodore L. and Annie E. Cuyler," died at the age of four of scarlet fever: "A few hours of illness closed his lovely life on sabbath evening April 19th 1868." Carved on the base of this spectacular memorial is a sentence from *Matthew,* "The one shall be taken and the other left," a reference to Precious Georgie and his twin brother Theodore, who lived to be eighty years old. Carved on one side of the base is this:

He looked up at his mother and whispered "Does Jesus love me? What will he say when he sees me?"
                    All through this April sabbath
                        With head on the mother's breast
                    The sweet child murmured of Jesus
                        Till the sun was low in the west.
                    Then the door of Heaven opened
                        That had been ajar all day
                    And our darling alone could answer
                    "What will Jesus say."

Soon after Precious Georgie's death, his father, a prolific writer, wrote *The Empty Crib* in an effort to deal with his grief. But tragedy would visit Theodore Cuyler and his wife again six years later. Mathiot, a son, was born on Christmas Day, 1874; he died twelve days later, and is buried under a small stone that reads, simply, "Our Christmas Gift."

The experience of HORACE GREELEY (1811–1872), the well-known publisher of the *New York Herald* and advocate of a host of reform ideas, was typical of that experienced by many nineteenth century parents: he and his wife had seven children, but only two survived infancy. Faced with these tragedies, Mrs. Greeley philosophized, "I didn't raise my children for this world but for the next."

"Our Christmas Gift."

The Victorians, in an effort to soften the horror of infant death (which in many years accounted for more than half of all deaths), created a symbolism in their cemeteries that memorialized children as innocents, untouched by the corruption of the world, as lambs, as little angels, as asleep. Empty furniture was associated with infant death: empty seats, cradles, and bassinets were allusions to children who were gone but not forgotten. A well-known song of the time, *Cradle's Empty, Baby's Gone,* and a poem, *The Vacant Chair,* referred to domestic objects that continued as repositories of memories of the departed child.

This marble monument, typical of many others that memorialized children in the nineteenth century, depicts a child at rest, asleep on a marble pillow. As one inscription at Green-Wood Cemetery reads, "He is not dead, he is just asleep."

Many parents who lost their child were comforted by the belief that their loved one would quickly ascend to heaven. This is one of many marble depictions at Green-Wood Cemetery of that ascension.

This marble chair dates from the 1870's. A monument to Mary Rosekrans Adsit, who died in October, 1869, at the age of fifteen months, it shows a cloak thrown over a chair, with an empty shoe on it, as if Mary is about to return momentarily. Symbolically, the cloak is the youthful equivalent of a shroud, and the shoe is the equivalent of an urn, both allusions to Mary's ascension to heaven.

DOING THINGS ON A GRAND (PIANO) SCALE

IMMIGRATING to New York City from Germany with his family in 1851, HENRY ENGELHARD STEINWAY (1797–1871) soon put his piano-making skills to good use, starting his own piano manufacturing business. By the 1860's, his Steinway & Company had become the leading piano manufacturer in America. At its huge new factory at Park Avenue and 53rd Street, which took up almost a square block, workers produced beautifully-crafted instruments which regularly won international competitions.

In 1866, Henry Steinway built Steinway Hall on 14th Street. Designed by architect JOHN KELLUM (1809–1871), it contained the firm's offices and showrooms on the first floor, and a large auditorium upstairs which soon became one of the centers of New York music and culture. It was there, in the winter of 1868, that novelist Charles Dickens thrilled New Yorkers with his lectures.

The Steinway Tomb at Green-Wood Cemetery, built in the 1870's at a cost of $80,000 (the equivalent of $1.5 million today), is the cemetery's largest, with room for between 150 and 200 interments. It was designed by John Moffitt, who advertised himself as a "Sculptor and Builder of Vaults, Tombs, Monuments, Altars, Fonts & Tablets." Nehemiah Cleaveland, nineteenth century chronicler of Green-Wood Cemetery, was not impressed, commenting, "There it is. Look at it and pass on."

In 1880, Henry Steinway's son, WILLIAM STEINWAY (1836–1896), continuing this penchant for large-scale building, bought 400 acres on the west end of Long Island, including half a mile of land fronting on the East River. There, adjoining Long Island City, he established Steinway, Long Island. This company town contained the firm's factories, worker housing,

The nineteenth century was a difficult time for children, even those who managed to survive a host of life-threatening childhood diseases. Thousands of children, abandoned by their parents, wandered New York City's streets, sleeping wherever they could.

Painter JOHN GEORGE BROWN (1831–1913) captured these street urchins on canvas (see opposite page). Born to a poor family in Durham, England, Brown served a seven-year apprenticeship to a glass cutter, then studied painting at the Edinburgh Royal Academy in Scotland before heading off to London to earn his living painting portraits. At a music hall there, in 1853, he was so moved by the songs of well-known entertainer Henry Russell about the wonders of life in America that he left for the United States. Settling in Brooklyn, Brown went to work as a glass cutter. His employer, William Owen, was so impressed with Brown's stained glass designs that he arranged for him to study with painter THOMAS C. CUMMINGS. Brown married Owen's daughter Mary (and after she died, he married her older sister Emma), and went on to study at, and became a member of, the National Academy of Design.

In 1860, Brown began to paint at New York City's famous Tenth Street Studio Building, and he continued to paint there for the next half-century. His sentimental paintings of street children, often newsboys and bootblacks, earned him national prominence. Brown explained his choice of subject: "I do not paint poor boys solely because the public likes them and pays me for them, but because I love the boys myself, for I was once a poor lad."

Brown's warmhearted depictions of urban and rural children, workers, and everyday middle class scenes, as well as his paintings of old age, made him a wealthy man with an annual income of $40,000 to $50,000 (about $700,000 to $900,000 in today's currency), much of which he invested in New York real estate. He was elected president of the National Academy of Design in 1869 and served as vice president of the Water Color Society.

The Steinway Tomb, circa 1890.

The Vanderbilt Steinway, an art-case concert grand piano, was built in 1893, then sent to Paris, where it was decorated in white and gilt for Cornelius Vanderbilt. After years in the Vanderbilt mansion, it was inherited by Flora Whitney Miller, longtime president of the Whitney Museum of Art. Photograph © 1987 Sotheby's, Inc.

a church, a free circulating library, model free kindergarten, public baths, a park, and schools. Within a few years of this town's establishment, over 1000 workmen were employed there. In 1990, the Steinway firm, still there, made its 500,000th piano.

THE HOT DOG

CHARLES FELTMAN (1841–1910) made his fame and fortune as a Coney Island restaurateur. Born in Germany, Feltman was intimately familiar with the frankfurter, named for Frankfurt-am-Main in his native land. In an effort to improve his Brooklyn business, Feltman came up with a better idea: sandwich a frankfurter in a specially-made elongated roll which could conveniently be held and eaten on the street or at the beach. Feltman called his 1869 creation, first served at the corner of East New York and Howard Avenues, the Coney Island red hot, and it was soon the eating rage. Henry Collins Brown, a New York historian, explained its attraction:

This painting, Best Friends, *is typical of John George Brown's sentimental depictions of street children. Courtesy of Christie's Images.*

This turn of the century post card vividly shows that the suspicions of some of Feltman's customers about what was in his "dog" still persisted thirty years after he created it.

It could be carried on the march, eaten on the sands between baths, consumed on a carousel, used as a baby's nipple to quiet an obstreperous infant, and had other economic appeals to the summer pleasure seeker.

However, it took some time for the public to decide what to call Feltman's creation. Frankfurter, sausage, Coney Island red hot; none of them really captured the public's imagination. Coney Island chicken and weenie (from the Austrian wienerwurst) both had their proponents. But it was popular uncertainty about exactly what kind of meat was in these casings that ultimately determined that it would be called "hot dog."

Feltman's Deutscher Garden was only one of his restaurants at which the rows of tables seemed to stretch off toward the horizon. German bands played at the Deutscher Garden in lederhosen, beer flowed freely, and signs urged customers not to argue.

A lot of hot dogs and dinners had to be sold at Charles Feltman's huge Coney Island restaurants to pay for this elaborate tomb.

Just across the road from the Durant Mausoleum is another unusual monument memorializing an individual's accomplishments. It describes the life of R. H. McDonald, '49er "who crossed the plains on pack mules," and lauds him as a "total abstainer" from liquor.

JOHN MCKANE, the Czar of Coney Island, expressed the widespread suspicion when he decreed that the small stands that sold Feltman's creation had to pay a $200 license fee, explaining: "We cannot dictate to a man what he must sell, but we can make it hard for him to carry on the business. Nobody knows what is in the sausage." When investigators for the Brooklyn Board of Health discovered that a sausage factory in Greenpoint, catering to the Coney Island trade, was paying a character appropriately known as "Jack the Skinner" $5 for the meat of each horse he delivered, so long as he removed the skin and hoofs first, the suspicions held by many about the ingredients of Feltman's Coney Island red hot were confirmed. It was only a small jump, of course, to speculation concerning other species of meat, and to what became the name of choice, the "hot dog."

THE CAISSONS GO ROLLING ALONG

IN 1850, ECKFORD WEBB (1825–1893) started Webb and Bell's shipyard in Greenpoint, Brooklyn. He later founded one of the best-known schools of naval architecture in America, the Webb Academy at Fordham. But Eckford Webb believed that his greatest accomplishment was his work on the Brooklyn Bridge. It was Webb who constructed the caissons, using ship-making techniques, which allowed the Great Bridge to be built. The caissons were huge wooden boxes with their open side down and an iron shoe attached to the lower edge of the sides. Launched into the East River, they were carefully floated into place where the bridge's towers were to rise.

Eckford Webb's granite ship announces his shipbuilding profession to passersby.

Eckford Webb was proudest of his work on the caissons upon which the towers supporting the Brooklyn Bridge were built. Two caissons were made, one for each of the bridge towers. Construction of the Brooklyn caisson (shown here) began in October, 1869, and was completed by the following spring. On May 3, 1870, this caisson was filled with compressed air to help keep it afloat and was towed from Webb and Bell's Greenpoint shipyard to the basin which had been built for it near the Fulton Ferry slip. The bridge's chief engineer, Washington Roebling, and its contractor, William Kingsley, were joined by several others as they rode it down the East River.

The granite stones for the towers were then placed on top of the caissons, and their weight gradually forced the caissons toward the bottom of the East River. Pressurized gas was then pumped into the caissons to keep the river water out, and workmen descended through air locks into the hollow interior of the caissons in order to dig them down toward bedrock.

Eckford Webb's granite monument contains a magnificent carving of a ship under construction on its front. On its back, the Brooklyn Bridge's caissons, huge wood and iron boxes that allowed workers to dig the foundations for the bridge's towers, are identified as Webb's greatest work.

The Durant Mausoleum.

DRIVING THE GOLDEN SPIKE

Tнoмas Clark Durant (1820–1885) emerged in the early 1860's as the chief figure in the promotion, funding, and management of the Union Pacific Railroad, part of the mammoth project to unite America's Far West with its East. As the Union Pacific stretched west from Omaha to meet the Central Pacific somewhere east of California, it was Durant's job to raise the funds for what would be hailed in both America and Europe as "The Great Work of the Age!"

Durant brought creativity and enthusiasm to this task. When the rails reached the 100th meridian of longitude, a point on the prairie in the middle of nowhere, he decided it was time for a fund-raising gala. Politicians, financiers, journalists, and royalty were loaded onto an excursion train which chugged west until it came to a sign marking the spot "247 MILES FROM OMAHA." In a luxurious version of frontier life, they camped in tents and were entertained with Indian war dances, a mock Indian raid on their camp, a staged Indian battle, vaudeville acts, and a concert band. The festivities included a trip to the end of the tracks to watch the Irish track-

This is the largest of three sculptures by John Moffitt inside the Durant Mausoleum. Behind a locked iron gate and heavy granite door, they have been seen by only a few people in their more than one century of existence.

Thomas C. Durant and other officials posed for this historic photograph upon the completion of the Transcontinental Railroad. Durant is the very tall man standing in the front row, just to the left of the tracks.

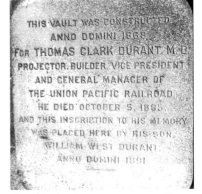

Surprisingly few monuments at Green-Wood Cemetery brag of the accomplishments of those they honor. Inside the Durant Mausoleum is a large plaque, put there by his son, which describes Thomas Durant's accomplishments.

layers as they worked feverishly. As the finale, a prairie fire was started for the amusement of the guests; it consumed twenty miles of grassland.

Using such promotions, Durant was able to raise the money needed to keep the tracks stretching west, and to deliver the political favors that kept the work going. But his task was never easy. In May, 1869, as Durant steamed toward Promontory, Utah, where the ceremonies marking the joining of the Union Pacific and the Central Pacific were to be held, his own workers held him hostage, refusing to let him go on until they received the five months of back pay that was owed them. Durant wired for $500,000, the men were paid, and he continued west to take part in the celebration which had been postponed awaiting his arrival.

On May 10, 1869, Durant, the senior representative of the Union Pacific there, drove The Golden Spike to complete the Transcontinental Railroad. As soon as he performed this honor, word of the historic event linking East and West was spread instantaneously throughout the United States by the first nationwide telegraph hookup, and celebrations erupted across the country.

THE SODA FOUNTAIN KING

JOHN MATTHEWS (1808–1870) trained in his native England to make devices that carbonated drinks, then immigrated to New York City, where he made carbonated drinks popular and created the elaborate soda fountain. Matthews long understood the importance of attracting children as his customers: "Youth, as it sips its first glass, experiences sensations which, like the first sensations of love, cannot be forgotten but are cherished to the last." When Matthews retired in 1865, his New York City manufacturing plant at First Avenue, between 26th and 27th streets, which produced the tin-lined cast iron soda fountains that he had perfected, was immense. By the time of his death, more than 500 establishments in New York City alone were using his products.

This Green-Wood Cemetery monument to the "Soda Fountain King" is the exuberant work of Karl Muller (1820–1887), whose name was prominently carved into the base of its central female figure. Born in Coblenz, Germany, Muller trained in a goldsmith's shop, then studied at the Royal Academy in Paris, where he won a gold prize for one of his statuettes. Around 1850, he immigrated to the United States, settled in New York City, and built a thriving business with his brother at Sixth Avenue and 49th Street, where they made plaster, terra cotta, and bronze statuettes, and cast white metal clock cases.

By 1868, Karl Muller was creating sculpture in terra cotta. The whimsical Matthews Monument, executed around 1870 in that material and marble for the then-huge sum of $30,000 (more than $500,000 today), is one of the few memorials at Green-Wood Cemetery that regularly elicits a smile. Voted the "Mortuary Monument of the Year" when it was first built, it is covered with likenesses of members of the Matthews's family, evange-

The monument to "Soda Fountain King" John Matthews dates from the early 1870's. This photograph was taken around 1890, and shows the monument, with its top section intact and stretching skyward 36 feet, surrounded by a wrought iron fence. Both that section and the fence have since been removed.

This photograph of a detail of the Matthews Monument dates from around 1875.

The terra cotta and marble Matthews Monument, as it appears today, is somewhat diminished, but still spectacular. Marble was also a key to Matthew's business success; the carbonic acid gas which carbonated his drinks was formed by mixing sulphuric acid (also called oil of vitriol) with marble chips. The enterprising Matthews bought up the marble scraps from the construction of St. Patrick's Cathedral, a supply sufficient to generate 25,000,000 gallons of carbonated drinks.

lists and various animals and plants. The faces of John Matthews's daughters grace its columns.

In the middle of the monument, a veiled statue, seated in a richly carved chair, typifies grief. Matthews himself is depicted in marble, lying on his back atop a sarcophagus, contemplating scenes from his life: learning how to make devices to create carbonic acid gas, bidding his farewell (at age of twenty-one) to his native Liverpool, and coming up with ideas for new soda water products. Gargoyles at each of the monument's corners spout rainwater channeled to them by the roof above Matthews's figure.

Though this monument is spectacular today, it was originally even more elaborate, before its top section began to deteriorate and was removed. Details of the decoration have been lost to weathering and well-intentioned, but poorly-executed, cleaning efforts. It is ironic that the chemical process that made Matthews rich, the reaction of acid and marble, is the same one which has caused the marble of his monument, exposed over the years to acid rain, to deteriorate.

THE DEFENDER OF ABUSED ANIMALS

HENRY BERGH (1813–1888) was one of those rare men who made a difference to many lives. In Bergh's case, the lives that he changed were those of animals in New York City and throughout the world. Impressed by the English example of an organization to protect animals,

Henry Bergh, who founded the A.S.P.C.A. and the S.P.C.C.

This illustration of Henry Bergh in action appeared in Harper's Weekly *on September 21, 1872, with this caption: "Mr. Bergh is doing a good thing for humanity as well as horseflesh by his efforts to stop the scandalous overcrowding of the street cars. On some of the lines leading to the upper part of the city scenes like the one depicted on this page are of too frequent occurrence. The car is packed and jammed with passengers until there is scarcely room to breathe, and the jaded team can hardly pull the load."*

In 2006, the Bergh Mausoleum was cleaned and restored by The Green-Wood Historic Fund. New plantings, designed by Superintendent Art Presson, were put in place and this sculpture, "Humility of Man Before a Group of Ageless Animals," was installed. By William Hunt Diederich and John Terken, it had hung on A.S.P.C.A. headquarters from the 1950's until 1992, when it was placed in storage because it was too heavy to hang on the A.S.P.C.A.'s new building. It was installed here, on permanent loan, in 2006 to honor Henry Bergh, founder of the A.S.P.C.A.

Bergh, in 1865, founded the American Society for the Prevention of Cruelty to Animals (A.S.P.C.A.) in New York, the first such organization in the United States. And Bergh was no mere functionary; he was always ready to take to the streets, risking his own safety, to protect animals from abuse.

Until Bergh came along, an animal was considered property, and its owner could do with it as he or she wished, free of any societal restraint. Henry Bergh changed that. Soon after the A.S.P.C.A. was chartered by New York State, he and a group of supporters went to Park Row, where several horsecar lines met, to check on the condition of the working horses. Bergh brought New York City's mass transit system to a halt as he stopped every horse that had a sore or ailment from working. He put himself between drivers and the horses they were beating, sometimes forcing the drivers to unharness the animals, other times making them lighten the load that was being pulled.

In Paris, streetcars were allowed to pick up passengers only if there were seats for them. New York City had no such law to limit the burden on its horses, but it did have Henry Bergh. Whenever Bergh came across overloaded horsecars, he would arrest the driver for abuse of his horses and make all the passengers get out and walk.

The man with a five-year contract to carry the United States Mail from the General Post Office to the railroad stations vowed that Bergh would not interfere with his horses. Taunting Bergh, he started to use lame horses to pull his wagons. When Bergh stopped these horses and unharnessed them, a large crowd gathered as the cursing driver proclaimed that Bergh was interfering with the U.S. Mail. Bergh answered that the mail was free to proceed, but the abused horses were not.

As a speaker, in the courtroom, before the legislature, and in the street, in the face of opposition, indifference, and ridicule, Bergh championed the rights of animals. His efforts resulted in improvements in the conditions of cattle being shipped, horses' working conditions, and milk purity. Bergh created an ambulance corps for the removal of disabled animals from the streets, and made available a derrick for rescuing animals that had fallen into excavations. He also invented clay pigeons to replace live birds for shooting practice.

Bergh toured the United States, laying the groundwork for animal protection organizations throughout the country and internationally. As a result of his efforts, thirty-four States, during his lifetime, enacted their first laws against cruelty to animals. In 1874, Bergh rescued a little girl from inhuman conditions, and this led to his founding of the Society for the Prevention of Cruelty to Children (S.P.C.C.).

His obituary in *The New York Times* was headlined, "Helpless Animals Losing Their Protector," and described him as "long and universally known as the defender of abused animals."

"MUTE ANIMALS SHARE HIS COMPASSIONATE BOUNTY"

A NATIVE of Rouen, France, Louis Bonard (1809–1871) left there in 1849, traded in South America and California, then settled in New York City, where he invested in real estate. Mechanically gifted, he was an eccentric individual who spent little and saved much. In his workshop, located in the cellar of a tenement he owned on Mulberry Street, he developed and patented a circular loom for hat weaving, a brick-making machine, and a machine for casting iron.

In 1871, knowing that he was on his death bed, Bonard sent for Henry Bergh, the founder and president of the American Society for the Prevention of Cruelty to Animals. When Bergh arrived at Bonard's tenement, he had no idea what awaited him. But things looked even less promising when Bergh entered a six foot by eight foot room containing a broken table, a trunk, and a mattress supported by boards and bricks. The room had no heat, heavy wooden bars guarded the dirty window, and bolts and bars protected the door.

Bonard told Bergh that he intended to leave his fortune to Bergh's pioneering animal rights organization. It is unlikely that Bergh, given the surroundings, was greatly enthused at this prospect. But Bergh did as he was told, and opened the trunk at the foot of the bed. To his amazement, it was filled with alternating layers of gold and silver watches, jewelry, and diamonds.

Bonard's relatives challenged his will. Their legal argument for negating his legacy to the A.S.P.C.A. was rather novel: Bonard, they claimed, was under an insane delusion that upon his death his soul would enter the body of an animal, and his will was therefore improperly executed with his own interests in mind, in the hopes of improving his future existence. This challenge failed, Bonard's estate of $150,000 (equal to about $1.8 million today) went to the A.S.P.C.A., and it erected a monument to Bonard in a prime spot near Green-Wood's Cemetery's main entrance.

TABLOID JOURNALISM

I N 1835, James Gordon Bennett (1795–1872), with a $500 investment, founded the *New York Herald*. Bennett was, at the time, his newspaper's entire staff. His office was in a cellar on Wall Street, and his desk was a wood plank supported by two flour barrels. But in the ensuing years, the *Herald*, known for its fictitious news, sensational opinions, reckless personal attacks, and disrespectful tone, became the most influential newspaper in America, with the largest circulation of any newspaper in the world.

Bennett aimed his appeal at the masses, summing up his philosophy by saying, "The newspaper's function is not to instruct but to startle." George Templeton Strong, New York's great nineteenth century diarist, felt that no man of his time had done more "to blunt the moral sense of the people"

The monument to Louis Bonard bears the A.S.P.C.A.'s seal on its front. Note the inscription on the right side: "MUTE ANIMALS SHARE HIS COMPASSIONATE BOUNTY."

James Gordon Bennett, who built the New York Herald *into a national and international power.*

Abraham Jacobi and Mary Jacobi, pioneering pediatricians. Mary Jacobi portrait, Dictionary of American Portraits, *Dover Publications.*

The marble Bennett Monument today.

than Bennett. Four times Bennett was beaten with canes by men who took exception to the scandalous stories he had published about them; each morning-after, Bennett entertained his readers with a first-hand account of his drubbing. Fearing that the enemies whom he had so richly cultivated would target his son, James Gordon Bennett Jr., he sent him off to Europe for his own safety to be educated there.

Bennett's Green-Wood Cemetery monument impressed Effie Brower, an early chronicler of the cemetery: "Nothing like this can be seen in the grounds, there is so much to please the eye and gratify the taste." It is of the finest Italian marble, and was sculpted for the Bennett family in Italy, then brought to this spot overlooking New York Harbor. According to a description in a nineteenth century New York guide, this monument is "a life-sized female figure, kneeling on a cushion in an attitude of prayer, commending her child, which is held in suspense by an angelic figure, to the Almighty Giver."

"THE BABIES"

D R. ABRAHAM JACOBI (1830–1919) specialized in the study of children's diseases, becoming one of the leading pediatricians in America. In the 1860's, he opened the first pediatric clinic in the United States. He taught medicine at New York Medical College, the University of the City of New York, and the College of Physicians and Surgeons, and served as president of the New York State Medical Society, the New York Academy of Medicine, the Medical Society of the County of New York, and the New York Pathological and Obstetrical Societies. Jacobi Hospital in the Bronx is named for him.

MARY CORINNA PUTNAM (JACOBI) (1842–1906) was the first female graduate of the New York College of Pharmacy in 1863. She received her M.D. the next year from the Female Medical College of Pennsylvania. During the Civil War, she volunteered at soldiers' hospitals in New York City, went to Louisiana in 1863 to treat her brother who had been stricken with malaria, and the next year went to South Carolina to

"The Babies," a memorial erected by pioneering pediatricians Abraham and Mary Putnam Jacobi to their children. Three children who were stillborn and two others who died at the age of one day are buried in this lot.

care for her sister, who had contracted typhoid while teaching at a freedman's school.

Unhappy with the level of her medical training, she applied to the Ecole de Medecine in Paris, and was admitted by the Minister of Public Education over the protests of faculty members who did not want a female student enrolled. When she graduated, in 1871, with high honors, she was the first woman to receive a degree from that school.

Returning to New York City in 1871, Mary Putnam worked at Mount Sinai Hospital, was hired by Columbia Medical School as the first professor of pediatrics in the country, taught at the Women's Medical College of the New York Infirmary, and organized and was president (1874–1903) of the Association for the Advancement of the Medical Education of Women. With broad formal training, extensive clinical skills, and many published papers, she was the leading woman physician of her era. She was also in the forefront of early theories on the contribution of environmental factors to disease. Ironically, though she was a member of many medical societies, she was denied membership in the Obstetrical Society.

Abraham Jacobi and Mary Putnam married in 1873 and had several children. But, despite the training and expertise of these pioneering pediatricians, only one of their children survived infancy. Those who died are memorialized by a granite monument, on which is starkly inscribed "The Babies."

THERE'S NO PHAROAH IN THIS TOMB

O NE OF THE largest and most elaborate tombs at Green-Wood Cemetery is that of CORNELIUS KINGSLAND GARRISON (1809–1885). Garrison could well afford the expense. He acquired his first fortune building and operating Mississippi River steamboats out of St. Louis. When the California Gold Rush began in 1849, Garrison went to Panama, where he established a successful banking house. Shortly thereafter he became the San Francisco agent of the Nicaragua Steamship Company, earning the then-phenomenal yearly salary of $60,000 (equal to $1.8 million today).

In 1853, after developing a reputation in San Francisco for financial genius and honesty, Garrison was elected its mayor. A reformer and activist, he opposed public gambling and Sunday performances, called for an "African" school to educate blacks, advocated giving blacks the vote, had new schools built, introduced a city beautification program, and brought gaslights to the streets. Garrison was also an early proponent of the transcontinental railroad and telegraph. He used his own money to pay for the construction of some schools, and donated his mayoral salary to orphanages. His mayoralty was one of the most memorable and productive in San Francisco history. However, Garrison was defeated in his reelection bid by the Know-Nothing Party's anti-Chinese candidate. San Franciscans, in appreciation of Garrison's service, gave him a $10,000 gold dinner set.

Cornelius Garrison, banker and mayor of San Francisco.

The impressive Garrison Tomb, seen in this circa 1870 photograph, was designed by architect Griffith Thomas in Moorish Revival style. The elaborate stone fence has since been removed.

Fanny Palmer, in a circa 1860 photograph. Courtesy of the Museum of the City of New York. Her grave is unmarked.

Almost thirty years before her burial at Green-Wood Cemetery, Fanny Palmer sketched and published this scene of the original cemetery entrance.

In 1859, Garrison moved to New York City, where he became a well-known financier and speculator, particularly in gas, railroad, and steamship companies. His involvement in shipping earned him the title "Commodore." During the Civil War, he placed many of his ships in service for the Union and funded the Union Navy's expedition against Butler's Ship Island. He later served as president of the Missouri Pacific Railroad and was an owner of New York City's first elevated railroad, which was on Greenwich Street.

Garrison's tomb, designed by noted architect GRIFFITH THOMAS (1818–1878) in Moorish Revival style, likely dates from the early 1870's. It is ironic that Thomas's own marble monument at Green-Wood Cemetery is of modest simplicity, particularly when compared to the lavish work he designed for Commodore Garrison.

FANNY PALMER: NINETEENTH CENTURY CAREER WOMAN

WOMEN in nineteenth century America were expected to maintain the home, not work outside it. FRANCES FLORA BOND (1812–1876) had different plans; she wanted a career. Born in England, she was raised to be an upper middle class woman. She studied art as a "polite accomplishment" and took lessons in painting at the school of Miss Mary Linwood, a practicing artist who soon became Frances's role model.

At the age of twenty-two, Fanny married EDMUND SEYMOUR PALMER (1809–1859), who listed his profession as "gentleman." In Leicester, they went into the lithographic printing business, a process in which the artist drew directly on a special stone and the stone was then inked to make prints, with Fanny as artist and Edmund as "director." Her work was described by a local newspaper critic as "distinguished by a boldness and freedom not often exhibited by a female pencil." But the Palmers's business failed, and in 1844, with their savings gone, they immigrated, along with members of the Bond family, to New York City. There they again set up a lithographic business, drawing and publishing advertisements, sheet music illustrations, and architectural renderings. When this business floundered, NATHANIEL CURRIER bought it out, and Fanny went to work as a staff artist for his leading print publishing business.

During the next two decades, Fanny Palmer created hundreds of scenes of riverboats, trains, clipper ships, bridges, the country, farms, and hunting, for Currier and then Currier and Ives (JAMES IVES became a partner in 1857). More than 200 of their prints were signed "F. F. Palmer," but she worked on many others. Though Fanny never traveled more than 100 miles from New York City, she relied upon photographs, sketches, and prints to draw panoramic views of Virginia, California, the Hudson and Mississippi Rivers, the Mexican and Civil Wars, and westward migration. Her prints decorated more homes in nineteenth century America than those of any other artist.

Wild Duck Shooting *was one of the Long Island Series "drawn from nature" by Fanny Palmer, in 1852, and published by* NATHANIEL CURRIER. *Her husband Edmund, who considered himself a gentleman, is the model here for the upper crust hunter, and is accompanied on the hunt by their son. Courtesy of the Museum of the City of New York.*

Architect Griffith Thomas designed many New York buildings, including the St. Nicholas Hotel (left) at Broadway south of Spring Street, which opened in 1853 (and sections of which still exist), and the Domestic Sewing Machine Building, at the southwest corner of Broadway and 14th Street, which was completed in 1873, but was torn down many years ago.

Fanny Palmer worked to support her family. Her husband Edmund, never a success in business, opened a tavern, "The Woodcock" (this name reflecting his upper class pretensions), near Brooklyn's City (now Borough) Hall. On March 7, 1859, perhaps under the influence of intoxicants, he fell down the stairs at his establishment and was fatally injured.

Unfortunately, their son, EDMUND S. PALMER, JR. (1834–1867) modeled himself after his father, and never held a job. He died in 1867, at the age of thirty-three, of tuberculosis.

Fanny Palmer, virtually the only skilled female artist in the man's world of print-making, rose to the very top of her profession. Nearly one-third of what are today considered to be the "Fifty Best" prints issued by Currier and Ives were drawn by her.

COLONEL FISK'S MURDER

JIM FISK, "Prince Erie," parlayed his brashness and impudence into one of the largest fortunes in America. Widely regarded as a public enemy for his manipulation of stocks, particularly that of the Erie Railroad, his massive schemes often left hundreds of investors financially ruined and the American economy staggering. Fisk's personal life was no more exemplary; one account describes him as "Fisk, now a fat, jovial, brassy voluptuary, [who] was leading a life of half-barbaric prodigality." Fisk's end was every bit as flashy as his life. After going through a series of mistresses, he chose unemployed actress Josie Mansfield as his favorite. From 1870 until 1872, she was the best-kept woman in New York, living lavishly at Fisk's expense.

EDWARD STILES STOKES (1841–1901), a handsome young sportsman and man-about-town who often placed big bets on the wrong horse,

Born on the Isle of Wight, England, Griffith Thomas came to New York City in 1838, and entered the architectural office that his father, Thomas Thomas, had already established there. Thomas Thomas had a clientele that included the Astors and other prominent New Yorkers. Griffith, though only twenty years old, was already a skilled draftsman when he arrived in New York City, and designed buildings for his father, then later in his own practice, in the classical and Palladian styles.

By 1860, Thomas and Son was one of the busiest architectural firms in the country. In the six years from 1868 to 1873, they designed thirty-three large buildings for offices, insurance companies, and banks, in New York City. During a practice spanning forty years, Griffith Thomas was so popular and prolific that, incredibly, the blocks on Fifth Avenue from its southern beginning up to Central Park averaged three buildings by him. His most important structures were Pike's Opera House on Eighth Avenue at 23rd Street, the Tweed Courthouse (extant), Mount Sinai Hospital, the Fifth Avenue, St. James, and St. Nicholas Hotels, Arnold Constable's on Canal and Mercer Streets and on Broadway at 19th Street (both extant), Lord & Taylor's Store at the northeast corner of Broadway and Grand Street (the first iron commercial building, it was described as "more like an Italian palace than a place for the sale of broadcloth"), the Domestic Sewing Machine building on the southwest corner of Broadway and 14th Street, and Dr. Spring's Brick Church on Fifth Avenue.

Colonel Jim Fisk, whose pretensions and financial manipulations were legendary. In 1868, Fisk purchased Pike's Opera House, at 23rd Street and Eighth Avenue, renamed it the Grand Opera House, and installed lavish offices where he produced elaborate dramas and opera. He leased the Academy of Music, on 14th Street, to put on grand opera, appeared in public as the "admiral" of the Fall River and Bristol steamboats, named the largest ferryboat on the Hudson the "James Fisk," and paid cold cash to become colonel of the New York Militia's 9th Regiment. Thereafter, that outfit was widely and derisively referred to as the "Opera House Army" or "Fisk's Footmen."

was known to spend two hours of every day grooming himself. Stokes, Fisk's business partner, began hanging around Fisk's Opera House, and Fisk made the mistake of introducing him to Josie Mansfield. Stokes soon developed a fondness for Josie, and Josie, at the very least, felt that Stokes might be handy in making Fisk jealous. But, at least initially, Fisk did not feel threatened by this rival; as he wrote to Josie about Stokes's prospects as a provider, "how beautiful you are to look at, but nothing to lean on." That soon changed, however, and Fisk and Stokes vied in earnest for Josie.

Months went by as Fisk and Stokes attempted to settle their love and business interests. Josie twice called on BOSS TWEED, asking him to intercede, but Tweed knew that there were some problems that even he couldn't fix. Fisk, tormented by the thought that Josie might be passing along to Ned Stokes some of the money that he had given her, canceled the Erie Railroad's deal with Stokes's refinery, wiping out Stokes's only income.

Stokes, hoping to restore the substantial income that allowed him to pursue his twin passions of gambling and women, met Fisk at fashionable Delmonico's Restaurant for dinner, and proposed that they let Josie choose between them. Fisk agreed, but when they took a hansom cab to her residence, and put the question to her, she suggested that they could all be friends. Fisk, who had made his fortune in railroads, was unconvinced: "It won't do, Josie. You can't run two engines on one track in contrary directions at the same time."

Edward S. Stokes, who battled Fisk in business and love, then killed him.

Fisk decided to keep the financial pressure on Stokes. When he learned that Stokes had collected $27,500 which was owed to their refinery, and had kept it all for himself, he swore out a warrant for Stokes's arrest for embezzlement. Stokes, after spending the weekend in the Ludlow Street Jail, vowed to get even. Acquitted at his embezzlement trial, Stokes then hired armed men to seize the refinery. But Fisk hired more men, and they captured it in an assault.

Stokes, however, was far from finished. He and Josie went to the press with threats against Fisk of exposure and blackmail. The press played it as farce, headlining "How Fisk and Stokes Quarreled, Fought and Did Not Bleed About a Lady Fair with Jet Black Hair." Stokes offered Fisk the latter's incriminating letters to Josie, at the modest price of $200,000.

On January 6, 1872, Stokes decided that he had had enough. As Fisk climbed the stairs at the Grand Central Hotel on Broadway, Stokes stepped from the shadows, revolver in hand, exclaiming, "I've got you

Josie Mansfield, who was well-kept and wanted them all to be friends.

now," and fired two quick shots. Fisk shouted, "For God's sake, will anybody save me?," and managed to stay on his feet until a doctor arrived.

Stokes was grabbed by hotel employees as he tried to get away, and was taken to the wounded Fisk, who identified him. Fisk, however, was concerned with more important matters; he wanted to know if he was going to die. His doctor assured him he was not going to die that day, and probably not the day after that either. His doctor was half-right: Fisk, despite treatment by seven doctors, lived through the first day, but died the next.

As Stokes was escorted to the Tombs to be jailed awaiting trial, he was unrepentant, pointing out to reporters that it was exactly one year since Fisk had had him arrested for embezzlement. Stokes lived in style while imprisoned: he carpeted his jail cell, and his meals were ordered every day from fashionable Delmonico's. Several bottles of scented bath water kept him company. One reporter who visited Stokes in custody found him wearing a handsome frilled shirt, three magnificent diamond studs, a velvet dressing gown, silk stockings, and gold laced slippers.

Ned Stokes stood trial three times for the murder of Jim Fisk. At his first trial, in June, 1872, Josie Mansfield, described in newspapers accounts as "a modern Desdemona" and "a magnificent Medusa," and by the prosecutor as "a harlot," was called to testify by the defense. According to the *New York Herald*, as she entered the courtroom, she "took a long, tender look at Stokes, and seemed for a moment to drink in his every feature." Josie told the jury that Fisk had often threatened Stokes's life. The defense offered the jury three alternatives: Stokes acted in self-defense, he had been driven insane by Fisk's persecution, or Fisk's doctors had killed him (with either excessive probing into his wounds or lethal quantities of morphine). Stokes testified, claiming that it was only by coincidence that he met Fisk on the night of the shooting. According to Stokes's account, Fisk pulled a pistol on him, and he fired first to defend himself and save his life. The District Attorney demanded that Stokes be hanged, telling the jury that "his hands are stained with blood to the very shoulders." But the first trial ended when the jury could not agree on a verdict, as rumors circulated that a juror had been bribed, with seven jurors voting to convict of murder and five holding out for manslaughter.

Stokes was tried again, and this second trial ended when the jury, after only three hours of deliberations, found him guilty of murder. Stokes was sentenced to hang, but on appeal he was granted a new trial. His third trial ended with a less-serious manslaughter conviction, and Stokes served four years at Sing Sing, where he was treated as an honored guest.

After his release from prison, however, Stokes was a haunted man. Fearing that he would be killed, he never slept in the dark, and always sat in public with his back against the wall. Stokes struggled with his demons for another thirty years, failing in several business ventures, then making a modest income from running two restaurants, before coming to his final resting place at Green-Wood Cemetery.

Edward Stokes's assassination of Colonel Jim Fisk, as depicted in a contemporary drawing.

Edward S. Stokes's hillside mausoleum.

Alice (top) and Phoebe Cary (bottom) were important nineteenth century literary figures. Alice was not in good health for many years, and Phoebe chose not to marry so that she could nurse her sister. When Alice finally succumbed in 1871, her funeral, according to Horace Greeley, was attended by more distinguished men and women, and a larger audience, than any other funeral of which he knew. Poet John Greenleaf Whittier, upon Alice's death, wrote "And birds and flowers are lost to her/Who was their best interpreter." Phoebe was in good health until her sister's death; her sorrow thereafter was so intense that, within five months, she joined Alice in their plot at Green-Wood Cemetery, where they are buried side by side.

FOR FIFTEEN YEARS, poet PHOEBE CARY (1824–1871), with her sister ALICE CARY (1820–1871), led "the Cary Salon," a New York cultural circle which met every Sunday evening at their 20th Street home in Manhattan. Regulars at what one participant called the "trysting place of Liberty" were women's rights advocates Susan B. Anthony and Elizabeth Cady Stanton, writer Fanny Fern, reformer HORACE GREELEY, newspaperman ROBERT BONNER (1824–1899), poet John Greenleaf Whittier, and showman P. T. Barnum. Barnum liked to drive around Central Park with Phoebe, often had her as a guest in his home, gave her tours of his museum, and shared many a laugh with her, whom he called the "wittiest woman in America."

This poem, by Phoebe Cary, reflects the nineteenth century resurrectionist view of death that was so central to Green-Wood Cemetery's character:

Examples of some of the symbolism on Green-Wood Cemetery monuments (left to right): entwined columns (symbolizing a husband and wife joined in death as they were in life), a shrouded urn (an allusion to resurrection), and a lamb (signifying that a pure and gentle child has passed on).

The resurrectionist view was repeatedly given voice by the funerary symbols that decorated the cemetery. Victorians touring the cemetery recognized the many variations on urns and shrouds as references to resurrection, symbolizing the body that remained after the soul had ascended.

Other symbols found on the monuments at Green-Wood Cemetery are roses (for a young woman who died while still in bloom), a cutoff column (symbolic of a young man who never had a chance to reach his full stature), entwined columns (representing a husband and wife who were joined in death, just as they had been joined in life), the obelisk (adopted from Egyptian design, and pointing toward heaven, a reference to ascension), handshakes (farewell to earthly existence), lambs (innocence of children), child asleep on a pillow or cloud (infant death), butterfly (youth), sheaves of wheat (the divine harvest, reaped at a mature age), down-turned torches (the line of descent continues despite death), anchor (either a seaman or an allusion to the Anchor of Hope), open Bible (piety), the Celtic Cross or the globe (God's unity and completeness), wings (resurrection), the Easter Lily (resurrection), and the weeping willow (mourning).

I am nearer my home to-day;
Nearer my Father's house, where the many mansions be;
Nearer the great white throne, nearer the crystal sea;
Nearer the bound of Life, where we lay our burdens down;
Nearer leaving the cross, nearer wearing the crown.
And brightly the other side breaks on a shore of light
Forever with the Lord.

NOT AN EASY JOB

JAMES HARPER (1795–1869), *the* Harper at Harper & Brothers (in his time the leading publishing house in the world, later Harper and Row, now part of Harper Collins, the world's fifth largest publisher), also served as mayor of New York City. That job must have seemed easy compared to some of his tasks at the publishing house.

One day, James Harper was in his office, entertaining an out-of-town clergyman who had stopped by, apparently for no other reason than so that he could tell the folks back home that he had visited the famous Harper Brothers. After several uninspired questions about the business, the clergyman pressed him on what exactly his job was: "You say that your brother John sees to the accounts, that your brother Wesley looks after the correspondence, and that your brother Fletcher receives authors and supervises the publication of new books and the *Monthly*, but you, Mr. Mayor, I have never been able to discover what you do."

James Harper assured him that his load was great: "Oh, they leave me an enormous amount of work; I have more to do than all of them put together."

The clergyman persisted, "Indeed! That is very curious. Allow me to ask what it is."

James Harper leaned forward, and, in a confidential whisper, replied, "I'll tell you, but you must never tell a soul. I entertain the bores."

The Harper Brothers Monument. As the stone in the foreground states, James Harper and his wife Rebecca were originally interred at the Sands Street Church; their remains were later brought to Green-Wood Cemetery. Fittingly, this monument is four-sided, with each side dedicated to one of the brothers and bearing his portrait.

AMERICA'S FIRST MATINEE IDOL

LOUIS MOREAU GOTTSCHALK (1829–1869) was born in New Orleans to a German-Jewish father and a Creole mother who was an accomplished singer. At an early age he showed musical ability, and went off to Europe to study the piano. But when he applied for admission to the Paris Conservatory, he was rejected without an audition, the director of classes explaining that his school was no place for someone from America, "the country of railroads but not of musicians."

Gottschalk managed to find a teacher in Paris, was befriended by Hector Berlioz, and toured Europe to acclaim. At the age of sixteen he played for Chopin, who was duly impressed, predicting Gottschalk would

A portrait of matinee idol Louis Moreau Gottschalk adorns this sheet of his music.

Louis Moreau Gottschalk's white marble monument was originally topped by an angel holding an open book, on which appeared the titles of six of his most famous compositions. Note the lyre, a musical instrument of ancient Greece, against the right leg of the angel. It is a reference to Gottschalk's musical career. Today, only the base of the monument remains. Green-Wood Historic Fund Collection.

"become the king of pianists." In 1853, Gottschalk made his American debut at Niblo's Garden in New York City, then toured the United States, Mexico, and South America. He was the first important American composer, was the first American musician with a national and international reputation, was the first from his country to popularize concert music, and was a brilliant pianist who shone playing his own very difficult compositions. Gottschalk's music combined Creole, black, minstrel, South American, Spanish, mariachi, West Indian, and Cuban sounds.

Though music critics were divided on Gottschalk's talents, his popularity in America was enormous, rivaled only by that of Jenny Lind, the Swedish Nightingale. At his concerts, he always wore white gloves, then dramatically removed them on stage one finger at a time. Female admirers would then storm the stage, tearing the gloves to pieces as they fought for souvenirs. A showman and a Don Juan, Gottschalk was fluent in five languages. Gottschalk, who never married, was run out of San Francisco for his romantic escapades, and was threatened by men throughout the country who believed that he had used his good looks and matinee-idol status to corrupt the morals of their wives.

A committed Unionist and abolitionist, Gottschalk toured Civil War camps, playing for the troops. On November 24, 1869, while leading 600 musicians in a performance of his own composition, *Morte!! (She is Dead)*, he fell ill, and succumbed a month later.

NO(E) WAY TO DIE

BRUSH MANUFACTURER JAMES H. NOE (1817–1875) was doing very well, thank you. Business was so good that he had plans drawn up for a new factory at 275 Greenwich Street in Manhattan. Construction began in the summer of 1875, and as it proceeded, Noe made it a habit to check on it every Sunday.

On August 22, Noe entered his new building and climbed to the roof on the ladders and temporary stairways. As he did so, he was unaware that Dandy Johnny Dolan, a well-known petty criminal, was at work up there, tearing away the newly-installed lead gutters to sell as scrap. Dolan, wearing an eye gouger on his thumb and his signature blue-bordered handkerchief around his neck, worked at his thievery as Noe approached.

Noe, brandishing his cane with a monkey carved in its handle, confronted Dandy Johnny, and forced him down to the ground floor. There, Dandy Johnny turned on the fifty-eight-year-old Noe, fracturing his skull with an iron bar. With Noe lying unconscious, Dandy Johnny, ever the thief, took Noe's gold watch and chain, the few dollars that he was carrying, and his cane. For unknown reasons, Dandy Johnny then tied his own handkerchief around Noe's face before fleeing. Noe, still alive when he was found, hung on for a week before succumbing to his injuries.

Dandy Johnny did little to cover his tracks. Rumor had it that he appeared at the haunt of the Wyos, a notorious New York City gang, with one of James H. Noe's eyes in his pocket. Noe's watch and chain soon turned up at a pawn shop on Park Row, and the owner identified Dandy Johnny as the man who had brought them in. Two prostitutes identified the handkerchief found on Noe as Dandy Johnny's. When detectives learned that Dandy Johnny was parading around New York City carrying a cane with a monkey carved in its handle, he was arrested.

Dandy Johnny Dolan, convicted after trial, was hanged on April 21, 1876, in the courtyard of the Tombs, New York City's prison.

TOO LATE FOR MARRIAGE

MARTIN KALBFLEISCH (1804–1873) would have been quite a catch. He was esteemed by his neighbors, who elected him mayor of the City of Brooklyn. And he was rich.

Late in his life, Kalbfleisch was sued for breach of promise to marry. It was indeed late in his life; while the suit was pending, he died. But, as Green-Wood Cemetery chronicler Effie Brower reports in her nineteenth century account of this affair, even after his death "there was an effort made to carry on the suit, but the old man could not appear, and so the farce ended."

THE BIRTH OF THE AMERICAN MUSICAL

IN 1866, a French ballet troupe, in New York City to perform at the Academy of Music, lost its engagement when the Academy was destroyed by fire. Marooned, the dancers soon found work in a melodrama that was already in production, the *Black Crook*. The first modern American musical, and fated to be the greatest theatrical hit of the century, it opened at Niblo's Garden. A spectacle in four acts running for five and

James Noe's monument reflects his family's resurrectionist attitudes towards his tragic death. Carved on its sides are a dialogue between Noe and his wife. First he speaks:

> Farewell loved wife and children,
> for me shed not a tear.
> I'm happy now with Jesus,
> And there's no weeping here.
> Though hard it seemed to tear me,
> From your fond hearts away.
> My savior called me to him,
> And I could no longer stay.

His wife, upon her death, responds:

> Reunited again dear husband,
> Where weeping indeed is no more.
> We will dwell together with Jesus,
> On his golden heavenly shore.
> The parting felt very keenly,
> My heart with sorrow was sore.
> But God in his infinite mercy,
> Now joins us to part no more.

Martin Kalbfleisch, before he was dead and could not keep his promise.

This portrait of William Wheatley, actor, theater manager, and producer, who helped give birth to the American musical, decorates his monument. The monument was recently cleaned and restored by The Green-Wood Historic Fund Collection.

One of the original Black Crook *show-girls, showing off her tights.*

one-half hours, mounted at the then-extraordinary cost of $50,000, it featured three hundred babies crawling across the stage, scores of singers, dancers, and musicians, and over one hundred beautiful women.

Produced by WILLIAM WHEATLEY (1816–1876) and Henry C. Jarrett, the *Black Crook* ran for 475 performances, making it the longest-running Broadway production up to that time, despite the dire warnings of clergymen and moralists. A great part of its success was a line of chorus girls appearing in flesh-colored tights, a scandalous display for the time, singing such catchy tunes as *You Naughty, Naughty Men*. As one critic enthused, "All that gold and silver and gems and light and woman's beauty can contribute to fascinate the eye and charm the sense is gathered up in this gorgeous spectacle."

Revivals of this "daring ballet-show, as nearly unclad as possible," were a staple of the American theatre into the twentieth century, including a production by Christopher Morley and Agnes de Mille in 1929.

COME STAY WITH US AT GILSEY HOUSE

I N 1868, PETER GILSEY (1811–1873) purchased the last remaining homestead in midtown Manhattan, the old clapboard house of Caspar Samlar and its surrounding flower beds, at the northeast corner of Broadway and 29th Street. Gilsey hired architect STEPHEN DECATUR HATCH (1839–1894) (whose remains, after a short stay, were removed from Green-Wood Cemetery) to design a cast iron hotel for him, and Hatch created a gem, in French Second Empire style, with mansard roof and clock. The first hotel with a cast iron facade in New York City, it was fabricated at the Architectural Iron Works foundry of DANIEL BADGER.

Gilsey House, circa 1875; this building still stands on Broadway at 29th Street.

Built during the post–Civil War boom at the then-phenomenal cost of $300,000 (equal to $5.3 million today), the Gilsey House was decorated by Garibaldi, New York's foremost interior designer, and its bar had silver dollars cemented into its floor. It opened with an invitation-only gala on April 15, 1871. Twenty-five hundred guests were entertained that evening by an orchestra as they dined on the "bounteous collation" and drank the finest wines and champagnes in the first-floor restaurants which ranked with the best eateries in New York. When Peter Gilsey was told that his guests had consumed all of his champagne, his reply was quick: "Send out and borrow some. Let them swim in it."

Catering primarily to coal magnates, railroad operators, Congressmen and military officers, the Gilsey House, soon after its opening, was described by *The New York Times* as "one of the most imposing of our metropolitan palace hotels." On the cutting edge, it was one of the first hotels in America to offer telephone service. Its commercial success was assured, soon after its opening, when New York City's theatre district moved uptown to the nearby stretch of Broadway. It was while staying at the Gilsey House that the elder Oscar Hammerstein won a bet by writing a three-act opera in two days.

The Gilsey House closed on December 10, 1904. The building, however, remains. It was converted into offices early in the century, and in the 1970's it became cooperative apartments. Its cast iron facade was refurbished and repainted in 1994, and the building is now known as 1200 Broadway.

GRAND CENTRAL DEPOT: THE END OF THE WORLD

The Gilsey Tomb, a sort of Gilsey House at Green-Wood Cemetery.

I N 1857, New York City enacted a law that made it illegal for steam locomotives, notorious for spewing cinders and panicking horses, to run south of 42nd Street. As a result, railroad magnate Commodore Vanderbilt decided to build his Grand Central Depot on the north side of that street, as close to his customers as possible. His plans were ridiculed by many: a terminus so far north of the residential center of the city, requiring a half day's travel to and fro, would be useless. One newspaper suggested that this station would more fittingly be called "End of the World," rather than Grand Central.

But Vanderbilt had not made his millions in ferries and railroads by being easily discouraged, and he hired prominent architect JOHN B. SNOOK (1815–1901) to design his depot. Of pressed brick topped by a mansard roof, it opened in 1871. Grand Central Depot included an immense train shed which could accommodate twelve trains, each twelve passenger cars and a locomotive long, under an iron and glass roof. In its heyday, only one building in America, the United States Capitol, had more visitors per year than Grand Central Depot. The Depot, remodeled in the 1890's, was torn down and replaced by Grand Central Terminal early in the twentieth century.

The elaborate drug store on the ground floor of Gilsey House, in this circa 1875 photograph, gives us some idea of the establishment's original splendor.

John Snook's Grand Central Depot, circa 1875. The doors at the far right were a key part of its operations. After a train came down Park Avenue and arrived in the train shed behind the terminal, the passenger cars were uncoupled from the locomotive. Horses then pulled the passenger cars through these doors and south along Park Avenue to a more centrally located station, where the passengers were discharged.

The Bethesda Fountain, sculpted by Emma Stebbins, is a Central Park landmark.

Those who are familiar with the history of Central Park know of the important roles played by co-designers Frederick Law Olmstead and Calvert Vaux, but the substantial contributions of the English-trained architect JACOB WREY MOULD (1825–1886) have largely been ignored. Mould was appointed Assistant Chief Architect of Public Works for New York City in late 1857, and during the Civil War years he designed some of the great landmarks of Central Park, including the panels that flank the grand staircases connecting the Drive and the plaza at the Terrace (left), Bow Bridge (right, designed with Calvert Vaux) and several other bridges, the Ladies' Pavilion, and the Music Stand.

EMMA STEBBINS (1815–1882) was born in New York City, where her father JOHN STEBBINS was a prominent Wall Street broker and president of the North River Bank. Raised in a cultured home, as a child she wrote verse and songs and painted. She studied with HENRY INMAN (1801–1846) (whose remains were removed from Green-Wood Cemetery nine years after his death), New York's leading portrait painter, and by 1843, she was so accomplished in her painting that she was elected an associate of the National Academy of Design.

In 1857, Emma Stebbins went to Rome to study painting, but soon turned to sculpture, and studied under Maine-born Benjamin Akers and an Italian master. Her bronze statue of Horace Mann was placed in front of the State House in Boston in 1865.

Her best-known work, *The Angel of the Waters*, today cherished as *Bethesda Fountain*, was unveiled in Central Park in 1873. It depicts the Biblical story of the angel who descended to the pool at Bethesda to stir the waters, giving them healing powers. Four cherubs, Temperance, Purity, Health, and Peace, support the angel. For this work, the first commission given to a woman for a major work in New York City, Emma Stebbins received the unprecedented sum of $60,000 (just over $1 million today).

Critics of the time were not impressed with *The Angel of the Waters*, suspecting that her commission was the result of the influence of her brother HENRY STEBBINS (1811–1881), who was president of Central Park's Board of Commissioners. However, over the years it has become a beloved New York landmark.

A BELOVED NEW YORKER

HORACE GREELEY (1811–1872), the founder and editor of the *New York Tribune*, was born in Amherst, New Hampshire, and apprenticed to a printer. When his master closed his business in 1831, Greeley set off, with $25 and his possessions in a handkerchief, for New York City. He worked a succession of jobs there, edited several publications, and in 1841, founded the *New York Tribune*, which he edited for the rest of his life. His aim was to create "a journal removed alike from servile partisanship on the one hand, and from gagged, mincing neutrality on the other." Widely known for his ideals and moral fervor, Greeley advocated many causes, including workers' rights, women's rights (though not woman suffrage), scientific farming, free distribution of government lands, and the abolition of slavery and capital punishment. By the late 1850's, the *Tribune* had a national influence as great as any other newspaper in the country, particularly in the rural North.

The *Tribune* was the first American newspaper to employ women reporters who wrote under their own byline. It introduced American readers to Charles Dickens, published Edgar Allan Poe's *The Raven*, and gave Karl Marx, Greeley's foreign correspondent in London, his first exposure in this country.

Greeley was known for his enthusiastic inconsistency. At the beginning of the Civil War, he criticized Lincoln for his "obstinate tameness" and urged him "Forward to Richmond" before Bull Run, the first battle of that war; only days later, after the defeat of the Union Army there, Greeley advocated armistice and the immediate disbandment of that army. After the Civil War, Greeley called for amnesty for Southerners and provided part of the bail to get Confederate President Jefferson Davis out of jail. Greeley coined the phrases "Know-Nothings" and "Copperheads," and told the unemployed during the Panic of 1837, to "Go West, young man, and grow with the country."

Greeley, who was long in the public eye, was admired by many and viewed with affectionate amusement by others. He was a familiar figure on New York City's streets, wearing a wrinkled white coat, his pockets stuffed with crumpled newspapers. But he always wanted very much to be a statesman. He served in Congress as a Whig for three months from 1848 to 1849, but ran unsuccessfully for the House of Representatives in 1850, 1868, and 1870, and for the U.S. Senate in 1861 and 1863.

The political career of "Old Chappaquack" (as he was popularly known) ended tragically with his campaign for President as the Democratic and Liberal Republican candidate in 1872. In that campaign, Greeley urged leniency for the South, equal rights for white and blacks, and thrift and honesty in government. For these positions, he was attacked as a traitor, fool, and crank, and was derisively referred to by noted cartoonist Thomas Nast as "Horrors Greeley." Greeley's wife of thirty-six years (whom he met at a vegetarian boarding house in New York City) died two weeks before the election, he was soundly defeated by Grant at the polls, and he returned to his beloved *Tribune* only to discover that its control had passed to Whitelaw Reid.

Weeks later, as Greeley lay on his deathbed, he looked up to see Whitelaw Reid, the man who had wrested control of his *Tribune* from him. Greeley, never one to mince words, could not restrain himself, snarling, "You son of a bitch, you stole my newspaper." Reid was later asked what Greeley's last words were. He diplomatically recalled them as "I know my redeemer liveth."

Horace Greeley's monument.

Greeley's funeral, held on December 4, 1872, was attended by President Grant, cabinet members, governors of three States, and an outpouring of mourners who remembered him as a beloved public figure.

Horace Greeley, a beloved New Yorker and national political figure.

Greeley wrote his own epitaph:

Fame is a vapor; popularity an accident; riches take wings; the only earthly certainty is oblivion; no man can foresee what a day will bring forth; while those who cheer today will often curse tomorrow; and yet I cherish the hope that the journal I projected and established will live and flourish long after I have mouldered into forgotten dust . . . and that the stone which covers my ashes may bear to future eyes the still intelligible inscription, Founder of *The New York Tribune*.

The *Tribune* published its last New York edition on August 15, 1966; an international edition is still published.

Greeley's monument was erected by America's printers. Topped by a bust of him, the pedestal has a bronze bas-relief on one side which shows Greeley as a youth, with composing stick in hand, standing over his type case. Another panel depicts a plow, an apparent allusion to the famous "Go West" statement. A pen and a scroll are carved in the granite.

SEW WHAT'S NEW?

This advertising card was distributed by a salesman for Elias Howe's sewing machines.

ELIAS HOWE, JR. (1819–1867) was born in Spencer, Massachusetts to an impoverished family. At the age of six he went to work, alongside his brothers and sisters, sticking wire teeth through leather straps. Marrying at the age of twenty-one, he struggled to support his wife and children with his mechanical skills. In 1846, his breakthrough came when he patented the first efficient sewing machine. It sewed at a rate of 250 stitches a minute, five times faster than the swiftest hand sewer. However, it was not all that efficient. The cloth had to be hung vertically, pinned to a baster plate, and the machine could only be advanced for the several-inch-length of that plate; then the cloth had to be unpinned, moved, and

This is the bronze bust of Elias Howe, sculpted by Charles Calverley.

repinned to the plate. The result was an inconsistent thread tension and slow, finger-pricking work. Nevertheless, even this primitive machine met resistance from seamstresses and tailors in America, who feared that it would put them out of work.

Howe, rebuffed in America, went to England to introduce his invention to the world. Two years later, when he returned destitute to the United States, he discovered that his invention had been pirated. After five years of litigation, he won his patent suit, gaining protection for his combination of the eye-pointed needle and a shuttle that formed a lock stitch. Thereafter, Howe received a royalty on every sewing machine that was manufactured in America. His annual income, which only a few years earlier was $300, soon grew to $200,000 (about $5.2 million today), and he became a millionaire.

During the Civil War, Howe enlisted as a private in the 17th Connecticut Regiment. However, failing health forced his resignation. When the financial strain of the war was heavy on the Union, Howe paid to outfit that regiment and send it into the field.

Howe's monument at Green-Wood Cemetery is in a prime location, at the intersection of Battle and Hemlock Avenues, and is surrounded by a granite curb. His bust was sculpted by Charles Calverley.

Near Tulip Path.

CHAPTER FIVE

The Centennial and Beyond (1876-1889)

FASHION IN FUNERALS

I SAAC HULL BROWN (1812–1880) wore many hats, and all of them were fashionable. He was the longtime sexton of Grace Church, "the most fashionable and exclusive of our metropolitan Courts of Heaven." As New York's first social arbiter, Brown collected intimate information on every household in his parish, and used that intelligence to advise his followers whom to invite and whom to snub. He knew the blood lines, financial affairs, and domestic troubles of everyone in New York society, and was only too anxious to pass his gossip along.

A hostess contemplating an entertainment event would send for Sexton Brown, and together they would choose the proper guests. Brown then made the arrangements and personally delivered the invitations. When the guests arrived, Brown, in trilby hat and huge overcoat, was on the sidewalk to greet them; for this he was known as "the connecting link between Society and the curbstone." If the hostess had invited certain guests despite Brown's disapproval, he greeted those he helped from their carriages with a whispered warning, "Very mixed, *very*."

It was Sexton Brown who made arrangements for New York City's 1860 gala ball in honor of the Prince of Wales. The good sexton also created Brown's Brigade, society's first male escort service, by compiling a list of presentable young men for hire, who would appear as needed for supper or dance in black swallowtail coats, white vests, and white cravats. His ultimate regret, however, was his limited reach: "I cannot undertake to control society above Fiftieth Street."

Brown was also in the undertaking and carriage-rental businesses. As he remarked, "The Lenten season is horribly dull, but we make our funerals as entertaining as possible." Just as in entertainment, funerals had their fashion. As one New York City guide wrote of Sexton Brown:

Fashion does not change more frequently in dress than in the method of conducting funerals in high life. What constituted a very genteel funeral last year would be a very vulgar one this. Cards of invitation are sent out as to a party. Sometimes the shutters of the house are closed, and the funeral takes place in gas-light. The lights are arranged for artistic effect. Parties who have the entree of fashionable life can tell, the moment they enter the rooms, what fashionable sexton has charge of the funeral. The arrangement of the furniture, the position of the coffin, the laying out of the body, the coffin itself, the adjustment of the lights, the hanging of the drapery, the plate-

How to explain why Sexton Brown is buried beneath this statue of Pythagoras? It is unlikely that Brown hoped to spend his eternity calculating the length of the hypotenuse of a right triangle. Rather, this unusual, perhaps unique, choice of a monument is in all likelihood related to the belief of Pythagoras (c. 580 B.C.–c. 500 B.C.) in the heavenly destiny of the soul and the possibility that it will rise to union with the divine. Pythagoras considered himself to be semidivine, with knowledge greater than that of others because he could remember his earlier incarnations; he rejected the idea that a human being lives only one life on Earth as the illusion of a lost memory. Salvation, according to his teachings, would be achieved through study of the cosmic order, and knowledge was the path to divinity. The idea that the soul lives in the body but can exist apart from it originated with Pythagoras's followers. It seems likely that Sexton Brown thought he knew more than anyone else about New York society, and that that knowledge just might be his ticket to heaven.

glass hearse, the number of horses, the size and quality of the plumes on the hearse and team, indicate the style of the funeral, and the wealth and social position of the family. Mourning has a style peculiar to itself, and the intensity of the grief is indicated by the depth of the crape.

One society lady honored stylish and bustling Sexton Brown with this verse:

> Oh, glorious Brown! thou medley strange
> Of churchyard, ball-room, saint and sinner!
> Flying by morn through Fashion's range,
> And burying mortals after dinner!
> Walking one day with invitations-
> Passing the next at consecrations;
> Tossing the sod at eve on coffins;
> With one hand drying the tears of orphans,
> And one unclasping ball-room carriage,
> Or cutting plum cake up for marriage:
> Dusting by day the pew and missal;
> Sounding by night the ball-room whistle,
> Admitted free through Fashion's wicket,
> And skilled at psalms, at punch, and cricket.

JOHN GENIN'S PEDESTRIAN BRIDGE ACROSS BROADWAY

ONLY A HANDFUL of people have ever heard of JOHN NICHOLAS GENIN (1819–1878), and his monument at Green-Wood Cemetery gives no hint of his fascinating life. A hatter by profession, Genin reached national prominence in the 1850's. Like P. T. Barnum, his neighbor on Broadway, Genin had a remarkable knack for using publicity to boost his business.

In 1850, at Barnum's urging, Genin made the winning auction bid of $225 for the first seat sold for the sensational cross-country tour by the singer Jenny Lind, the Swedish Nightingale, and reaped the tremendous publicity that followed. Every important newspaper in the country reported Genin's bid. Barnum wrote in his *Struggles and Triumphs* (1865) that "John N. Genin, the hatter, laid the foundation of his fortune" with this purchase. Throughout the country, men and women took off their hats to check whether they were wearing "a Genin."

When the Hungarian patriot Louis Kossuth came to New York City in 1851, Genin again seized the moment. He met Kossuth's ship off Sandy Hook, and gave him and his followers hats from his "dead stock," with black feathers added, for them to wear as they paraded up Broadway. Genin, as soon as the parade was over, briskly sold the rest of his "dead stock" hats.

In 1852, when Amelia Bloomer needed a hat to go with the Bloomer-pants outfit she had designed, she turned to Genin, who produced the first round hat for fashionable young women, giving them an alternative to the bonnet.

When public officials, in 1854, ignored public demands for clean streets, Genin took the bull by the horns, and hired, at his own expense, one hundred men and carts to do the work. For this act he was offered the nomination for mayor, but declined the honor, preferring to remain in the hat business.

But John Genin's greatest scheme was a pedestrian bridge across Broadway. From the late 1830's to the early 1860's, New York City's fashionable shopping area was on Broadway, near City Hall. That area, particularly where Park Row met Broadway, was a traffic nightmare, and only the most adventurous pedestrians even tried to cross the street there. One wag claimed that it took "more skill to cross Broadway than to cross the Atlantic in a clamboat." Things got so bad that a special squad of policemen was detailed to help shoppers get from one side of Broadway to the other.

In this Currier print of the controversial Bloomer costume, the headgear design is by hatmaker John Genin.

This print, engraved for the December 25, 1852, issue of Gleason's Pictorial Drawing-Room Companion, *shows "Genin's Bridge," his plan to make his hat store accessible to the fashionable shoppers who frequented Broadway's west side.*

The pedestrian bridge across Broadway at Fulton Street was finally built, in 1866, as Loew Bridge, but was torn down only two years later. Note St. Paul's Chapel at left, where George Washington worshipped during his Presidency, and which still stands.

Businesses on the east side of Broadway particularly suffered from this traffic problem. Stores on the west side of the street had their windows lit by the morning sun; as a result, that was the fashionable or shilling side, and the east side was the cheap or penny side. Shoppers who didn't want to fight their way across Broadway were likely to confine their shopping sprees to the more stylish shops on Broadway's west side.

John Genin, whose "Hat Shop for Gentlemen" was on the corner of Fulton Street, opposite St. Paul's Chapel, was one of the businessmen on Broadway's less-stylish east side. A creative man, Genin had a solution to his problem: a pedestrian bridge across Broadway. Genin agitated for four-

Hatter John Genin's monument.

teen years, until New York City's political leaders finally built Loew Bridge at Fulton Street and Broadway in 1866.

But the matter was not yet settled. The "Mad Hatters' Feud" followed, in which Knox, Genin's hat-selling competitor directly across Broadway, campaigned to have Loew Bridge torn down. Knox's argument, that the bridge was a nuisance which "has put my business in the shade" and attracted disreputable characters who lurked in its shadows, soon won out. In 1868, only two years after the cast iron bridge for which Genin had fought so long was built at a cost of $25,000 to city taxpayers, it was torn down at the additional public expense of $9,000 (together equal to more than half a million dollars in today's money).

THE TWEED COURTHOUSE: MONUMENT TO CORRUPTION

IT HAS BEEN estimated that during his reign of corruption, WILLIAM MARCY ("BOSS") TWEED (1823–1878), the "Tiger of Tammany," and his political cronies stole $200 million (the equivalent of about $3.5 billion in today's money) from the citizens of New York. Tweed, serving as New York State Senator, Democratic County Chairman, School Commissioner, Deputy Street Commissioner, and President of the Board of Supervisors, had untold schemes to put public money into his own pockets and those of his friends. But his greatest single thievery project was the New York County Courthouse on Chambers Street, described at the time as "The House that Tweed Built."

In 1858, the New York State Legislature approved "a sum not exceeding $250,000" (close to $6 million today) for the construction and furnishing of New York City's courthouse. This was a substantial sum in an era when school teachers were making only $300 per year. But that appropriation was nothing compared to what the Tweed Ring had in mind for their grandest exercise in graft. In an era in which all of the land for Central Park cost New York City $5 million, and the elaborate St. Patrick's Cathedral cost $2 million to build, the Tweed Courthouse wound up costing New York's taxpayers $12 million (equivalent to about $200 million today). More money was spent to build the Tweed Courthouse than was spent to construct the United States Capitol. In fact, the Courthouse was the costliest public building that had yet been built in the United States.

It is no mystery why the Tweed Courthouse cost so much to build: bills were, as the reformer ROBERT ROOSEVELT said, "manifestly fabulous," wildly inflated in order to provide generous sums for kickbacks. Billings for plaster work by Andrew J. Garvey, the grand marshal of Tammany Hall who was dubbed the "Prince of Plasterers," were $3 million; much of that was for Garvey's repairs of his own work. The final expenditure for brooms for the courthouse, $250,000, matched the total originally budgeted for the entire building. Enough carpet was ordered (close to $5 million worth) to cover all of City Hall Park three times, and many of the companies billing

Boss Tweed, who for years was the most powerful man in New York, was a frequent subject of Thomas Nast's cartoons. Tweed fully understood the damage that Nast's drawings did him, once remarking, "I don't care a straw for your newspaper articles; my constituents don't know how to read, but they can't help seeing them damned pictures." When Tweed was finally processed to begin his prison sentence, he was asked, for the record, to state his profession; his reply was "Statesman."

The Tweed Courthouse, a monument to corruption, pictured in Harper's Weekly *in 1871, when "work" was still in progress. This view looks east from Broadway; City Hall appears at the right. The Courthouse stairway was sheared off years later when Chambers Street was widened.*

for carpeting did not even exist. Thermometers for the courthouse cost $7,500. Three tables and forty chairs were billed at $179,729. Over $1 million was paid for plumbing work. The marble for the courthouse was purchased from a quarry in Massachusetts that Tweed himself just happened to have recently purchased; quarrying that marble cost more than it had cost to build an entire courthouse in Brooklyn.

Before the Tweed Courthouse was done, two of New York's most prominent architects, JOHN KELLUM (1809–1871), succeeded upon his

Boss Tweed's family plot is one of the few at Green-Wood Cemetery still surrounded by its original fence. His monument is at center rear.

death by LEOPOLD EIDLITZ (1823–1908), had labored on its design over the twenty years of its construction. Kellum designed the courthouse as a grand Italianate civic monument. Eidlitz later planned the southern wing in the style for which he was the chief proponent, Victorian medievalism, and modified Kellum's design for the rotunda.

After a campaign led by *The New York Times* and cartoonist Thomas Nast of *Harper's Weekly*, Tweed was arrested for his crimes in 1871, and the Tweed Ring was finally forced from power. Tweed went to trial in November, 1873; ironically, his trial was held in the still-incomplete courthouse. Tweed was convicted of 204 counts, but he escaped from custody and fled to Spain, only to be recaptured by Spanish officials who, relying on a Nast cartoon, recognized him. Tweed was brought back to New York City, spent some time in prison, and died in 1878.

In 1974, a task force appointed by Mayor Abraham Beame recommended that the Tweed Courthouse be torn down. It survives today (without its monumental stairway, which was sheared off in 1942 for the widening of Chambers Street) because preservationists convinced the powers that be that there could be no more lasting monument to political corruption than the Tweed Courthouse. Of the public buildings that have occupied City Hall Park over the years, only the Tweed Courthouse and City Hall survive. Both the interior and the exterior of the Tweed Courthouse are designated New York City landmarks.

GUILTY AS SIN

IN 1847, the Rev. HENRY WARD BEECHER (1813–1887) became the pastor of Plymouth Church in Brooklyn Heights. Within a few years, his sermons, spreading the "Gospel of Love," captivated the country. The Sunday morning ferries from New York City to Brooklyn, which brought thousands over to see "the Great Divine" preach in his emotional style, became known as "Beecher Boats." Beecher was the conscience of the country, an activist for abolition, the spokesman for liberal Christianity, and perhaps the most popular preacher in America. When rifles were sent to Bloody Kansas in the 1850's, to be used by Free Soilers in the fight against slavery, they were known as "Beecher's Bibles" in his honor. But the Rev. Beecher's affair with Elizabeth Tilton would topple Beecher from his exalted position.

ELIZABETH RICHARDS TILTON (1834–1897), a schoolmate of one of Beecher's daughters and a graduate of the Brooklyn Female Seminary, married Theodore Tilton in 1855. The holy ceremony was performed by Rev. Beecher. When Theodore Tilton went to work as a reporter, his first assignment was to stenographically record Beecher's sermons. Soon he and Beecher were working together at what was to become the leading religious newspaper in America, *The Independent*, with Theodore as its managing editor and Beecher as its editor-in-chief. Beecher was Tilton's father figure; Tilton loved Beecher "as he had no other man," and Beecher had no closer friend than Tilton.

Theodore Tilton toured the country, lecturing on popular topics, including abolition, Reconstruction, and women's rights. Together, Theodore Tilton, Henry Ward Beecher, and Henry C. Bowen (who owned *The Independent* and who had invited Beecher, in 1847, to lead the newly-formed Plymouth Church) were known as "the Trinity of Plymouth Church." Both Elizabeth and Theodore Tilton were active members of Plymouth Church, teaching Sunday school there and serving on church committees. Theodore was also the superintendent of the Plymouth Sunday School.

Though for a short time Elizabeth edited a poetry column in *Revolution*, a suffragist journal, and both she and her husband were prominent in the Equal Rights Association, she never felt comfortable with Theodore's intellectual circle. He once told a friend that "Elizabeth was undervalued in her intellectual character, she was so domestic and so quiet; but that she was the finest critic he ever had." At other times, such as when Theodore told her at a gathering of his friends that "I would give $500 if you were not by my side," the message was unmistakable that he was ashamed of her.

In 1863, as Lucy Bowen (Henry C. Bowen's wife) lay on her deathbed, she announced that she had a final confession to make: she and Rev. Beecher had had an affair. Soon thereafter, Henry Bowen wrote to Theodore Tilton: "One word from me would make a revolution in Christendom." Bowen, fearing that a scandal would kill his newspaper, decided to keep quiet. But he never again entered Beecher's house.

According to the court papers later filed, it was on October 10, 1868, with Theodore Tilton away on a lecture trip, that Elizabeth, after two years of repeated overtures, finally gave in to Beecher's urgings for "romantic love," and their affair began. (Earlier that same year Theodore, on one of his lecture trips, had had an affair of his own.) Theodore learned of Beecher's affair on July 4, 1870, when his wife confessed to him.

Henry Bowen and Theodore Tilton, working quietly behind the scenes, tried to force Beecher's resignation from Plymouth Church. But Beecher refused, and sought Theodore's forgiveness. As private negotiations continued into 1872, "free love" advocates (and sisters) Victoria Woodhull and Tennessee Claflin, hoping that Beecher would be forced to abandon his hypocrisy and publicly join their cause, broke the scandal in their newspaper. Though they invited Beecher to sue for libel if he dared, he filed no suit, hoping that his "policy of silence" would make the scandal go away. The sisters, however, were jailed by U.S. Attorney BENJAMIN FRANKLIN TRACY for sending obscene material (their newspaper account) through the mail. The charges against them, however, were soon dropped, and the scandal died down.

However, Theodore Tilton, rebuked by Beecher's supporters and dropped from Plymouth Church's rolls, decided in 1874 to go public and expose Beecher. Decades later it would still be referred to as "The Great Scandal"; no other event of the time was more written and talked about. Tilton filed a $100,000 civil lawsuit against Beecher for alienation of affection, promising not to take the money if he won. Elizabeth Tilton left her

Henry Beecher, Elizabeth Tilton, and Theodore Tilton, the principal players in "The Great Scandal."

PRICE, 25 CENTS.

YᴱTILT-
ON

ᴼᴿ Yᵉ
Muddle of yᵉ Mutual Friends,
A BURLESQUE IN VERSE.

This pamphlet, *Ye Tilt-on Beecher, Or Ye Muddle of Ye Mutual Friends, A Burlesque in Verse*, printed in 1874, is typical of the satire to which Beecher was subjected. Carrying on for twenty-four pages, it begins with this:

One day a great Preacher fell into a
    Puddle,
And some Mutual Friends found them-
    selves in a Muddle.
        But *what* was the Puddle,
        Or *where* was the Muddle,
Or *how* or *how deep* in the Muddle they
    fell,
Neither Preacher or Friends or Public
    could tell.
        "They had no idea;"
        But one thing was clear—
In the Puddle *he* was, and he could not get
    out;
In the Muddle *they* were, and they
    floundered about;
They tossed to and fro, just like tubs
    without handle,
And wallowed about in ye Pool of ye
    Scandal.

husband, and publicly denied the adultery. But Charles A. Dana of the *New York Sun* was among the many who were unconvinced: "Henry Ward Beecher is an adulterer, a perjurer and a fraud; and his great genius and his Christian pretense only make his sins the more horrible and revolting."

The trial, which captivated Brooklyn, New York City, and the nation for one hundred and twelve days, began in Brooklyn's Courthouse on January 11, 1876. Reporters from throughout the country packed the courtroom, ready to transmit instantaneously the latest developments back to their home offices by specially-installed telegraph lines. The top attorneys in the country battled for their clients. Opening and closing statements alone took two months. Roger Pryor, who had been a leading secessionist and a Confederate brigadier general, represented Theodore Tilton. Benjamin Franklin Tracy, Beecher's attorney, a former Union general and Civil War hero, attacked Theodore Tilton with purple prose like this:

> A staunch new vessel, launched upon an honorable voyage, sailing with prosperous winds over unruffled seas, has been transformed into a pirate by the wickedness of her commander, and wrecked by his folly, and now lies a stranded and battered hulk, the object at once of the curiosity and abhorrence of mankind.

As the trial proceeded, opera glasses were sold in the courtroom. So many bouquets were sent to the courtroom by Tilton and Beecher partisans that the trial became known as the "flower war." Beecher testified and denied the charges, claiming that Tilton was nothing but a blackmailer. The defense of "The Great Divine" was a simple one: he, the embodiment of American purity and virtue, was too good a man to have had an affair with Elizabeth Tilton. Elizabeth Tilton was never called as a witness.

After six months of testimony by over one hundred witnesses and a week of deliberations, during which reporters kept spyglasses trained on the jury room, the jury announced that it could not reach a verdict, and that it was deadlocked at nine to three in favor of defendant Beecher.

After the trial, Plymouth Church raised Beecher's yearly salary to the unheard-of sum of $100,000 (about $2 million today) to help him pay his legal bills. Elizabeth Tilton, who had testified at Congregational Council and Plymouth Church hearings that Beecher was innocent, lived on a $10,000-a-year payment (equal to $200,000 today) provided by Beecher and his supporters. But by April, 1878, she could take it no more, and publicly confirmed that she had had an adulterous affair with Beecher: "The lie I have lived the last four years has become intolerable." Shortly thereafter all payments from the trust ended, and she was excommunicated from Plymouth Church.

Elizabeth Tilton, ostracized by everyone except her daughter and a radical group known as the "Christian Friends," died lonely and blind in 1897, at her daughter's Brooklyn home. Theodore Tilton left the United States in 1883, and spent the rest of his life in Paris, living in an attic room, writing poetry and romantic novels, and playing chess, until he died impoverished in 1907. Henry Ward Beecher, though he remained a popular preacher, was no longer taken as seriously as a moral leader by the public. Sales of his sermons and books suffered, and he became the brunt of satire.

But Beecher was unrepentant. In 1884, during the Presidential election, he defended Grover Cleveland at a mass meeting in Brooklyn against revelations that Cleveland had fathered an illegitimate child: "If every man in New York State who has broken the seventh commandment voted for Cleveland, he would be elected by a 200,000 majority."

Today, in one of Green-Wood Cemetery's prime locations, on Battle Hill overlooking New York Harbor, there is a good-sized plot that has neither a central monument nor any marker naming the individuals buried in it. At the corner of the plot there is a granite stone, flush with the ground, marking the corner of the plot. It has but one word on it: "Tilton." A few feet away is another marker, again with only one word carved on its surface: "Grandmother." Nothing tells the passerby that this is the final resting place of Elizabeth Tilton, one of the principals in "the Great Scandal."

Henry Ward Beecher is buried not far away from Elizabeth Tilton, on another Green-Wood hillside; his stone, ignoring the point that Beecher was accused of doing evil, boldly proclaims "He thinketh no evil." Theodore Tilton is buried in France.

Henry Ward Beecher's granite monument bears the rather ironic epitaph, "He thinketh no evil."

GRANDPA AND HIS GRANDDAUGHTER

PETER LAWSON, "Grandpa," died in 1887, at the age of eighty-four. His granddaughter, JENSINE GOMARD, died the next year at the age of twenty-two. They are pictured together on this monument. She holds a rose, symbolic of a female who died too young.

"THE LIGHT WENT FROM MY LIFE FOR EVER"

IN 1884, Theodore Roosevelt (1858–1919) seemed to have it all. Born into a prosperous and respected New York family, he graduated from Harvard, married ALICE HATHAWAY LEE ROOSEVELT (1861–1884), the love of his life, and was elected to the New York State Assembly. As the legislative session ground on in Albany, he waited expectantly: their first child was due any minute.

On February 12, 1884, Theodore received a telegram in Albany telling him that Alice Roosevelt had been born, that she was fine, but his wife was "only fairly well." Perhaps that was to be expected after a first delivery.

Roosevelt's colleagues gathered around to congratulate him, to shake his hand, and he was all aglow. But soon a second telegram arrived, and his expression turned somber. He caught the first train back to New York City, but it crept painfully through the fog as it approached New York City. When Theodore finally reached the Roosevelt home at 6 West 57th Street, his brother Elliott met him at the door, crying "There is a curse on this house. Mother is dying and Alice is dying too."

Their mother, MARTHA BULLOCH ROOSEVELT ("Mittie") (1835–1884), who appeared to have been suffering from nothing more than a cold,

"Grandpa and His Granddaughter."

Theodore Roosevelt's wife, Alice Hathaway Lee Roosevelt (top), and his mother, Martha Bulloch Roosevelt (bottom), who died the same day. Portrait of Alice Hathaway Lee Roosevelt, Dictionary of American Portraits, Dover Publications.

now lay dying from typhoid fever. Theodore's wife Alice, only twenty-two years old, was so ill with Bright's Disease, a kidney inflammation, that she was barely able to recognize him. Rushing to his wife's bedside, he held her for two long hours, hoping that he could somehow give her strength. Told that he had to come immediately if he wanted to see his mother alive, he hurried to her room. Before the day was out, both his mother and his wife lay dead.

Theodore Roosevelt drew a large cross in his diary for February 14, and wrote beneath it, "The light has gone out of my life." Two days later his diary entry noted that "we spent three years of happiness greater and more unalloyed than I have ever known fall to the lot of others." He concluded, "For joy or for sorrow my life has now been lived out."

The shock of these two deaths, at a time when Roosevelt had been "full of happiness," threatened his ability to go on. Bewildered by the hand that fate had dealt him, he showed no interest in his baby, and was unable to communicate with his friends and relatives. Instead, he paced his room, red-eyed, trying to understand.

New York's leading newspapers somberly described these deaths. The *World* noted, "Seldom, if ever, has New York society received such a shock as yesterday in [these] sad and sudden deaths." The *Herald* remembered Roosevelt's mother, Mittie, for her "brilliant powers as leader of a *salon*" and her "high breeding and elegant conversation." Alice Hathaway Lee Roosevelt, noted the same newspaper, was "famed for her beauty, as well as many graces of the heart and head." The *Tribune* was worried about Theodore: "The loss of his wife and mother in a single day is a terrible affliction, [and] it is doubtful whether he will be able to return to his labors."

Two days later it dawned sunny, with temperatures in the twenties. The double funeral, which began at the Fifth Avenue Presbyterian Church and proceeded behind twin hearses bearing rosewood coffins to Green-Wood Cemetery, was attended by the political and social leaders of New York. Astors, Vanderbilts, Harrimans, and Roosevelts were all there. Theodore looked stunned and dazed.

After the funerals, Roosevelt briefly threw himself into his work in the Assembly. However, he soon found that he was unable to keep going and retreated to the Badlands of Dakota, staying there for two years in an effort to overcome his grief.

Theodore never spoke Alice Hathaway Roosevelt's name again, and never talked to his daughter about her mother. His autobiography, full of the joys of family life, contains no mention of his love who had died so young. But the summer after her death, Theodore gathered the text of the tributes to her, the funeral service, the speeches given in her memory by his colleagues in the Assembly, and newspaper clippings, added his own words, and sent it all off to be published privately as a memorial to Alice. On the first page he wrote of Alice:

. . . She was beautiful in face and form, and lovelier still in spirit; as a flower she grew, and as a fair young flower she died. Her life had been always in the sunshine; there had never come to her a single great sorrow; and none ever knew her who did not love and revere her for her bright, sunny temper and her saintly unselfishness. Fair, pure, and joyous as a maiden; loving, tender, and happy as a young wife; when she had just become a mother, when her life seemed to be but just begun, and when the years seemed so bright before her—then, by a strange and terrible fate, death came to her.

And when my heart's dearest died, the light went from my life for ever.

But life was far from over for Theodore Roosevelt. In 1886, he married his childhood sweetheart, Edith Carow. Elected governor of New York and Vice President of the United States, he became, in 1901, at the age of forty-two, the youngest man ever to assume the office of President of the United States.

The side by side monuments to Alice Hathaway Lee Roosevelt and Martha Bulloch Roosevelt. Carvings describe each of them as the "wife of Theodore Roosevelt"; the future President's father (who is buried a few feet away) was also named Theodore. President Theodore Roosevelt is interred in Oyster Bay, New York.

JAILED, DEAD AND BURIED, BUT STILL NOT SILENCED

A NATIVE of Springfield, New York, DE ROBIGNE MORTIMER BENNETT (1818–1882) attended school in Cooperstown, and at the age of fourteen joined the Shaker community in New Lebanon, New York. There, he worked in the seed gardens, learned herbal medicine, and became the community's physician. In 1846, he and others, including his sister and Mary Wicks, his soon-to-be wife, left the Shakers to rejoin "the world."

For the next twenty-seven years, Bennett went from place to place, earning his living as a nurseryman and druggist. His greatest financial success was as the purveyor of "Dr. Bennett's Quick Cure, Golden Liniment, Worm Lozenges, and Root and Plant Pills."

By 1873, Bennett had turned to freethinking, and was publishing the *Truthseeker* to spread his views. He wrote many books espousing his radical views, including *The World's Sages, Thinkers, and Reformers* (1876), *From Behind the Bars* (1881), and *A Truth-Seeker Around the World* (1882). From 1877 until his death, Bennett was persecuted for his opinions. His attacks on clergymen and the Bible were too much for that protector of civic virtue, Anthony Comstock, who three times tried to initiate criminal proceedings against Bennett. The first two efforts went nowhere; the third prosecution, before a judge friendly to Comstock, resulted in Bennett's conviction for sending indecent material through the mails. Bennett was sentenced to thirteen months in jail, and all efforts to spare him from prison, including a petition to President Rutherford B. Hayes signed by 200,000 citizens, fell on deaf ears. Bennett, sixty years old, served his time in jail, then upon his release was given a hero's reception in New York City by his friends. However, his health had suffered during his jailing, and after a short period of travel to spread his word, he died after a brief illness.

It was said of Bennett, "He was an amalgam of quack, crank, and ideal-

Theodore Roosevelt, in an 1885 photograph taken in the Dakota Badlands, where he went to forget the tragedies of the previous year.

The monument to freethinker De Robigne Mortimer Bennett shows how eager he was to spread his views. It is decorated with a quill subduing a sword, as in "the pen is mightier than the sword." Even in death, Bennett would not be silenced: the other three sides of his monument, erected by "one thousand friends," have "His Words," statements of his philosophy, carved in them.

ist. The quack and crank are somewhat excused by the hard conditions of his early life; the idealist, in spite of faults of taste and mistakes of judgment, was for almost a decade an effective popular spokesman for liberal ideas in religion and ethics." His monument at Green-Wood Cemetery, erected by fellow freethinkers, is covered with his statements.

YOU COULD DIE WAITING

EVEN IN THE 1880's, you could die waiting for a Democrat to be elected President, and GORDON WEBSTER BURNHAM (1803–1885) did just that. At the age of seventy-nine, Burnham decided to marry, but not just yet. He certainly could afford a wife; president of the Waterbury Clock, Waterbury Watch, and the American Pin companies, he had all the money he would ever need. But Burnham had sworn that he would not exchange marriage vows while there was a Republican in the White House. One day in 1885, Burnham went in his carriage to pick up his intended bride. The weather was nasty, and Burnham became ill as he waited. He died within days.

Burnham's monument at Green-Wood Cemetery is by the prolific sculptor John Moffitt. It is not surprising that Burnham chose a prominent sculptor for this work, for Burnham was long a patron of such art. In 1863, he gave the statue *Eagles and Prey* by Christian Fratin to New York City, and in 1876 he presented New York City with Thomas Beall's heroic bronze statue of Daniel Webster. Both still grace Central Park.

The Burnham Family monument is by prominent sculptor John Moffitt, who created several other works at Green-Wood Cemetery. This monument and the rest of the lot were cleaned and restored, with funds from the family, in 2006.

The makeshift morgue for the Brooklyn Theatre Fire victims, in a contemporary woodcut. Only one other disaster in New York City history, the burning of the steamship General Slocum, *claimed more victims.*

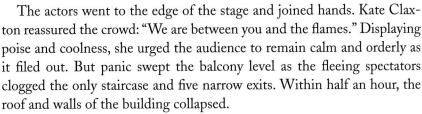

Kate Claxton as Louise in The Two Orphans. *After the fateful evening in 1876, she was known as "Kate Claxton of the Big Brooklyn Fire."*

THE BROOKLYN THEATRE FIRE MONUMENT

ON TUESDAY NIGHT, December 5, 1876, the Brooklyn Theatre, on the southeast corner of Johnson and Washington Streets in downtown Brooklyn, was packed with one thousand patrons. They were there for a performance of the phenomenally popular *The Two Orphans*, starring KATE CLAXTON (1848–1924) as the blind girl Louise, who triumphed over repeated misfortunes. Everything went smoothly until shortly after 11:00 p.m., just minutes before the play's end, when Claxton, on stage performing, heard whispers of "fire" from backstage. Looking into the wings, she and her fellow-actor could see what the audience could not: flames engulfing scenery which had been ignited by a kerosene lamp. When her fellow-actor hesitated in his lines, Claxton whispered "Go on, they will put it out, there will be a panic—go on." But the stagehands were unable to contain the fire, and the audience soon discovered it.

Flames consume the Brooklyn Theatre in this contemporary woodcut.

The actors went to the edge of the stage and joined hands. Kate Claxton reassured the crowd: "We are between you and the flames." Displaying poise and coolness, she urged the audience to remain calm and orderly as it filed out. But panic swept the balcony level as the fleeing spectators clogged the only staircase and five narrow exits. Within half an hour, the roof and walls of the building collapsed.

The next morning, firemen began to sift through the rubble, expecting to find only a few bodies. It was then, as they came across victim after victim, that the incredible loss of life became apparent. By the time the digging was done, 278 victims had been counted.

Kate Claxton was found that morning, dazed and badly burned, wandering in New York City's City Hall Park, unable to recall that she had crossed the East River by ferry from Brooklyn.

The Brooklyn Theatre Fire Monument, in a photograph circa 1890. The fence is no longer there.

Born Kate Eliza Cone in Somerville, New Jersey, Kate Claxton became a star actress. Both her grandfather and her father had dabbled in acting, but when she chose acting as a career, it was over her family's objections. She made her professional debut in Chicago in 1869, then came to New York City the next year to join Augustin Daly's company at the Fifth Avenue Theatre.

After disaster struck in 1876, while she was on stage at the Brooklyn Theatre, she was thereafter known as "Kate Claxton of the Big Brooklyn Fire." Soon after that fire, she was in the Southern Hotel in St. Louis when it also caught fire and burnt. Thereafter, many superstitious theatregoers refused to attend her performances.

Claxton acquired the rights to *The Two Orphans* in 1877, and toured nationally with it, playing her trademark role, Louise, until 1903. As an actress, Kate Claxton was known for her sweetness, beauty, and refinement, and was often referred to as "the Sarah Bernhardt of America." She was also successful as a businesswoman, managing her own stage productions for many years. She retired from the stage in 1904, the year that her son, Harold Stevenson, committed suicide.

Actress Kate Claxton in a celebrity photograph by NAPOLEON SARONY.

In 1878, Kate Claxton married Charles Stevenson, an actor in her company. While they were working apart, he secretly obtained a divorce and married another actress. When Claxton learned of this, she sued and had that divorce set aside, then had her marriage to Stevenson annulled. Given her marital troubles, it seems strange that her epitaph identifies her as "Wife of Charles A. Stevenson."

This contemporary woodcut shows the unclaimed victims of the Brooklyn Theatre Fire being placed in a common grave at Green-Wood Cemetery.

The City of Brooklyn went into mourning, and arrangements were made for a mass burial at Green-Wood Cemetery of those whose families could not afford to pay for burial or whose remains had been burnt beyond recognition. Within a few days of the tragedy, cemetery workers dug a circular trench seven feet deep for a common grave, and the hearses and undertakers' wagons lined up to unload the donated silver-trimmed caskets. Twelve Green-Wood employees lowered 103 coffins into the freshly-dug earth, arranging them with the victims' heads toward the center.

Two thousand mourners huddled together against a bitterly cold wind as sixty German singers lent their voices to Abt's *Repose*. After two hours of speeches and ceremonies were completed, forty-two diggers shoveled the soil over the coffins, and a floral crown and cross was placed on the freshly-dug earth by the Germania Theatre Company. A granite obelisk, carved with inscriptions describing the disaster, was later put in position atop the mound that marks the victims' final resting place.

SPIRIT RAPPERS

JOHN FOX knew a bargain when he saw one. Because neighbors were convinced that a farmhouse near Rochester, New York, was haunted by the spirit of a peddler who had been murdered there, he, his wife MARGARET (1797–1868), and their family rented it cheaply.

Shortly after they moved in, however, the strange occurrences began. On March 31, 1848, the Fox family was awakened by rapping sounds coming from the bedroom of daughters Kate and Margaret, ages twelve and nine. Mrs. Fox, investigating as Kate snapped her fingers three times, heard three knocks on the wall from "Mr. Splitfoot." Questions were asked about the ages of family members; correct answers were given with a knock for each year.

Anne Leah Fox (1818–1890), the oldest of the sisters who breathed life into Spiritualism. Dictionary of American Portraits, *Dover Publications.*

Word of these "spirit rappings" spread rapidly, and hundreds of people, hoping to communicate with departed loved ones, rushed to the house. Witnesses claimed that they saw tables lift off the floors, and mirrors and crockery shatter for no apparent reason.

ANNE LEAH FOX (1818?–1890), Kate's and Margaret's older sister, took them to her home, and invited neighbors to witness these strange events. The spirits mastered an alphabetical code, and rapped out long messages.

As news of these "Rochester Rappings" spread, the Fox sisters quickly became a national sensation. Millions of Americans were convinced by the sisters' experiences that there was an afterlife, and Spiritualism became the country's fastest-growing religion. James Fenimore Cooper, William Cullen Bryant, Frederick Douglass, and First Lady Mrs. Franklin Pierce, saw the sisters demonstrate these rappings, and left convinced of their supernatural abilities. The governor of Wisconsin, through Margaret and Kate, spoke with the ghosts of John C. Calhoun and Benjamin Franklin. HORACE GREELEY was also convinced: "We believe . . . that these singular sounds and seeming manifestations are not produced by Mrs. Fox and her daughters nor by any human connected with them." "Spiritualist circles" were formed throughout the country.

In 1850, Anne Fox brought her sisters to New York City, where they charged $100 (the equivalent of close to $3000 today) and up to conduct seances. Musical instruments and creaking ships were heard, and peculiar lights were seen. Kate recorded "spirit letters" backward and left-handed. "Rapomania" swept the country. During the Civil War, Spiritualism became even more popular as grieving parents paid mediums (most of whom were women) to help them speak one last time with their sons who had died in battle and had "passed over." Mary Todd Lincoln invited spiritualists to the White House, and President Lincoln attended their seances.

Kate toured England, married, and had a child who supposedly demonstrated the powers of a medium at the age of three months and wrote in Greek even before he could talk. Anne, the most active sister in promoting Spiritualism, continued to insist that her sisters' performances were beyond their control.

On October 21, 1888, forty years after the first rappings, Margaret confessed that their actions had been a hoax, telling her audience at the Academy of Music in New York City that "Spiritualism is an absolute falsehood from beginning to end." She explained that she and her sister had started their "rappings" to tease their superstitious mother, using an apple swung on a string to make the rapping sound. As her audience watched, Margaret then climbed onto a table to demonstrate the alternative technique of dislocating her big toe to make rappings. She explained that she had perfected this trick as a child and had taught it to her sister Kate. The headline in the *New York Herald* the next day summed it up: "HER BIG TOE DID IT ALL."

Margaret, in her confession, maintained that her older sister Anne was fully aware of the hoax. In fact, she said, Anne had herself tried to imitate the rappings, but was unable to do so because she could not throw her own big toe out of joint. Margaret's confession, published in her book, *The Death-Blow of Spiritualism*, had a devastating impact on Spiritualism, an impact from which it never recovered.

"MILE-A-MINUTE" MURPHY

WHEN BICYCLIST CHARLES M. MURPHY (1871–1950) bragged in the 1880's that "there is not a locomotive built which could get away from me," everyone laughed except Long Island Rail Road publicist Hal Fullerton. Fullerton realized the promotional windfall that would occur if Murphy could set a world bicycle record by pedaling sixty miles an hour behind a wind-screened pace coach pulled by a L.I.R.R. locomotive. He contacted Murphy, who was confident that he could do it, and agreed to give it his all.

Mile-A-Minute Murphy Training on a Bicycle Machine, *Courtesy of the Suffolk County Historical Society.*

While railroad workers worked at laying a smooth wooden track between the rails on a level three-mile straightaway stretching from Farmingdale to Babylon on Long Island, Murphy trained for his race against the clock.

On June 30, 1889, at 5:10 p.m., with the president of the Amateur Athletics Union, reporters, and photographers looking on, Murphy mounted his Tribune Racer "Blue Streak" and took his position behind the pace locomotive and the hooded railroad car. The train began to chug, using the first mile of the course to reach full speed, with Murphy right behind. As they crossed the starting line, Murphy, pumping away furiously, was just behind the train. He held even with it for the first quarter mile, then began to fall behind. Murphy himself now takes up the tale:

Mile-A-Minute Murphy Behind The Locomotive During Preparations For The Mile Long Run, *Courtesy of the Suffolk County Historical Society. Murphy bends over his bicycle and checks the track in final preparation for his historic ride.*

Charles Murphy, known as "Mile-A-Minute" Murphy throughout his life, obviously loved that nickname; he is buried beneath it.

Fred Burns (an official) asked me through the megaphone what was the matter. I raised my head from the bent position on the handlebars to reply. Quick as a flash I fell back fifty feet. With all the energy and power at my command I tried to regain the lost ground. It was no use. I was doomed to failure. . . . The suspense became maddening. I saw ridicule, contempt, disgrace, and a lifetime dream go up in smoke. O! how I suffered.

Somehow, Murphy reached down, closing the gap with a final burst and crossing the finish line only inches behind the coach. The officials on the back platform, hearing the locomotive engineer blowing his whistle to signal that the end of the plank way was rapidly approaching, reached down and pulled Murphy (and his bicycle, around which he had wrapped his legs) onto the still-roaring train. Exhausted and fearing he was about to die, Murphy asked to be carried back to his wife. Instead, he was slapped on his back and told that his time for the mile was 57.8 seconds, a world record.

Charles M. Murphy's performance that day is considered by many to be the most remarkable ever by a bicycle racer. He would be known as "Mile-A-Minute" Murphy for the rest of his life.

SNATCHING DEFEAT FROM THE JAWS OF VICTORY

WHEN HE WAS INVITED, during the last days of the 1884 presidential campaign, to give a speech at a reception for the Republican candidate James G. Blaine, SAMUEL DICKINSON BURCHARD (1812–1891) was the obscure pastor at New York City's Houston Street Presbyterian Church. Burchard, in his oration, attacked the Democrats as the party of "Rum, Romanism, and Rebellion." Democratic candidate Grover Cleveland seized on this attack, charging that Blaine was anti-Catholic, and used it to turn the election in his favor. Cleveland carried New York State by the narrowest of margins, 1047 votes, and it was New York's electoral votes that were the difference in the election.

Samuel Dickinson Burchard, the obscure minister who cost his candidate, James G. Blaine, "The Man from Maine," the 1884 Presidential election. Dictionary of American Portraits, *Dover Publications.*

THE STEWART BRONZES

IN THE LAST QUARTER of the nineteenth century, if you wanted to hire the best team of artists available to design a sculpture or funerary monument, you hired Stanford White and Augustus Saint-Gaudens. White was the greatest architect and designer of his time, and Saint-Gaudens was a master sculptor. Together they created such acclaimed works as *The Farragut Monument* (1879–1880) in New York City's Madison Square Park, *The Peter Cooper Monument* (1894) just south of Cooper Union Institute, *The Puritan* (1886) for Springfield, Massachusetts, and The *Standing Lincoln* (1887) and *The Logan Monument* (1897) for Chicago. They also collaborated on a few cemetery pieces, including *The Adams Memorial* (1890–1891) in Washington, D.C.'s Rock Creek Cemetery and the design for New York Governor Edwin Morgan's tomb, which was planned for Cedar Hill Cemetery in Hartford, Connecticut.

In August, 1884, just as the work on the Morgan Tomb was about to begin, the shed where the sculpted pieces were stored went up in flames, destroying them and ending that project. As it had been planned, it featured three robed angels at the foot of a Greek cross, with one angel shown playing the harp, another plucking the lute, and the third praying.

The bronze reliefs adorning the tomb of coal and steel magnate DAVID STEWART (1810–1891) (father of Isabella Stewart Gardner, who founded the Boston art museum that bears her name) are remarkably similar in spirit to what was intended for the Morgan tomb. They date from 1883, the year before the Morgan figures, and also feature robed angels.

Though to the modern eye there is nothing controversial about the designs for the Stewart mausoleum, that was not the case when they were created. The idea of depicting death in anything other than a gloomy way was not universally accepted at that time. Indeed, when Stanford White saw the musician-angels Saint-Gaudens had planned for the Morgan tomb, he urged Saint-Gaudens to write to Morgan to prepare him for its daring approach to death: "Some people are such God damned asses they always think of death as a gloomy performance instead of a resurrection."

The Stewart Tomb is decorated with resurrectionist bronzes by Augustus Saint-Gaudens.

INVENTING THE TUXEDO

PIERRE LORILLARD (1833–1901), tobacco merchant, sportsman, and race horse breeder, wanted to make the 1886 gala opening of the Tuxedo Park Club, his members-only 6000-acre enclave for the rich, an affair to remember. Deciding that something less formal than a full-dress tail coat would do for his male guests, Lorillard designed and introduced a new style, the tailless jacket, thereafter known as the tuxedo.

Peter Cooper, the man who founded Cooper Union and to whom all benefactors were compared.

A MAN of many talents, PETER COOPER (1791–1883) made his fortune in iron mills and glue factories. His philanthropy was legendary: the generosity of other New Yorkers was measured against his. At a cost of $1 million (equal to about $23 million today), Cooper financed Cooper Union, which opened in 1859 as a unique free trade school for men and women offering courses in science, engineering, and art to "people who must earn their bread." Cooper Union also featured a free library and a hall for public lectures.

But perhaps Cooper's greatest contribution was his invention of a locomotive that made railroads in America practical. Cooper, in the 1820's, had invested in land along the route of the recently established Baltimore and Ohio Railroad. But his investment was faring poorly because locomotives imported from Europe could not handle the sharp curves that characterized American terrain, and the railroad was unable to move its passengers and freight efficiently. Various schemes were tried, including huge sails (which, not surprisingly, worked well only when a strong wind was blowing) and horse-propelled treadmills, but none did the job.

Finally, Cooper decided that it was time to put his own inventive genius to work. In 1830, working at his New York City foundry, he designed and built the *Tom Thumb*, the first locomotive ever constructed in the United States. Combining a short and flexible wheel base and an advanced upright boiler design, it worked well in America's rough terrain. Cooper built the *Tom Thumb* using five musket barrels for the Railroad boiler tubes, then sent it to Baltimore for use on the Baltimore and Ohio Railroad, where he personally put it through its paces. Though early on the *Tom Thumb*, with Cooper at the helm, lost a race to a horse when its blower belt slipped, Cooper's invention soon demonstrated its worth, saved the Baltimore and Ohio, and made railroads in America practical.

This 1831 lithograph shows the Tom Thumb, *the first locomotive made in the United States.*

This marble monument, placed in position in the late nineteenth or early twentieth century, describes Peter Cooper's accomplishments.

A LEADING FEMALE DOCTOR

Homeopathic physician, women's rights activist, and reformer, Clemence Sophia Harned Lozier (1813–1888) did not have it easy. Born in New Jersey to a Quaker mother who cared for the sick and a father who was a farmer, she was orphaned at the age of eleven. Five years later, she married Abraham Witton Lozier, a carpenter and builder in New York City. Soon thereafter, his health failed, and she opened a girls' school in their home on West 10th Street to support her family. Urged on by her doctor-brother, she studied medical books, then taught her pupils anatomy, physiology, and hygiene, becoming one of the first to instruct female students in these subjects.

After her husband died in 1837, she became a "visitor" for the New York Female Moral Reform Society, which campaigned to end prostitution and to reclaim the fallen, and she began to care for the sick. In 1844, she left New York City, and married again shortly thereafter. This marriage was an unhappy one, and she proceeded with the unconventional act of seeking a divorce, which was granted in 1861.

After applying to several medical schools, only to be rejected because of her sex, she enrolled at the Central New York College of Rochester in 1849, and graduated from its successor, the Syracuse Eclectic College, in 1853. Returning to New York City to specialize in obstetrics and gynecology, she offered women what was a rare opportunity at that time, the chance to be treated by a female doctor. Patients sought her out, and she began a series of very popular lectures at her home to educate women about medical matters. She excelled in obstetrics and general surgery, and her income soared to the top of her profession.

Convinced that women could not be educated properly in a male-dominated medical school, Dr. Lozier planned one for women. On April 14, 1863, with the help of her friend, women's advocate Elizabeth Cady Stanton, she founded the New York Medical College and Hospital for Women, the first medical school devoted to training female doctors in New York State. During its first year of operation, Dr. Lozier personally guaranteed all of its expenses. Touring Europe after the Civil War, she studied hospital construction and administration, then returned to reorganize her school and hospital, serving as dean and professor of gynecology and obstetrics until her death. Her school was a great success, graduating two hundred women physicians during her lifetime, including two of her daughters-in-law. In 1918, Dr. Lozier's school and hospital became part of the New York Medical College of the Flower and Fifth Avenue Hospitals.

Dr. Lozier was the first woman to present a paper to the New York State Homeopathic Society. She wrote popular health books for women, including *Child-birth Made Easy* (1870), and was prominent in the woman suffrage movement, serving as president of the National Woman's Suffrage Association (1877–1878) and the New York City Woman Suffrage Society

This column, which began its existence as a decorative element of Tiffany's Fifth Avenue store, was purchased by Mrs. Hewitt and was installed in the Cooper-Hewitt family lot many years ago. It was subsequently removed to Cooper Union's Hewitt Annex, then returned to Green-Wood in 2007.

Dr. Clemence Lozier, the pioneer doctor.

(1873–1886). Lozier also was active in Sorosis (the New York women's club) and the National Working Women's League, was president of the Moral Education Society of New York and the local Woman's Christian Temperance Society, and was vice president of the Universal Peace Union. Her home was a meeting place for opponents of slavery and advocates of prison reform, international arbitration, and Indian rights.

On the day Dr. Lozier was laid to rest at Green-Wood Cemetery, more than forty female doctors, all of whom had graduated from her school, were there to bear witness to her accomplishments. Elizabeth Cady Stanton eulogized her with this: "As a mother, wife, physician, friend, and reformer we cannot too highly exalt her virtues."

BUILDING THE BROOKLYN BRIDGE

WILLIAM C. KINGSLEY (1833–1885) was always building. After settling in Brooklyn in 1856, he worked as the contractor for the Brooklyn water works. In subsequent years, his construction firm, Kingsley and Keeney, was given large contracts to build Prospect Park and the Hempstead Reservoir.

But, undoubtedly, Kingsley's greatest project was the Brooklyn Bridge. A contractor, in order to stay in business, needs work, and the ability to create projects for himself doesn't hurt. By the mid-1860's, Kingsley was convinced that a bridge between New York City and Brooklyn was feasible and, perhaps most importantly, would be great for his business. He became the driving force behind that project, hiring Colonel JULIUS WALKER ADAMS (1812–1899), a civil engineer who had worked with him on the Brooklyn sewers, to come up with a design and to prepare cost estimates. However, though Adams had previously dabbled in bridge designs, and though he had many influential friends, he had never built a bridge of any consequence. His role was to come up with a lowball estimate of the cost of the bridge, allowing Kingsley and its other promoters to gain the necessary approvals from public officials. Adams concluded that the Brooklyn Bridge could be built for $5,000,000; ultimately it would be built by John and Washington Roebling for three times that amount.

When the New York and Brooklyn Bridge Company was organized in 1867, Kingsley became one of its major shareholders. Soon he was named its superintendent, and a motion, proposed by none other than BOSS TWEED and passed by the other trustees, authorized payment to Kingsley of 15% of all construction costs. This was an unheard-of percentage for such a large contract; in 1870 alone, it amounted to $175,000 ($3 million today) for Kingsley. In 1873, after Tweed had fallen from power, Kingsley's contract with the Bridge Company was renegotiated, and his payment was slashed to a relatively piddling flat fee of $10,000 (equal to $182,000 today) per year.

In 1875, Kingsley joined the board of trustees of the Brooklyn Bridge, and succeeded HENRY CRUSE MURPHY as president of the board in 1882, upon Murphy's death. Kingsley held that position on May 24, 1883,

William C. Kingsley, the Brooklyn Bridge's contractor, as he was depicted on the front page of the July 5, 1873, edition of Frank Leslie's Illustrated Newspaper. *By 1873, the Tweed Ring had been forced from power, and those who had profited from its largess, including Kingsley, were fair game. Fowler, on the left, was a Commissioner of the Brooklyn Board of City Works; he was involved in yet another scandal with Kingsley involving the latter's work on the Hempstead Reservoir.*

William C. Kingsley's monument is made from granite that was once a part of the Brooklyn Bridge.

This is the entrance to the Brooklyn Bridge's wooden catwalk, circa 1880. Note the large circular traveler at left, used to spin the cables in place, a crucial operation which McNulty supervised. The catwalk was open to the public; anyone so inclined could walk across it. Note the sign from Engineer-in-Charge Washington Roebling, discouraging behavior which might cause a collapse: "Safe for only 25 men at one time. Do not walk close together nor run, jump or trot. Break step!"

the day that the Brooklyn Bridge opened.

William Kingsley's monument at Green-Wood Cemetery was cut from a granite stone that was once a part of the Brooklyn Bridge, and was placed there by the bridge's Board of Trustees to honor his role in making the dream of a bridge between the great Cities of New York and Brooklyn a reality.

A BROOKLYN BRIDGE ENGINEER

GEORGE W. McNULTY (1850–1924) graduated from the University of Virginia, worked as a surveyor, then applied to work on the great engineering project of his time, the Brooklyn Bridge. When McNulty's application for a position was unceremoniously rejected, perhaps because he was then just twenty years old, he offered to work for free. Colonel Washington Roebling, who was in charge of the bridge project, was so impressed by McNulty's proposal that he hired him with pay.

McNulty, who soon developed a reputation as one of the ablest men working on the bridge, was the assistant engineer assigned to lay the first stone courses of the Brooklyn tower, build the Brooklyn approach to the bridge and the Brooklyn anchorage, prepare the mechanical paraphernalia necessary for the cable making, and design the big, curved terminal on the Brooklyn side.

After completing his work on the Brooklyn Bridge, McNulty worked as a contractor in New York City, installing the Broadway cable system, building the subway from Times Square to Columbus Circle, constructing the Sunnyside Yard for the Pennsylvania Railroad, and helping to build many other subway lines. He also served in the National Guard, reaching

George McNulty was also responsible for the construction of the anchorage on the Brooklyn side of the Brooklyn Bridge. Fulton Street is the main thoroughfare curving to the right in this circa 1875 photograph.

In this photograph of many of the men who played key roles in the construction of the Brooklyn Bridge, Henry Murphy, president of the East River Bridge Company, is in the group standing at left, with his arms crossed. George McNulty is in the right foreground, wearing a top hat and leaning on his elbow against the eyebars which would connect the cables to the anchorage. ORESTES P. QUINTARD, *the secretary of the Bridge, standing second from the left, is also buried at Green-Wood Cemetery.*

the rank of major, and was a governor of the Engineers' Club. One of his sons was named Washington Roebling McNulty in honor of his mentor. McNulty is buried in an unmarked grave at Green-Wood Cemetery.

SO CLOSE, AND YET SO FAR AWAY

Henry Cruse Murphy may have been just one vote away from the Presidency.

HENRY CRUSE MURPHY (1810–1882) led a distinguished life. A lifelong resident of Brooklyn, he graduated with honors from Columbia College in 1830, was admitted to the bar, and soon became City Attorney and Counsel to the Corporation of the newly-formed City of Brooklyn. In 1835, Murphy and his partners launched a law firm which, in the ensuing years, had such complete control of the local Democratic Party that Brooklyn historian Henry Stiles would later comment that to write a history of that firm "would be to write the political history of Brooklyn from 1835 to 1857."

In 1841, Murphy became proprietor and one of the editors of the *Brooklyn Daily Eagle*, and the next year, still only thirty-one years old, was elected mayor of Brooklyn. Murphy was elected to Congress in 1842 and 1846, and from 1857 until 1861 he served as United States Minister to Holland. Upon his return from that post, he was elected to six consecutive terms in the State Senate, serving there from 1861 until 1873. It was largely through Murphy's efforts that the Third Senatorial Regiment and the 159th New York State Volunteers were raised and equipped during the Civil War.

Murphy was the unsuccessful Democratic candidate (at the time the Democrats were the minority party in New York State) for U.S. Senate in 1867 and 1869, and lost a bitter struggle for the Democratic nomination for governor in 1868. He played an important role in the erection of the Brooklyn Bridge, drafting and securing passage of the necessary authorizing legislation, then serving as president of the East River Bridge Company from its creation in 1867 until his death in 1882. For this role he was compared to Moses, who led his people to the promised land but was denied admission; Murphy led the Bridge Company for fifteen years, only to die six months before the bridge's grand opening. Murphy helped to found the Long Island Historical Society (which fairly recently changed its name to the Brooklyn Historical Society) and the Brooklyn City Library, played a prominent role in the development of Coney Island, was president of the Flatbush & Coney Island Railroad, and built the Brighton Beach Hotel.

Despite these tremendous accomplishments, Murphy is little remembered today. This, however, would not have been the case if Murphy had gotten only one more vote in the most important ballot of his life. When the Democratic National Convention deadlocked in 1852, the Virginia delegation caucused to select a compromise Presidential candidate. The choices came down to two: Franklin Pierce of New Hampshire and Henry Cruse Murphy of Brooklyn. Pierce defeated Murphy in the Virginia caucus by one vote, went on to win the Democratic nomination, and was elected President of the United States.

AMERICA'S PRINTMAKERS:
MR. CURRIER AND MR. IVES

CURRIER AND IVES, printmakers for the American people, are fondly remembered today for their nineteenth century lithographs. Their impact is so substantial that, a century after their heyday, a phrase in our everyday language refers to their work: pastoral farm and winter pictures are still referred to as "Currier and Ives scenes." Both NATHANIEL CURRIER (1813–1888) and JAMES IVES (1824–1895) chose Green-Wood Cemetery as their final resting place.

Nathaniel Currier was born in Roxbury, Massachusetts, and as a boy apprenticed in Boston to the first lithographic printing company in the country (printing from drawings on stone). In 1833, Currier established his own printing company in New York City near City Hall. His first print, issued in 1835, was *The Ruins of the Merchants' Exchange.* During the next seventy years, more than 7000 lithographic titles reflecting all facets of nineteenth century America were issued by his firm, including city and landscape views, shipping, railroading, planting, harvesting, hunting, and horse racing scenes, cartoons, "darktown comics," battle, Indian, and flower pictures. Millions of copies were sold. Currier's prints were the first illustrated news extras and the first political banners.

These scenes were created by artists, drawn on stone and printed, then hand-painted by German immigrant working girls who copied the color

Nathaniel Currier (top) and his partner, James Ives (bottom), sold their lithographic prints across America. Courtesy of the Museum of the City of New York.

scheme from a sample. The prints sold cheaply, from 20 cents apiece for small folios up to $3 for larger ones, as wall decorations for the mass market. Street hawkers, men with push carts, harness shops, barrooms, and general stores all were outlets for these prints. In 1857, Currier took James Merritt Ives as a partner, and all prints issued thereafter bore the famous Currier and Ives imprint. Two of their best artists were FANNY PALMER and NAPOLEON SARONY; EASTMAN JOHNSON, Arthur Fitzwilliam Tait, George Henry Durrie, and GEORGE CATLIN were just a few of the painters who created original art for them. The firm of Currier and Ives, "Publishers of Cheap and Popular Prints," continued in business until 1907 when, with both of its original partners dead, and faced with increasing competition from photography and chromolithography, its inventory was sold for little more than the cost of the materials. Sadly, thousands of their printing stones were destroyed at that time.

By the 1920's, however, "the Currier Craze" had begun as collectors scrambled to find Currier and Ives prints. Harry T. Peters, the pioneer in the field, issued his book. Publicity from auction sales, escalating prices, and the discovery of new scenes, made the prints increasingly attractive. In 1932, Harry Shaw Newman, the owner of the Old Print Shop in New York City, organized a jury to select Currier and Ives's "Fifty Best" of large folio prints. The *New York Sun* got into the act, issuing copies of one print each day at the beginning of 1933. Later, a "Fifty Best" of small folios came out. And, in 1991, the American Historical Print Collectors' Society offered the "New Fifty Best." The work of Currier and Ives, produced for a mass market, is very collectible today.

THE ROAD.-WINTER.

The sketch for The Road—Winter, *showing Nathaniel Currier and his first wife in a sleigh, was originally a Christmas gift to Nathaniel Currier from his employees. Currier was so impressed by it that he quickly ordered prints made, and it became a bestseller. First issued as a lithograph in 1853, this scene continues to this day to be a popular Christmas card. In 1974, the United States Postal Service reproduced it as a Christmas stamp. Courtesy of the Museum of the City of New York.*

Though he had acted on stage and managed theatres in his native England, HENRY JAMES MONTAGUE (1840–1878) came to America unheralded. Montague almost immediately joined the famed stock company of LESTER WALLACK (1820–1888) and made his stage debut in his adopted country on October 6, 1874. Overnight, Montague became the matinee idol of the American stage:

> He was handsome, gentle and gentlemanly—a perfect specimen of refined English manhood. New York had seen nothing like him before; he had the faculty of making most other leading men seem boorish, ill-dressed, and possibly a bit vulgar . . .

Young women adored him, young men copied his manners, and his picture was displayed on dressing tables and in shop windows throughout New York City.

Four years after his American stage debut, while performing on a stage in San Francisco, Montague suffered a lung hemorrhage, recovered briefly, only to be fatally stricken two days later. Knowing his fate, he gasped his last words to his friends who had gathered around, "It's no use. I am going boys, God bless."

Montague's remains were sent east by train, and were met at Grand Central Depot by a delegation from the Lambs Club, of which he had been Shepherd. Funeral services, with admission by ticket only, were held in New York City at the Church of the Transfiguration ("the Little Church Around the Corner"), and the streets were thronged with mourners. A memorial service was also held in San Francisco. Montague, only thirty-eight years old, was interred at Green-Wood Cemetery, with a large crowd looking on, in the plot of Lester Wallack, the man who had given him his first acting chance in his adopted country.

During Montague's short life, his favorite flower was the violet, one of which always dangled from his lips as he promenaded on Fifth Avenue. For two years an anonymous admirer had sent Montague a bouquet of violets every Saturday. Even when Montague toured, the violets continued to arrive at his stage door. Though Montague tried to find out who his secret admirer was, he apparently never solved this mystery. On the day of his funeral a huge bouquet of violets appeared anonymously on his grave. Even today, Ocean Hill, where he is buried, is covered in early spring with violets.

Fellow actors Henry Montague (top) and Lester Wallack (bottom). Note the violets in Montague's lapel.

Lester Wallack and Henry Montague were buried under twin memorials erected by the Lambs Club in honor of its first and second Shepherds.

Stone portraits of Frederick and Magadelana Friederike Rollwagen.

This photograph, circa 1860, shows the stone yards which clustered near Green-Wood Cemetery's main entrance at Fifth Avenue and 25th Street.

A LOVELY BUD

FRIEDRICK ROLLWAGEN (1807–1873) came to America from Alsace, France, prospered in his adopted country, and became a substantial landowner on the Lower East Side. But his success was of no help to his granddaughter, MAGDALENA FRIEDERIKE ROLLWAGEN (1873–1876), who succumbed to whooping cough at the age of two and one-half years on February 26, 1876. Busts of Friedrich and Friederike stand side-by-side, and on her granite monument a poem is carved which compares her to a bloom never allowed to flower:

> This lovely bud so young so fair
> Called hence by early doom.
> Just came to show how sweet a flower
> In paradise would bloom.

Though stone yards and monument makers clustered near the entrances to Green-Wood Cemetery, hoping to attract customers, surprisingly few of these makers chose to advertise their finished work by signing it. One of the few exceptions is John Feitner, a marble worker at 24th Street and 5th Avenue in Brooklyn, just outside Green-Wood's main gates, who proudly marked his efforts on these monuments. His firm continued to create monuments at Green-Wood well into the 1930's.

MORGAN CITY, LOUISIANA

LEAVING his Connecticut farm at the age of fourteen for New York City, CHARLES MORGAN (1795–1878) worked as a grocery clerk and later opened a provision shop. Trading with the South, he gradually began to buy steamships, and by the eve of the Civil War had a virtual monopoly on shipping along the Gulf of Mexico. After the war, Morgan had the distinction of owning more ships than anyone else in America, and his monopoly extended to control of railroading in the Gulf ports area.

Shipping magnate Charles Morgan's hillside mausoleum is topped by his bust.

Few residents of Morgan City, Louisiana, know that the person for whom their town is named is buried in Brooklyn, New York. Note the symbolic joining of the shrimp and the oil rig in the symbol on the right of Morgan City's welcome sign.

[156]

Morgan City, Louisiana, on the Atchafalaya River at the terminus of one of his railroads, was named in his honor. Now with a population of 15,000, the town is primarily Cajun. Morgan City once called itself the "Jumbo Shrimp Capital of the World." However, oil was discovered off-shore in 1947, and the petroleum industry has now become dominant there. Morgan City celebrates the oddly named "Shrimp and Petroleum Festival" every year over the Labor Day weekend.

CHARLES CALVERLEY'S
GREEN-WOOD CEMETERY SCULPTURES

OF THE THOUSANDS of sculptures in Green-Wood Cemetery, surprisingly few can be attributed to known artists. Two important signed works by sculptor Charles Calverley adorn Green-Wood Cemetery.

Charles Calverley (1833–1914) was born in Albany, New York. On his thirteenth birthday, he went to work, later writing that he was

> bound in the old-fashioned way for seven years to the marble cutting trade—in a one horse marble shop . . . and the first job I was set to do was to clean out the stove and make a fire—and my salary for the first year was one dollar a week and bound myself (that is, my mother fed and clothed me).

Calverley's talents were discovered by the well-known sculptor Erastus Dow Palmer, who was greatly impressed by a rose that he had carved on a headstone. In 1853, Palmer bought Calverley out of his apprenticeship, took him into his studio, and taught him for the next fifteen years, ten hours a day, to sculpt in marble.

Calverley specialized in portraits of famous men, creating medallions of Abraham Lincoln, James A. Garfield, Henry Wadsworth Longfellow, and PETER COOPER. He also sculpted busts, and his full size bronze statue of Robert Burns (in Washington Park, Albany, New York) is considered his masterpiece.

In the late 1860's, Calverley left Palmer's Albany studio to set up his own sculpture business in New York City. It was while working there that Calverley gained commissions for the two busts that he created for placement at Green-Wood Cemetery: that of the founder and longtime editor of the *New York Tribune*, HORACE GREELEY (completed in 1876), and that of the inventor of the sewing machine, ELIAS HOWE (completed in 1884). Both of these bear Calverley's signature. In addition, the delicate marble cameo of Precious Georgie at Green-Wood Cemetery has been attributed to Calverley.

Calverley created several other elaborate cemetery works. His own family's memorial at Albany Rural Cemetery in Menands, New York, dating from the 1890's, is decorated with his self-portrait bust and bronze reliefs of his brother John, his wife Susan, and his mother Elizabeth. His bronze *Meditation*, a large-scale figure, was completed for the Boulware family in 1902, and is also at that cemetery.

Sculptor Charles Calverley's self-portrait stands above his grave at the Albany Rural Cemetery in Menands, New York.

Charles Calverley's busts of Horace Greeley (top) and Elias Howe (bottom) adorn Green-Wood Cemetery.

The Sculptor Angel.

CHAPTER SIX

The Gay Nineties
(1890–1899)

THE KING OF THEATRICAL PHOTOGRAPHS

BORN IN Quebec, Canada, NAPOLEON SARONY (1821–1896) came to New York City as a youth and learned the art of lithography. Sarony became a prominent lithographer and pioneered in the printing of theatrical posters.

After the death of Sarony's first wife, he sold his business and left for Europe, where he learned photography from his brother. Opening his own photographic studio in Birmingham, England, he specialized in portraiture. Sarony returned to New York City in 1865 to market two of his brother's inventions: a device to hold the subject still in unusual poses for the then-necessary long exposures, and a photographic paper.

Sarony opened his New York photographic studio at 680 Broadway, and soon became the most fashionable photographic portraitist of his time. Anybody who was somebody was posed by Sarony and had his or her picture snapped by Sarony's camera operators; during his career, Sarony photographed over 200,000 "notables." From the late 1860's until his death, he was the photographer of choice for theatrical and society portraits. More than 30,000 actors and actresses posed in front of his lens. His unparalleled compositions were characterized by dramatic posing, innovative use of a variety of backgrounds and props (including a stuffed crocodile, Egyptian mummies, Russian sleighs, and Chinese statues), and unusual lighting and shadows, which "lifted cabinet card photography to unmatched heights of photographic grandeur."

Advancing large payments against royalties for exclusive rights to the likeness of his sitters, Sarony soon had a monopoly on the images of the

The theatrical Napoleon Sarony, with fez, mustache, boots, and sword.

A few of the famous theatre people who posed for Sarony and are buried at Green-Wood Cemetery: (left to right) MALVINA PRAY FLO-RENCE *(1830–1906) (known professionally as Mrs. W. J. Florence),* WILLIAM J. FLORENCE *(1831–1891),* HENRY J. MONTAGUE *(1840–1878),* ADA REHAN *(1860–1916), and* ANNE GILBERT *(1821–1904) (known professionally as Mrs. G. H. Gilbert).*

The monument to Napoleon Sarony, photographer to nineteenth century stars, is a gem. Though its top section is gone, and Sarony's name does not appear on it, this monument, based on its location and its imagery, unmistakably belongs to the great portraitist. The combination of the painter's brush and palette with the box camera, carved in stone across the front, are clear references to both of his exceptional careers.

During James Stranahan's twenty-two years as Brooklyn's Parks Commissioner, over $9 million of public money was spent under his supervision. When his term ended, and it was discovered that $10,604 was unaccounted for, he sent the comptroller a personal check for that amount.

famous. Those who aspired to fame, but had not yet attained it, often paid him to market their likenesses. His portraits of actors and actresses, visiting dignitaries, lecturers, prize fighters, politicians, wrestlers, writers, and the notorious, were more widely disseminated in American homes than those of any other photographer, and were as popular in Paris as they were on Broadway. Lillie Langtry, Oscar Wilde, Buffalo Bill Cody, Sarah Bernhardt, Edwin Booth, Grand Duke Alexis of Russia, Union Generals William Tecumseh Sherman, Philip Sheridan, and Winfield Hancock, and every President from Abraham Lincoln to Theodore Roosevelt, were only too happy to pose for Napoleon Sarony's lens.

Five feet tall, Sarony was known for his trademark getup of high cavalry boots, military-cut tunics and capes, black beard and huge mustache, topped by a Turkish fez. His second wife was also known for her elaborate costumes: every day she promenaded along the Ladies Mile, New York City's fashionable shopping district, wearing a new outfit; each one was then returned to its maker the next day.

"THE FIRST CITIZEN OF BROOKLYN"

KNOWN AS "the First Citizen of Brooklyn," JAMES S.T. STRANA-HAN (1808–1898) played a key role in virtually every great civic project in Brooklyn during the second half of the nineteenth century, including Ocean and Eastern Parkways and the Atlantic Docks. But Stranahan's greatest contributions were to the movement to unite the great Cities of New York and Brooklyn.

Late in the nineteenth century, New York City was the largest city in America, and Brooklyn was the third largest. First as president of the Union Ferry Company, then later as trustee of the Brooklyn Bridge (he deserves credit for his insistence that the bridge be modified to accommodate trains), Stranahan did everything in his power to join these two municipalities. In 1883, just weeks before the Brooklyn Bridge opened, Stranahan explained his motivations in a speech before the New York Chamber of Commerce:

> The Thames flows through the heart of London, and the Seine through the heart of Paris. But in neither case have you two cities. It is London on both sides of the Thames, and Paris on both sides of the Seine. The corporate unity is not dissevered by either river. Numerous bridges make the connection between the two sides in both cities, and it is best for both that it should be so. The population on neither side would be advantaged by being split up into two municipalities.
>
> Here, however, we have our New York City and our Brooklyn with the East River rolling between them. They are distant cities in immediate contiguity with each other and separated by a water highway. Is this distinctness of municipality any advantage to either? I think not. Would the consolidation of these two cities into one municipal corporation be any harm to either. I think not. The people are the same people, have the same manners and customs, and have common com-

mercial and social interests; and one municipal government would serve them quite as well as two, and at far less cost. I know of no reason why this distinctness should be continued other than the fact that it exists; and I confess I see no good reason why it should exist at all. I may be mistaken, but I think that the public sentiment of Brooklyn would cordially welcome consolidation of the two cities under the title of New York. The East River Bridge, now superadded to the ferry system, will, as Brooklyn hopes, so facilitate their mutual intercourse that both, without any special courtship to either side, will alike ask the legislature of the state to enact the ceremony of a municipal marriage; and if this shall be done, then I venture to predict that each will be so happy and so well content with the other that neither will ever seek a divorce.

Stranahan lived to the ripe old age of ninety, surviving long enough to see the campaign to unite New York City and Brooklyn, in which he played such a central role, succeed. His funeral cortege was the first ever permitted to pass through Prospect Park. That was indeed a fitting final tribute to the man who, for years, headed Brooklyn's Parks Commission, and was hailed as the "Father of Prospect Park."

James S.T. Stranahan, who contributed so much to his beloved Brooklyn, was honored during his lifetime with this statue at Prospect Park's north entrance, paid for by grateful citizens.

DID THEY EVER RETURN, NO THEY NEVER RETURNED

L ATE ON THE EVENING of August 26, 1893, a special Manhattan Beach train chugged back from Coney Island, jammed with a tired but happy group of singers who had performed at Sousa's Festival that day, concertgoers, and sunbathers. If this train had not been delayed by another train in front of it, the carnage could have been avoided. But after some delay, as the Manhattan Beach train got just past the Laurel Hill station, a Rockaway Beach train, running at full throttle of fifty miles per hour, was mistakenly allowed on the same track by the switchman in the nearby tower.

Though the Rockaway Beach train whistled a last second warning, allowing a lucky few to jump clear of the ill-fated Manhattan Beach train, it could not stop, and plowed full speed into the last car of the doomed train. Of the six open wooden cars on the Manhattan Beach train, the last two were cut in half. The locomotive on the Rockaway Beach train was crushed.

Immediately after the crash, passengers tried to help those who had been most seriously injured. People from nearby houses who had heard the crash ran to the scene to do what they could. Though there were at least six doctors in the first car of the Manhattan Beach train, its first four cars had become separated from the last two, and had been pulled some distance up the track; none of them knew of the carnage that had taken place behind them. Instead, after they were assured by railroad employees that no one had been injured, they were taken from the scene. One doctor, assured that the train had just run over a cow, later lamented what might have been:

Why in the name of all that is human did not that train run back

Detail of the monument erected by the Dietzel family.

to the wrecked cars so that help could have been given to the suffering? Why in the name of common sense and humanity was not some inquiry made among the crowd of passengers in the forward cars as to whether there were any doctors on that train? Had we gone to the wreck and started the work of relief then, what a great amount of suffering we could have saved, and perhaps we might have saved lives.

As it was, the first treating doctor did not arrive at the scene until forty-five minutes after the disaster, and the rescue train, loaded with as many doctors as could be found, did not get there for an hour and a half. In all, sixteen people died from the crash and dozens were injured.

Two of the dead were MAGGIE B. DIETZEL (1870–1893) and OSCAR DIETZEL (1862–1893) of 122 East 114th Street in New York City. Maggie Dietzel, who apparently died instantly, was later identified by a wedding ring on her left hand on which was inscribed, "O.D. to M.D., 26th of May, 1892." Oscar Dietzel, a partner in the firm of Dietzel & Grossenbach, manufacturers of braid on East 39th Street in New York City, was alive when he was pulled from the wreck and rushed to St. John's Hospital. *The New York Times* described what happened there:

> One of the saddest scenes of the day was about the bedside of Oscar Dietzel, who subsequently died. In his delirium he held out his arms and piteously called for his wife. She was then lying dead in Skelton's morgue in Newtown.

SOCIETY AS I HAVE FOUND IT

The Washington Centennial Ball.
Ward McAllister as the Count De La Nolle, Lover of Marguerite
of Valois. Hot stuff.

Ward McAllister dressed as Count De La Nolle for the 1889 Washington Centennial Ball.

WARD MCALLISTER (1827–1895), born to privilege in South Carolina, made some money as a lawyer in San Francisco, then married the daughter of a Georgia millionaire. Retiring from work at the ripe old age of thirty-two, he came to New York City in 1859, determined to spend the rest of his life guiding the rich to new heights of elaborate and exclusive entertainments. McAllister launched himself into this passion by hosting champagne picnics in Newport, Rhode Island, where his friends were coached out to the country, then danced on a platform built for the occasion as rented sheep grazed bucolically nearby.

By the late 1860's, Ward McAllister had become the self-appointed social arbiter of New York City. McAllister won this position unopposed, though not without effort; one writer described him as

> the only man of his day willing to give his days and nights to the study of heraldry, books of court etiquette, genealogy, and cooking, to the getting up of balls and banquets, to the making of guest lists and the interviewing of ambitious mothers with debutante daughters. . . . These things he came to love as a miser loves his gold.

In 1872, McAllister organized the Patriarchs, twenty-five of New York's richest men, who were allowed to invite "four ladies and five gentlemen" to a series of fashionable balls. He authored *Society As I Have Found It* in 1890, in which he maintained that "a fortune of only a million is respectable

Ward McAllister's funeral cortege was met with indifference as it proceeded along Fifth Avenue.

The interior of the Catacombs.

poverty." McAllister, in 1892, coined the phrase "The Four Hundred," observing, after he learned that that was the number who could be accommodated in Caroline Schermerhorn Astor's ballroom, that there were "only about four hundred people in New York Society," and appointing himself to choose who was "in" and who was "out" amongst the richest of the rich.

McAllister had no set rules as to whom could take a place in "society." Even the nouveau riche might qualify: "four generations of gentlemen makes as good and true a gentleman as forty." McAllister's views about the society over which he presided are well-summarized in this passage from his book:

> New York society turned over a new leaf. Up to this time, for one to be worth a million of dollars was to be rated a man of fortune, but now, bygones must be bygones. New York's ideas as to values, when fortune was named, leaped boldly up to ten millions, fifty millions, one hundred millions, and the necessities and luxuries followed suit. One was no longer content with a dinner of a dozen or more, to be served by a couple of servants. Fashion demanded that you be received in the hall of the house in which you were to dine, by from five to six servants, who, with the butler, were to serve the repast. The butler, on such occasions, [was] to do alone the head-work, and under him he had these men in livery to serve the dinner, he to guide and direct them. Soft strains of music were introduced between courses, and in some houses gold replaced silver in the way of plate, and everything that skill and art could suggest was added to make the dinners not a vulgar display, but a great gastronomic effort, evidencing the possession by the host of both money and taste.

Ultimately, McAllister managed to alienate the society he had so wished to control. His *Society as I Have Found It* angered the Four Hundred, who became targets of ridicule when their self-indulgence was committed to print. For the last two years of his life, Ward McAllister was ostracized.

The McAllister coat of arms decorates the doorway of their crypt.

When he died, Mrs. Astor, the Mystic Rose whom he had made queen of New York society, saw no reason to cancel the dinner that she had scheduled for the next day. Though McAllister's funeral cortege proceeded down Fifth Avenue, the street of his greatest triumphs, few paid it any heed. Only five of his Patriarchs and fewer than twenty of the Four Hundred bothered to come to his funeral at Grace Church.

It is ironic that Ward McAllister is interred in the Catacombs at Green-Wood Cemetery. The Catacombs were built into a hillside in the late 1850's as a structure for relatively modest family interments. Unlike elsewhere at Green-Wood, the Catacombs offered no opportunity for the ostentatious display of wealth. If Green-Wood is seen as a community, then the Catacombs are the equivalent of a rather small, unassuming apartment building. Yet, despite McAllister's pretensions, expressed in gems such as "A man with a million dollars can be as happy nowadays as if he were rich" and "If you wish to be fashionable, always be in the company of fashionable people," he wound up in neither an elaborate freestanding tomb nor a fashionable hillside mausoleum, but rather in the unpretentious Catacombs.

It is a further irony that McAllister is the most famous individual in the Catacombs; in his lifetime he was often the least famous of those around him, basking in their reflected glory. Clearly, however, Ward McAllister never lost his concern for status: his crypt is the only one of the thirty that make up the Catacombs with a coat of arms on its gate.

It is appropriate, however, that Ward McAllister is interred at Green-Wood, surrounded by so many of those from the society he cultivated. Indeed, nearby are the Bradley Martins, whose extravagant and controversial ball two years after McAllister's death was but the logical outgrowth of his life.

THE "HEROIC WIFE" OF AN IRISH PATRIOT

The monument to Matilda Tone traveled with her remains and those of her son from Georgetown to Green-Wood Cemetery.

T HE IRISH PATRIOT, Theobald Wolfe Tone (1763–1798), tried to establish, with other members of the United Irish movement, a democracy in Ireland joining Catholics, Protestants, and Dissenters, as Irishmen. But Tone, for his efforts, was forced into exile in 1794. With his wife, MATILDA TONE (1769–1849), he lived for a short time in Princeton, New Jersey, then sailed to France, where he was commissioned a French officer. Tone, advised by the American Ambassador to France, James Monroe, planned and executed two ill-fated invasions of Ireland. Tone was captured after the second of these, and was tried and convicted of treason. Sentenced to be executed, he died in jail under suspicious circumstances.

Matilda Tone was as committed as her husband to their cause. She joined him in France in 1797, and the next year was left a young widow with three children. Two of her children died of tuberculosis in 1806. In the ensuing years she lived on a pension from the French Army and on funds from Napoleon and Tallyrand. But when they were ousted from power in

1815, Matilda Tone's days in France were numbered. Coming to New York City in 1817, she lived there, then joined her son in Washington, D.C., where he was working in the War Department. She appears to have played a role in the publication of *The Life of Wolfe Tone*, which was edited by her son and published in 1826.

Upon her death, Matilda Tone was interred in the Old Presbyterian Cemetery in Georgetown. In 1891, when that cemetery was sold, Matilda's great-grandchildren had her and her son's remains brought to Green-Wood Cemetery. On the eve of All Saints' Day, they were interred under the white marble monument that had stood over them in Georgetown, and a wreath of ivy was laid atop the newly-dug soil.

That marble monument, cleaned, recarved, and sealed in 1996, under the auspices of the New York Irish History Roundtable and the Irish-American Labor Coalition, was rededicated by Ireland's President Mary Robinson on October 8, 1996, as a steady rain fell. Theobold Wolfe Tone is interred in Bodenstown, County Kildare.

ST. PATRICK'S CATHEDRAL, GRACE CHURCH, AND MORE

JAMES RENWICK, JR. (1818–1895) had a long and distinguished career as an architect. At the tender age of twenty-four, Renwick won the design competition for Grace Church (constructed during 1845 and 1846), which he created for New York City's wealthiest and most fashionable congregation, and which is today a Broadway landmark. Renwick is best known for his design of St. Patrick's Cathedral (constructed from 1858 to 1879), still standing opposite Rockefeller Center on Fifth Avenue. At the time of its dedication, St. Patrick's was the eleventh-largest church in the world.

Renwick was the architect of many other public buildings, including New York City's Calvary, St. Bartholomew's, and St. Stephen's churches, the Church of the Puritans, the Y.M.C.A. Building (1869), Booth's The-

This is the architectural monument to architect James Renwick, Jr.

Of all of the buildings designed by architect James Renwick, Jr., during his illustrious career, St. Patrick's Cathedral, shown in an 1869 woodcut, is the best known.

Renwick also designed Grace Church (left), on Broadway in New York, the Corcoran (now Renwick) Gallery (center) across Pennsylvania Avenue from the White House, and the Smithsonian Castle (right), on the mall in Washington, D.C. All three of these buildings, shown in circa 1870 photographs, have survived.

atre, the Free Academy, the Clarendon, Albemarle, and St. Denis Hotels, La Farge House, the Masonic Temple and the New York Stock Exchange Building of 1880–1881, Brooklyn Heights's St. Ann's Church, Washington, D.C.'s Smithsonian Institute (the "Castle") and Corcoran (now Renwick) Gallery, and Vassar College in Poughkeepsie, New York. Renwick Triangle, at the intersection of East 10th and Stuyvesant Streets in Manhattan, is named for him.

THE BRADLEY MARTINS' BALL TO END ALL BALLS

FOR MANY YEARS, MRS. BRADLEY MARTIN, nee CORNELIA SHERMAN (1845–1920), had insisted that "she would some day give a ball to surpass" any that New York had ever seen. Her father, lumber magnate ISAAC SHERMAN (1818–1881), made her dream possible when he left her $7 million (a fortune equal to $135 million in today's money) in his will. With the country in a deep depression, she and her husband, BRADLEY MARTIN (1841–1913), decided to hold a fancy dress ball on February 10, 1897, at the Waldorf Hotel to stimulate the economy. "It will give impetus to trade," Mrs. Bradley Martin declared.

Renting the lower part of the Waldorf, including fifteen rooms for the guests to dress themselves and two ballrooms for the festivities, they planned the first society ball to be held in a New York City hotel, and the most elaborate entertainment in New York history. Invitations were sent out only a few days before the ball so that the guests would not have time to send off to Paris for their costumes, and would have to use American designers and seamstresses.

The Marine Band, brought up from Washington, D.C., and a Hungar-

Two generations earlier, in the 1850's, MRS. WILLIAM COLFORD SCHERMERHORN decided that it was time to give a memorable society ball. After all, her home at Broadway and Great Jones Street had just become the first in the city to be done over by a decorator. And, given that the new decor was Louis XV, it was only logical that all the guests appear in costumes of the French court. However, a problem soon arose when the male invitees learned that by royal decree all of the courtiers at that court had been clean-shaven. Intermediaries implored Mrs. Schermerhorn to change her mind, but she was adamant; her servants would be in historically-accurate period attire, and no less could be expected of her guests. But as the costume ball drew closer, a man about town discovered that at the French court the King's musketeers had been allowed to wear beards and mustaches. New York society's facial hair was saved; nearly every man came to Mrs. Schermerhorn's ball costumed as a musketeer.

A contemporary print of the costumed guests at the Bradley Martins's ball. Mrs. Bradley Martin, who fulfilled her dream with this ball, is framed at upper left.

ian band, were hired to play. The 750 guests were directed to appear in costumes copied from 16th, 17th, and 18th century English, French, and German fashions. As the excitement built, *The New York Times* published a list of the guests in alphabetical order, with a description of the costume each would be wearing. August Belmont, Jr. hired a local costumer, for $10,000 ($231,000 today), to make him a splendid suit of gold-inlaid armor.

However, even before the ball was held, critics attacked the idea of such lavish entertainment. The Rev. Dr. William S. Rainsford, rector of St. George's Protestant Episcopal Church, felt "this affair will only draw attention to the growing gulf which separates the rich and poor, and serve to increase the discontent of the latter needlessly . . . , that such display now will furnish additional texts for sermons by the socialistic agitators." The Bradley Martins' plans became the target of comics and newspapers. Oscar Hammerstein produced a burlesque, *The Bradley-Radley Ball*, satirizing them. Some defended the plans of the Bradley Martins, pointing out that thousands of seamstresses were working because of the extravagant costumes that would be *de rigeur*. But as the evening of the ball approached, rumors circulated that anarchists planned to attack the guests. Police, led by Commissioner Theodore Roosevelt, ringed the Waldorf-Astoria to repel any mob action.

Mrs. Bradley Martin came to her ball dressed as Mary, Queen of Scots, wearing the ruby necklace that had once decorated Marie Antoinette's famous neck, and received her guests from a raised throne. Bradley Martin was costumed as Louis XV.

In an era when the typical New York breadwinner was earning $10 a week, the Bradley Martins spent the unfathomable sum of $389,000 (more than $8 million in today's money) to entertain their guests that night. For this expenditure, Mr. and Mrs. Martin were lambasted by the press, clergy, and social reformers. The tax collector got into the act, suddenly taking an interest in the financial affairs of the host couple, and doubled their tax assessment to more closely match their social aspirations. Hounded and enraged, the Bradley Martins fled the country, spending their remaining years abroad, only returning to their homeland to be interred at Green-Wood Cemetery.

SQUANDERING A FORTUNE
(WHICH WASN'T EVEN HIS)

HENRY HILTON (1824–1899), a lawyer, judge, and close friend of "BOSS" TWEED, spent his life destroying the accomplishments of others. When Tweed had him appointed treasurer of the New York City Parks Commission, Hilton busied himself with laying waste to as many of Frederick Law Olmstead's Central Park vistas as he could. But only one of the numerous buildings that Hilton wanted to pack into Central Park was ever built; it is now the Tavern on the Green.

In 1864, Hilton began working on A. T. Stewart's legal affairs. Stewart

A. T. Stewart's Retail Store (top), on Broadway at 8th Street, and the Park Avenue Hotel (bottom), at 32nd Street, both by architect JOHN KELLUM, were part of the empire that Henry Hilton took over and destroyed. In the photograph of the hotel, note the railroad cars along Park Avenue.

Henry Hilton's monument.

was then the third wealthiest man in America, behind John Jacob Astor and Commodore Vanderbilt, and had an annual income of $2 million (almost $34 million in today's currency). Hilton was treated as a favorite son by the childless Stewart, whose own children had died in infancy.

When Stewart died in 1876, leaving the largest fortune yet amassed in a single lifetime in America, Hilton was heavily in debt. Though Hilton was left $1 million (equal to close to $20 million today) in Stewart's will and was appointed its executor, he immediately made his move. Drafting an agreement to pay Stewart's widow $1 million in cash in exchange for $50 million in holdings, he had her sign it on the day of Stewart's funeral. Stewart's widow survived for ten years, but Hilton never paid her the $1 million. Rather, adding insult to injury, he loaned her money for her expenses and turned a profit by charging her interest.

Hilton also did an uncanny job of ruining Stewart's businesses by provoking boycotts of them. In 1877, Hilton was involved in the first widely-publicized anti-Semitic incident in America. On Hilton's own order, Joseph Seligman (a friend of U.S. Grant) and Seligman's family were barred from Hilton's Grand Union Hotel in Saratoga, even though they had vacationed there each of the previous ten years. Hilton explained his policy with the observation that Christians did not like to be around Jews, and that Jews were bad for business. As a result of this incident, a boycott of Stewart's Department Store, then under Hilton's control, was organized.

The next year, the Park Avenue Woman's Hotel, which had been planned by A. T. Stewart with feminist support as a place for working women to live, was closed down by Hilton after only 53 days of operation, and converted into a business hotel. A storm of protest followed, led by New York City's women and newspapers, and pledges were signed not to shop at A. T. Stewart's Department Store. These boycotts, provoked by Hilton, took their toll, and four years later A. T. Stewart's Department Store went out of business.

Hilton also played a key, but unhelpful, role in the efforts to recover Stewart's remains from extortionists. In 1878, Stewart's casket and remains were stolen from the St. Mark's-in-the-Bouwerie Churchyard, and were held for ransom. Hilton refused to pay the demanded $200,000, and instead counteroffered $25,000 for Stewart's remains. But it was not until Mrs. Stewart intervened, and negotiated a $20,000 payment, that a gunny sack containing her husband's bones was turned over to her.

Hilton lived lavishly with the money from the Stewart Estate. He poured money into Woodlawn (today that property is owned by Skidmore College), his immense estate of over 1400 acres with thirty miles of paved roads just north of Saratoga Springs, New York. By the time of his death, Hilton had managed to dissipate virtually all of A. T. Stewart's immense fortune.

THEY MAY NOT BE BREATHING,
BUT THEY STILL CAN VOTE

KNOWN AS THE "Czar of Coney Island," JOHN Y. MCKANE (1840–1899) reigned over the political machine that controlled what came to be known as Sodom-by-the-Sea. One of McKane's favorite tricks for staying in power was padding voter registration lists. His operatives were regularly sent to copy names off tombstones at Green-Wood and Washington Cemeteries, and the names of the dead were then registered as voters, who invariably, from their graves, cast their ballots for McKane's candidates.

In 1892, when special election inspectors were sent to Coney Island to prevent another round of Election Day fraud, McKane had them assaulted and arrested on trumped up charges that they were drunk and vagrant. When these inspectors tried to serve a court injunction on McKane to prevent further chicanery, he proclaimed that "Injunctions don't go here." That statement came back to haunt McKane, for it became the *Brooklyn Eagle*'s headline as it launched its attack on his corrupt regime, and the story became national news. A mass meeting was held at Brooklyn's Academy of Music, and public-spirited individuals raised money to bring McKane to justice. With BENJAMIN TRACY (who years before had successfully defended Henry Ward Beecher against adultery charges) prosecuting, McKane was convicted, and sentenced to six years in Sing Sing Prison.

On March 1, 1894, crowds lined the streets of Brooklyn to watch as McKane was driven through the streets on his way to prison. The same man turned up on corner after corner, shaking his fist at McKane. That man was PETER TILYOU (1838–1919), who built the first amusement park on Coney Island, battled McKane for years, and fathered the Steeplechase's GEORGE TILYOU. With McKane's fall from power, George Tilyou was named Justice of the Peace. McKane, after serving four years in jail, returned to Coney Island, but his power was gone, and he made his living selling life insurance.

THE BOWERY . . . I'LL NEVER GO THERE ANYMORE!

BY THE LATE nineteenth century, the Bowery, stretching from Chatham Square north about one mile to Cooper Square, was associated with cheap lodging houses, saloons, brothels, and tramps. It had a magnetic pull on sailors, who were only too willing to dedicate their shore leave and their pay to enjoying the nickel museums and live entertainment featuring women in various states of undress.

In 1892, the Bowery received a further blow to the little honor it had managed to retain when Charles M. Hoyt wrote the words, and PERCY GAUNT (1852–1896) set them to music, for *The Bowery*. Their song told the story of a rube beset by the thieves, thugs, and others who populated that thoroughfare. This is a typical verse:

John McKane, who ruled Coney Island with violence and fraud.

John McKane's monument.

The Bowery had an international reputation for seedy attractions.

I struck a place that they called a "dive,"
I was in luck to get out alive;
When the policeman heard my woes,
Saw my black eyes and my battered nose,
"You've been held up!" said the copper fly.
"No, sir, but I've been knocked down!" said I.
Then he laughed, to' I couldn't see why!
I'll never go there any more!

And then the chorus, much to the consternation of those honest few who were still trying to make their living on that street of ill repute, repeated:

The Bow'ry, the Bow'ry!
They say such things
And they do strange things
On the Bow'ry, the Bow'ry!
I'll never go there any more!

"JEROME (NOT THE SAINT BUT THE STOCKJOBBER)"

LEONARD W. JEROME (1817–1891), born on a farm near Syracuse, New York, graduated college and became a lawyer in Rochester. But Wall Street, "a jungle where men tear and claw," beckoned, and he answered its call, spending the rest of his life making and losing several fortunes as a Wall Street speculator.

Jerome often hosted lunches for the financial editors of the *Herald* and the *Tribune*, at which he let slip tidbits that, when published, helped his investments. One of his speculations lost close to a million dollars in two hours; he made and spent $10 million in his lifetime. As one observer said of Leonard Jerome, "He dazzled New York Society with the glitter and novelty of his carriages and the costliness of his blooded horses. He excited its dubious admiration by his extravagance and assurance; his fantastic speculations; his scandalous love affairs; his incredible parties." George Templeton Strong, New York's best nineteenth century diarist, referred to him, none too admiringly, as "Jerome (Not the Saint But the Stockjobber)."

Jerome's partner in many of his schemes was William Travers, who also shared Jerome's love of horses. Together they helped to found the Saratoga Racing Association, and along with August Belmont they founded the American Jockey Club in the 1860's.

Leonard Jerome, who made and lost several fortunes on Wall Street.

In 1866, Leonard Jerome opened his racetrack, Jerome Park, on 230 acres in the Bronx, land today occupied by Jerome Park Reservoir and Lehman College. The "Daddy of Horse Racing in the United States," it was the first flat race track in America, with a grandstand seating 8000, an elaborate ballroom, and a fancy dining room. Facilities for polo, trapshooting, sleighing, and ice skating were also available. Jerome Park soon became the fashionable place for New York's upper crust to be seen during the spring and fall. It flourished until 1894, when it finally closed its gates.

Leonard Jerome also built the boulevard running from Macomb's Dam

WILLIAM HOLBROOK BEARD (1825–1900), who studied painting in Dusseldorf and Rome before settling in New York City, was well-known for his genre pictures, architectural studies, and allegorical works. But his most popular works were his satiric paintings of animals engaged in human activities. In early 18th century London, a term developed for stocks with little or no value: "bears." It was not long before the term "bull," for an individual optimistic about the rise in the stock market, developed. And, by mid-19th century, these terms were in common use in the United States. Perhaps Beard's best-known painting is *The Bulls and the Bears in the Market,* completed in 1879. It is unclear which of these animals, whether bull or bear, Leonard Jerome was. Another prominent Wall Street force who chose Green-Wood Cemetery as his final resting place was JOHN M. BRADSTREET (1815–1863), who founded what was to become the oldest and largest agency in the world supplying credit information and ratings on all types of businesses. J. M. Bradstreet and Son's Improved Mercantile Agency was founded in 1876 as the Bradstreet Company; it merged with R. G. Dun & Co., in 1933, to form Dun and Bradstreet.

to Jerome Park; though Jerome Park is long gone, Jerome Avenue still carries his name. As Jerome Avenue became a substantial thoroughfare, CLARA HALL JEROME (1827–1895), his wife, learned that a move was afoot to rename it for a New York City alderman. Unwilling to sit idly by, she had bronze street signs cast with "Jerome Avenue" on them, then supervised hired men as they hung the signs along the street. That did the trick, and the plans to change the name of the street that honored her husband were quietly dropped.

Leonard Jerome and his wife had three daughters, all of whom married Englishmen. The most famous of these marriages was that of their daughter Jennie to Lord Randolph Churchill. Winston Churchill, born from that marriage, led Great Britain through the darkest days of World War II.

Leonard Jerome's home, at Madison Avenue and 26th St., designed by

Coaches At Jerome Park on a Race Day *appeared in* Harper's Weekly *in 1886.*

The Beard Bear was donated in 2002 by sculptor Dan Ostermiller to mark the grave of anthropomorphic painter William Holbrook Beard. Here the bear wears a ribbon in honor of the A.S.P.C.A. and its founder, Henry Bergh (a permanent resident of Green-Wood).

The Leonard Jerome Mansion was one of New York City's great residences when it was photographed circa 1865.

The Jerome Mausoleum.

THOMAS R. JACKSON (1826–1901), was built in 1859 for lavish entertaining, and was one of the first and most distinguished French Second Empire mansions in New York City. It had a theatre seating 600, on the stage of which Jerome gave young and attractive female singers, with whom his relations were notorious, an opportunity to perform. As his sister once said of him, he had "much sense of honor and hardly any sense of sin." The adjoining stables were carpeted and paneled in black walnut. It was from these stables that Jerome introduced four-in-hand driving (four horses and a coach) to America. At the first ball held at his mansion, one fountain circulated champagne, the other eau de cologne. A meeting in his mansion led to the founding of The Metropolitan Museum in 1869. The mansion, after it ceased to be a residence, became the University Club, and then the Union League Club. It was designated a New York City landmark in 1965, but was torn down in 1974, after its owner (intentionally or otherwise) failed to repair a badly-leaking roof, allowing water damage to destroy the place.

Jerome actively supported the Union during the Civil War. He paid the expenses for the first great Union meeting at the Academy of Music. In the wake of the 1863 Draft Riots, he helped to finance a relief fund for its victims. He also gave $35,000 (slightly more than $800,000 today) for construction of the ship *Meteor*, which was designed to capture the Confederate ship *Alabama*.

PROGRESS AND NOT MUCH POVERTY

HENRY GEORGE (1839–1897) certainly came a long way. Born into a religious, middle class household in Philadelphia, his formal education ended when he left school at the age of fourteen to become an errand boy. He then worked at a series of jobs, including foremast boy on a sailing ship, seaman, farm laborer, apprentice typesetter, and newspaper editor. He quit some, was fired from others, and was always penniless. With his wife pregnant, and no food or money to his name, he decided to go out and get money from the first person he met: "I stopped a man—a stranger—and told him I wanted $5. He asked what I wanted it for. I told him that my wife was confined and that I had nothing to give her to eat. He gave me the money. If he had not, I think I was desperate enough to have killed him."

Starting in 1865, George began to write for a living, and his fortunes turned. His eulogy of President Lincoln was published, and he was hired as editorial writer and then managing editor of the *San Francisco Times*. But the theme that consumed him, and on which he spent years writing, was the widening post–Civil War gap between rich and poor, and the drastic reforms that he felt were needed in the free enterprise system.

In 1879, George achieved worldwide fame as the author of the landmark *Progress and Poverty*, "an inquiry into the cause of industrial depressions and of increase in want with increase in wealth," in which he championed a "single tax" on land as the core of his plan to reform America's economic system in order to alleviate post–Civil War inequities.

Getting his book into print was quite a struggle for George. Despite every effort, he was unable to find a publisher for his work on such a dry topic. Finally, George made arrangements with Appletons Publishing: he would set the type for his book, and they would print and bind a few hundred copies. George got permission from his employer to use their type, and he worked evenings for two years to set his book.

Though *Progress and Poverty* hit the market at the then-enormous price of $7.50 ($150 today), it was an immediate and sensational hit. Edition after edition sold out, and in the first year nearly two million copies were sold. George's book, propelled by its sincerity, fervor, and detail supporting a simple theory, soon became the second-best selling book of the day, eclipsed in sales only by the Holy Bible. World leaders such as Sun Yat-sen, George Bernard Shaw, and Leo Tolstoy were strongly influenced by it.

Because of the arrangements George had been forced to accept from Appletons in order to get his book published, he ultimately received virtually all of the profits from it. With virtually no expenses, these profits were staggering. George was almost instantly transformed into a wealthy man by the system that he so vehemently criticized.

In 1880, Henry George moved to New York City, where he became immensely popular. He spent the next few years on speaking tours through Ireland, England, Scotland, and Australia. Then, in 1886, George ran as the United Labor Party candidate for mayor of New York City, rejecting the Tammany Hall political machine's secret offer of a seat in Congress if he withdrew. Although he was portrayed as an "apostle of anarchy" and lost resoundingly to ABRAM HEWITT, George did receive more votes than Republican candidate Theodore Roosevelt.

Henry George was a very well-known and popular man. Henry George souvenirs were hot items in the years after his death: this paperweight bearing his portrait and the 1898 post card of his Green-Wood Cemetery monument are examples.

Henry George's monument was cleaned and restored recently by the Green-Wood Historic Fund.

Henry George died of a stroke while campaigning for New York City mayor in 1897. More than 100,000 people came to pay their respects at his bier, and thousands accompanied his body to its burial place at Green-Wood Cemetery. George has been called the most influential and important American reform theorist of the late nineteenth century. He was also the grandfather of Agnes de Mille, the famous dancer and choreographer.

By Sylvan Water.

CHAPTER SEVEN

Into the Twentieth Century (1900-1935)

THE *GENERAL SLOCUM* ON FIRE

WEDNESDAY, JUNE 15, 1904, was a warm spring day. Hundreds of German-immigrant mothers and their children from St. Mark's Lutheran Church on the Lower East Side boarded the steamship *General Slocum* at its pier on East Third Street while a band lent a festive air to the day with a lively polka. Everyone looked forward to a day away from the tenement life of their neighborhood, the area then known as Little Germany or Kleindeutschland; they were to steam up the East River into Long Island Sound, then east to enjoy a country picnic at Locust Grove on Huntington Bay. As the ship set out on its cruise, no one could have known the horror that awaited them.

Within a half-hour of leaving the pier, as the *General Slocum* passed 125th Street, a boy on board spotted smoke coming from the bow area, and ran to find a crewman. As passengers saw flames leap up, one witness recounted, "No one screamed. No one cried out. Not at first. No one went haywire. Faces just froze." By the time the ship was off 130th Street, the fire, which had started in a paint storage locker, had spread through the lowest of the three decks. When the crew tried to fight the rapidly-spreading flames, fire hoses burst in their hands, and frantic hands grabbing for sand buckets found them to be empty. Mothers grabbed life jackets, put them on their children, and threw them into the hoped-for safety of the river, only to watch in horror as the jackets disintegrated in the water and the children went under. Some passengers jumped overboard, only to be killed by the churning paddle wheels.

Captain William van Schaick, who only the year before had received an award for safely carrying 35 million passengers in his career, did not turn to the left, towards the nearby Bronx shore, for fear of igniting the oil tanks and lumber yards there, and was unable to head right because of rocks in the water. But, instead of just stopping his ship, he inexplicably continued full speed ahead, feeding oxygen to the fire and spreading it rearward, where many desperate passengers had fled, until he ran his ship aground on a sand bar near North Brother Island. By then, the flames had spread through the whole vessel, collapsing its upper deck, and dropping passengers into the flames.

Two inmates on a Rikers Island work detail rowed out to help, and managed to save fifteen people. But the loss of life was horrendous. Though all but one crew member survived, of the 1,335 passengers, 1,051 perished and

The twisted wreck of the General Slocum *after it was raised and towed to shore.*

The General Slocum *victims were displayed for identification in this makeshift morgue.*

Carrying the dead from the General Slocum *tragedy out of the morgue.*

Black ribbons announce one family's mourning for the victims of the General Slocum *disaster.*

The Hartung Monument at Green-Wood Cemetery bears the names of five family members who died on June 15, 1904, in the General Slocum *disaster.*

another 124 were injured. The fire that consumed the three-deck wooden side-wheel steamboat *General Slocum*, the "Queen of the Excursion Steamers," claimed more lives than any other disaster in New York City history.

When the disastrous news reached Little Germany, quiet descended and crepe hung over that Lower East Side neighborhood "like black leaves." On June 17, the *New York Herald* ran three full pages of "In Memoriam" notices. So many people were dead that coffins, hearses, and carriages had to be brought in from as far away as Philadelphia for all the funerals. The price of black ribbon, only five cents a yard before the tragedy, soared to five times that price as New York mourned.

Of the fatalities, the names of forty-six appear in Green-Wood Cemetery's burial ledgers. Many of them were children. One family, the Hartungs of East 21st Street, buried five of its own at Green-Wood: LOUISA (forty-seven years old), FRANCIS (seventeen), MILIE (who would have turned thirteen three days later), CLARA (ten), and ELSIE (six). Another 156 victims were interred at Lutheran Cemetery in Middle Village, Queens. It was there that those who had managed to survive the flames and the water, the members of the Organization of the General Slocum Survivors, met yearly to remember this tragedy.

Captain van Schaick, who insisted that he had done everything that was humanly possible to save lives, was acquitted of manslaughter, but was convicted of failure to train his crew in fire drills, and served three years in Sing Sing Prison. After a massive petition drive, Van Schaick was pardoned by President William Howard Taft. In the wake of the tragedy, new efforts were made to enforce safety measures on steamboats, and a marble monument to the victims of the *General Slocum* was dedicated in Tompkins Square Park. On it was engraved, "They were earth's purest children young and fair."

The man in whose honor this excursion steamer was named, General HENRY SLOCUM, Civil War hero, is himself buried at Green-Wood Cemetery.

THEY'LL ALWAYS NEED TOYS

Frederick Augustus Otto Schwarz (1836–1911) left Germany for New York City, where he founded Schwarz's Toy Bazaar. There he sold toys, novelties, dolls, and fancy goods to New Yorkers of all ages. Little could he have foreseen, when he started his business, that his firm would one day become the best-known toy store in the world, with its Fifth Avenue store the anchor of a national chain.

F.A.O. Schwarz's grave at Green-Wood Cemetery.

"HE LOVED NATURE"

The monument to Alfred Van Der-werken, Jr.

A cemetery monument, to be noteworthy, need not be elaborate, nor need it be dedicated to someone famous or notorious. This diminutive memorial to Alfred Van Der-werken, Jr. (1870–1906) is a joy in its simplicity. It uses a common conceit of monument makers of the time: carving stone (in this case, granite) to look like some other material (here the wooden trunk of a tree). This memorial is a unique variation on the oft-seen cutoff column; both symbolize a male life ended, or cut off, in its youth. Alfred died of pneumonia at the age of thirty-five.

TILYOU'S STEEPLECHASE PARK

George C. Tilyou (1862–1914) was Coney Island's master promoter. At the age of fourteen, he sold souvenir boxes of sifted sand and bottles of sea water for a nickel or a dime. It was Tilyou, at the ripe old age of seventeen, who wrote in the newspaper that he published to promote his real estate sales that "If Paris is France, then Coney Island, between June and September, is the world."

In 1892, recognizing a good thing, Tilyou went to the World Exposition in Chicago and offered to buy George Ferris's Wheel on the spot. Ferris refused to sell, but Tilyou was undaunted. Tilyou had a "Ferris Wheel," half the size of the one he had tried to buy, built on Coney Island. He then put up a sign, announcing that the world's largest Ferris Wheel was soon coming to that spot, rented the surrounding space, and with the proceeds financed the installation of the largest Ferris Wheel in the world.

Tilyou opened his famous amusement place, Steeplechase Park, in 1897. Its featured attraction was a racecourse over which wooden horses raced "half a mile in half a minute and fun all the time." It was the perfect attraction for turn-of-the-century New York youth. As one observer noted, "Young men like it because it gives them a chance to hug the girls; girls like it because it gives them a chance to get hugged."

F.A.O. Schwarz's toy store has grown into a national chain. This sign is outside its Fifth Avenue store.

Showman George Tilyou. Courtesy Steeplechase Amusement Park and Dictionary of American Portraits, *Dover Publications.*

This is the famous Steeplechase ride, with its horses off and running, in a photograph from the 1930's.

Riders leaving the Steeplechase found themselves on the stage of the Blow Hole Theater. As packed crowds roared with uncontrollable laughter, jets of air blew the skirts of unsuspecting females into the air, and a dwarf with a cattle prod chased others across the stage. These attractions were so popular that the stage periodically had to be darkened; only then would the spectators leave their seats and allow the next audience to come in and enjoy the entertainment. Performances at the Blow Hole Theater ran for seventy years.

In 1907, Tilyou's Steeplechase Park was destroyed by fire. Tilyou, ever the resourceful promoter, didn't miss a beat. The next day, he posted a sign in front of the still-smoldering ruins:

> To inquiring friends: I have troubles today that I did not have yesterday. I had troubles yesterday that I have not today. On this site will

If you couldn't afford a cottage in Newport, a villa along the Hudson, or a lodge in the White Mountains, the place to escape New York City's summer heat was Coney Island. As one immigrant wrote to his family, "America has a custom, every Sunday we take vacation and go to Coney Island." Starting around 1880, and continuing into the 1920's, steamers left from Manhattan's Pier One at Battery Place and docked at the Iron Pier at Coney Island one hour later. In this 1886 scene, drawn by THURE DE THULSTRUP (1848–1930), considered by many to be *Harper's Weekly's* best woodcut artist, these proper New Yorkers, serenaded by a three-piece ensemble, are "On the Way to Coney Island."

be erected shortly a better, bigger, greater Steeplechase Park. Admission to the burning ruins 10 cents.

Steeplechase Park was rebuilt and reopened for business nine months later.

George Tilyou, the "first impresario of controlled chaos," died in 1914. His epitaph at Green-Wood Cemetery, strangely enough for someone who achieved such great success in the business of making people laugh, and who managed to turn his initial investment of $1000 into a fortune of $2,000,000 (equal to $32 million today), reads, "Many Hopes Lie Buried Here."

Steeplechase Park remained in business for another half-century after George Tilyou's death, finally closing in 1964.

The entrance to the Steeplechase, The Funny Place, as it appeared in 1910.

George C. Tilyou's monument bears a strange inscription for someone who made millions of dollars amusing the public: "Many Hopes Lie Buried Here."

Peter F. Dailey often performed with minstrel BILLY WEST (1853–1902); he is buried in West's plot, beneath this marker.

"HE LAUGHED AND THE WORLD LAUGHED WITH HIM."

PETER F. DAILEY (1861–1908) starred as a comedian on the New York stage. His eulogy read: "Inimitable Peter! Born comedian, the quickest-witted man that ever used grease paint; splendid voice; an acrobat and agile dancer despite his two hundred and fifty pounds; no performance ever the same; needing neither lines nor business, but only to be given a stage." Dailey's epitaph, in a very different spirit from that of George Tilyou, reads, "He laughed and the world laughed with him."

WILLIAM F. MANGELS (1866–1958), working in Coney Island, played a key role in the creation of the great American amusement parks at the turn of the century. Mangels was one of the leading manufacturers of carousels in America. He invented the Whip ride, and designed the wave pool at Palisades Amusement Park in New Jersey. Other rides that he invented were copied throughout the world. But it was Mangels's Tickler that prompted P. G. Wodehouse, apparently as he fought nausea and bruises, to pick up his pen and write:

> The principle at the bottom of Coney Island's success is the eminently sound one that what would be a brutal assault, if administered gratis, becomes a rollicking pleasure when charged for at the rate of fifteen cents per assault. Suppose one laid hand upon you and put you in a large tub; suppose he then proceeded to send the tub spinning

One of William Mangels's most popular creations, the Whip, is shown in the foreground of this 1920 post card of Coney Island's Luna Park. The Whip is still in use in many amusement parks.

The Tickler, one of William Mangels's inspirations, was forty seconds in a tub as it crashed and twirled on casters down an incline. One observer described the ride as to "be packed in a monster barrel and be rolled incontinently down a hill.... There are milder things than that barrel shown in European museums in execration of the Spanish Inquisition."

down an incline so arranged that at intervals of a few feet it spun around and violently bumped into something. Next day he would hear from your lawyer. But in Coney Island you jump into the Tickler and enjoy it; you have to enjoy it because you have paid good money to do so. Being in America, Coney Island is thought a little vulgar; if it were in France we would have written how essentially refined the Tickler and the Human Roulette Wheel were, and with what abundance and polish the French people took its pleasure.

THE ASSASSINATION OF MAYOR GAYNOR

I N A U G U S T, 1910, New York City's Mayor W I L L I A M J. G A Y N O R (1848–1913) decided that he had earned a vacation. Booking passage to Europe, he was scheduled to sail on August 9 from Hoboken aboard the *S.S. Kaiser Wilhelm der Grosse*. But, as the ship was being readied for departure, Gaynor was approached by fired city worker James J. Gallagher, who shot him in the throat at point blank range. Gallagher was then wrestled to the ground by Big Bill Edwards, the Street Cleaning Commissioner and a former Princeton football player, who held him for the police.

Gaynor's own description of the shooting is dramatic:

Bill Warnecke, a photographer for the New York World, *was running late that day, and arrived to photograph the mayor's departure after all the other news photographers had completed their work. Warnecke, in this classic photograph, captured the immediate aftermath of the assassination attempt, as just-wounded Mayor William Gaynor struggled to survive.*

My next consciousness was of a terrible metallic roar in my head. It filled my head, which seemed as though it would burst open. It swelled to the highest pitch, and then fell, and then rose again, and so alternated until it subsided into a continuous buzz. It was sickening, but my stomach did not give way. I was meantime entirely sightless.

I do not think I fell, for when I became conscious I was on my feet. I suppose they saved me from falling, and they were supporting me. My sight gradually returned, so that after a while I could see the deck and the outlines of the crowd around me. I became conscious that I was choking. Blood was coming from my mouth and nose and I tried all I could to swallow it so those around me would not see it. But I found I could not swallow and then knew my throat was hurt. It seemed as though it was dislocated. I struggled to breathe through my mouth, but could not, and thought I was dying of strangulation. I kept thinking all the time the best thing to do.

In some way I happened to close my mouth tight and found I breathed perfectly through my nose. I then believed I could keep from smothering. . . . They wanted me to lie down on the deck, but I said no, I would walk to my stateroom. I could now see faces, and I wanted to get away from the crowd. I could not bear to have them looking at me in the plight I was in, especially the crowd of newspaper men, and especially those with cameras. Two of them rushed up from the line where they all stood and put their cameras right in my face and snapped them. I finally put my hand up and I think I said, "don't." I hope these pictures were not published. The other newspaper men acted decently, as they always do.

We were on the opposite side of the ship, and I was supported

This unusual granite circle memorializes Mayor William J. Gaynor.

through the gangway down a few steps, and then up the same number, and my stateroom was there. As we were crossing, I said to Commissioner Thompson on my right hand to send for two of the best surgeons of the city, and be sure and tell them not to discourage me. I had difficulty to make him understand me, but he finally did. Finding that my wound was not immediately mortal, I had determined to make a fight for it, and did not want any one to come near me who would discourage me.

The doctors decided to leave the bullet in Gaynor's throat, but it left him with a chronic cough and a rasping voice. When he returned to work, almost two months after the attack, he was cheered by a crowd of 10,000 citizens. He became a national figure, and there was talk of "Gaynor for President." But that bullet changed his temperament; he became vindictive and irascible, alienating the reformers who had supported him. On the first anniversary of the shooting, he said what others had been thinking, that perhaps it would have been better if he had resigned.

When Tammany Hall announced in 1913 that Gaynor would not receive its renomination for mayor, he accepted the nomination of an independent citizen's committee, then left on a cruise to rest for the upcoming campaign. But this cruise only completed what the earlier one had begun: Gaynor's son found him dead on the ship's deck, apparently the victim of the bullet still lodged in his throat and the rigors of being mayor.

The funeral procession for this immensely popular man was the largest New York City had seen since that of President Abraham Lincoln.

THE "FATHER OF BASEBALL"

NO MAN did more to popularize baseball than HENRY CHADWICK (1824–1908). A British-born newspaperman, Chadwick immigrated to America as a youth, and made Brooklyn his home. In 1847, at Elysian Fields in New Jersey, Chadwick played his first baseball game, then dedicated the rest of his life to the promotion of the sport which he helped to become the national pastime. Chadwick was convinced that the relatively quick pace of baseball was just right for Americans: "What they do, they want to do in a hurry." He persuaded *The New York Times* and other dailies that baseball was news fit to print, and became the country's first baseball editor, working at the *New York Clipper* and then the *Brooklyn Eagle* for the next half-century.

Chadwick assigned numbers to each of the positions in the field to create the baseball scoring system that is still in use today and introduced the newspaper box score, a statistical summary by which the performance of players could be compared. He coined many of baseball's most-enduring phrases, including "assist," "base hit," "base on balls," "cut off," "chin music," "fungo," "white wash," "double play," "error," "goose egg," "left on base," and "single." He also edited and published baseball guides and yearbooks, chaired the Rules Committee of the National Association of Base Ball Players, and supervised the annual game, at the beginning of every

Henry Chadwick, who was dubbed the "Father of Baseball" by President Theodore Roosevelt. There is some irony in Chadwick's induction into the Baseball Hall of Fame; it is located in Cooperstown, N.Y., based on the claim that the game was invented there. But Chadwick never believed in what he called the "Cooperstown Myth." A native of England, he long-maintained that baseball descended from the English game of rounders. Courtesy of the National Baseball Hall of Fame and Museum, Inc., Cooperstown, New York.

baseball season, at Brooklyn's Capitoline Grounds, where rules changes were demonstrated.

Chadwick firmly believed that baseball should remain a sport of gentlemen characterized by clean and honest play. He feared that, unless care was taken, greed would take over the game he loved.

In the spring of 1861, Chadwick went to Richmond, Virginia, to organize a baseball club there. His efforts, however, were interrupted by the outbreak of the Civil War. Chadwick's statement as war loomed expressed his prayer for peace in the terms he knew best, those of baseball: "God forbid that any balls but those of the Cricket and Base Ball field may be caught, either on the fly or on the bound."

Though suffering from a fever, Chadwick attended opening day of the 1908 baseball season at the Polo Grounds. Pneumonia soon set in, and on April 20, 1908, Chadwick lay unconscious in his bed. When he regained consciousness, he asked which team had won the game that day between his beloved Brooklyn team and the New York Giants. Told that the Giants had won, Chadwick expressed his regrets and lapsed into an unconsciousness from which he never emerged.

It was President Theodore Roosevelt who honored Chadwick, in 1904, as the "Father of Baseball." In 1938, Henry Chadwick was elected to the Baseball Hall of Fame. His plaque at Cooperstown reads, "Baseball's preeminent pioneer, writer for half a century, inventor of the box score, author of the first rule-book in 1858, chairman of rules committee in first nationwide baseball organization."

Chadwick's monument at Green-Wood Cemetery was paid for by contributions made to a committee chaired by that other great Brooklyn baseball man, CHARLES EBBETS. It cost a bargain $600 (equal to about $10,000 today) to erect, and its dedication, originally scheduled for the first anniversary of Chadwick's death, was, in the parlance of baseball, rained out. The four corners of his lot are marked by stones carved to look like bases. Attached to the central monument are bronze versions of a catcher's mask, a baseball glove, and crossed-bats. It is topped by a granite sphere carved to look like a baseball. Appropriately, the plaque memorializing Chadwick is in the shape of a baseball diamond; after all, it was Chadwick who coined that phrase to refer to the shape of a baseball infield.

THE FORT HAMILTON PARKWAY "BATHTUB"

Locals often ask about the "bathtub" monument that they see while driving along Fort Hamilton Parkway near the Eastern Entrance to Green-Wood Cemetery. However, exhaustive examination of the area has failed to disclose any monument suitable for bathing. Apparently these inquiries pertain to the sarcophagus, a carved stone coffin that does look very much like a Victorian bathtub. The ancient Greeks used the term sarcophagus to refer to a type of stone that was used for coffins and supposedly consumed the flesh of corpses.

Granite bases mark the four corners of Henry Chadwick's lot.

The remarkable monument to Henry Chadwick, the "Father of Baseball." For years in the early 20th century, CHARLES EBBETS, owner of the Brooklyn Dodgers, led an annual pilgrimage by baseball's faithful to Chadwick's grave, where they laid a wreath in his honor. Appropriately, Ebbets is buried on a nearby hillside. This monument was cleaned and restored by the Green-Wood Historic Fund in 2004.

Contrary to a popular misconception, it's a sarcophagus, not a bathtub.

THE BROOKLYN ENIGMA: THE PSYCHIC MARVEL OF THE NINETEENTH CENTURY

THOUGH HER GIVEN NAME was MARY J. FANCHER (1846–1916), she was to become famous as Mollie Fancher. When she was still a girl, her family moved to Brooklyn, and she was educated at the Brooklyn Heights Seminary. But a few weeks before her graduation, intestinal problems forced her to leave school. Unfortunately, this was only the first in what was to become a lifetime of medical tribulations. On May 10, 1864, Mollie was thrown by her obstreperous horse, and landed on her head. Knocked unconscious, it took her two months to recover from a concussion, double vision, and two broken ribs. But that was nothing compared to what awaited her.

In early 1865, Mollie was engaged to be married to a man of wealth and social position. On June 8, 1865, she went to see her doctor, then was off to do some shopping. Boarding the Fulton Street streetcar, she was loaded down with packages. When the streetcar reached her stop, she began to step down. But as she did so, the operator, who thought she had already gotten off, started the car forward. Mollie's skirt snagged on the car, and she was dragged a block before frantic passersby were able to get the car to stop. Again unconscious, with her ribs once more fractured, she had this time also suffered severe injuries to her spine and brain.

On February 3, 1866, after months of treatment, she was put into her bed at 160 Gates Avenue, Brooklyn, never to leave it again for more than a few minutes at a time during the rest of her life. Her eyesight began to fail, and the pain in her spine intensified. When her left lung failed, and no pulse or breathing could be detected, the doctors agreed that she was dying and her friends bade her good-bye. Her reverend was summoned, and a doctor pronounced her dead. But pronouncements of her death were very much premature. Though her eyesight, hearing, speech, and sense of touch deserted her, she clung to life. For nearly nine years after her accident, she went from one trance to another. Her body was wracked by spasms, with her right arm twisted behind her head, her hands rigidly closed, and her legs twisted around each other. The "treatments" inflicted on her by her befuddled doctors, which included packing her spine in ice, shaving and blistering her head, and putting her in hot sitz baths, only increased her suffering.

In May, 1866, Mollie Fancher discovered that she could see without using her eyes. According to her aunt, Susan Crosby, who was constantly by her side, Mollie was able to tell time by passing her hand over a watch. She could read letters that were still folded and sealed in their envelopes, could differentiate colors by touch, could predict fire bells and thunderstorms, could tell who was at the downstairs door, and could see her friends as they traveled about or were in their homes. Many believed that her physical pain had brought her clairvoyance. As one of those who believed in her special gifts wrote, in an effort to explain her abilities:

> The question has arisen, and will naturally be suggested, how does

Mollie Fancher at the age of sixteen.

Mollie Fancher in a trance, 1887.

Miss Fancher see beyond the walls of her room, by which she is environed? . . . Is it by spiritual sight? Does her spirit, while still retaining sufficient relation to the body to maintain its seat and hold upon the material forms, pass out through this to other material substances, and, by the use of her spiritual vision, discern what is transpiring? The affirmative would certainly seem the only that can be made. . . .

Louis Sherk, one of those who often visited Mollie, recounted this example of her gift of sight:

MOLLIE

MOLLIE FANCHER KNEW THE SECRET OF LIFE.
HALF A CENTURY IN HER BED, HER DAUNTLESS SPIRIT,
CHEERFUL PATIENCE AND UNFAILING SYMPATHY, INSPIRED
MANY WITH COURAGE TO MEET LIFE'S PROBLEMS.
FORGETFUL OF HER OWN SUFFERING, SHE CARRIED
THE BURDENS OF HOSTS OF FRIENDS.
THRU A LIFE OF INDUSTRY, GOD GRANTED HER PRAYER:
"LET ME NOT LIE WITH FOLDED HANDS."

FANCHER

This description of Mollie Fancher's life is carved on her monument.

Upon another time I sent a man to her house to hang her picture in the front room, but did not inform him who occupied the house. I gave him instructions where to hang it if no one should be in the room. It so happened that no one was in the front room, and as he reported to me, the folding doors between the front and back room were closed. In the midst of his work he heard somebody severely criticizing him as to the manner in which he was hanging the picture. He looked around, saw nobody, and proceeded with his work, when he was again interrupted. He became alarmed, looked under the piano and back of the chairs, saw nobody in the room, went back to his work, when he was further criticised. He hastily finished his work and left the house. He told me that he would not go back to that house for any money, for he did not want to come in contact with the devil. I then informed him that this devil was Miss Fancher, and that many wealthy people would gladly pay a large sum to have had the experience which he had. The explanation to the whole thing being, that Miss Fancher from her bed in the back room, saw what he was doing, and had something to say as to the manner in which the work was done; but to see him she had to see through the partition intervening.

As early as 1866, Mollie Fancher's story began to draw public attention. It was in that year that the *Brooklyn Eagle* ran a story, without mentioning her name, headlined, "A Remarkable Case," with these subtitles: "Terrible Condition of a Patient–The Nerves in Rebellion–A Continuous Trance–Persistent Muscular Rigidity–The Gift of Second Sight-Physic Baffled–The Sufferer Lives Seven Weeks Without Food."

In the ensuing years, the claims of those who were convinced of her special powers appeared in various newspapers, often answered by skeptics. The *New York Herald*, in 1878, editorialized sympathetically, hoping that further inquiry would prove her powers genuine:

> While the intelligent public will wish the lady good riddance of the swarms of inquirers who beset her without respect for her feeble health, it will also hope that some competent person or persons may be allowed opportunity for investigating a case which, if all that is said to be, is of exceptional importance in its relations to physical and mental science.

At the same time, the *New York Sun* was even more enthusiastic, printing an article entitled, "Dead and Yet Alive! The Extraordinary Case of Miss Fancher of Brooklyn. Facts Verified by Abundant Testimony. A Mental Sight That is Not the Clap-Trap of Clairvoyance." It was said that "in Brooklyn, not to know about this famous lady is to prove one's self unknowing."

Though scientists, clergymen, reporters, and citizens came to see Miss Fancher, she refused to press any claim that she had special powers. She declined all offers to act as a medium. P. T. Barnum sent his agent to hire her for exhibit, but she turned him away. When she refused to be tested by investigators, her supporters explained that the stress of testing would mask her gift.

However, she was quite capable of personally handling the occasional skeptic who might appear. One gentleman, who prided himself on his superior wit, attempted to needle her about her supposed powers of second-sight with this inquiry: "When you are away on any of your occult perambulations, do you ever come across *me*?" She quickly answered, "Oh, yes; frequently!" "Well," he came back, "that is very interesting. Do you ever see anybody around me?" "Very often," was her reply. "Ah, indeed!" continued the gentleman. "And can you give me any idea what they look like?" "Creditors," came the reply.

Mollie Fancher was driven, in the last year of her life, by the desire to reach the fiftieth anniversary of her bedridden existence. She underwent two serious operations during that final year; her doctors were convinced that her recovery from them was the result of her desire to celebrate February 3, 1916. On that date, her friends and relatives gathered at her bedside to share her triumph. But nine days later she was dead. Her obituary in *The New York Times* was headlined, "Mollie Fancher, Fifty Years in Bed, Dies: Psychic Invalid Recently Celebrated Golden Jubilee of Her Imprisonment."

MINERVA AND THE ALTAR TO LIBERTY

THE BATTLE OF LONG ISLAND, the "first battle of the nation," fought in August of 1776, was the first time after the adoption of the Declaration of Independence that the Continental Army took to the field against British troops. During that engagement, in which 2000 American troops under General Lord Stirling engaged in a retreating action against 6000 British troops under General Grant, fighting occurred across a ridge that would later be known as Green-Wood Cemetery's Battle Hill. A group of American riflemen, fighting for their new country, were surrounded and killed there, then buried where they had fallen.

Minerva *salutes her sister, the* Statue of Liberty, *in New York Harbor. Charles Higgins's mausoleum is at far right.*

The crowd gathers for the 1920 dedication of Minerva and the Altar of Liberty. *Courtesy of the Brooklyn Historical Society.*

CHARLES M. HIGGINS (1854–1929), whose "Higgins' American India Ink," glues, and pastes were made at his Ninth Street factory in Brooklyn, had a lifelong desire to elevate this battle to what he considered to be its proper prominence in American history. Higgins provided the impetus for *Minerva and the Altar to Liberty*, which were unveiled in front of his mausoleum on August 27, 1920, the 144th anniversary of the Battle of Long Island.

The statue is of the Roman goddess Minerva, goddess of battle and protector of civilized life, who was born from Zeus's head full grown and in armor. She was sculpted by Frederic Wellington Ruckstall (1853–1942), cast in bronze, and stands atop Brooklyn, saluting her sister the *Statue of Liberty* in the harbor, while laying a wreath with her other hand at the *Altar to Liberty*. A poem by schoolgirl Sarah Day, the winner of a writing competition, adorns the altar.

Arbor Water, circa 1900. Just a few years later, it was drained for the erection of the Chapel. Note the planters atop the mausoleum in the foreground, and how well-maintained they were.

THE CHAPEL

WHEN GREEN-WOOD CEMETERY was first laid out, land was reserved for the construction of a chapel. However, when it became apparent that there was no great public demand for a mortuary chapel at the cemetery, the lots on Chapel Hill were sold off.

As the twentieth century began, Green-Wood Cemetery's directors decided that it was time to erect a chapel, and solicited plans from the leading architects of the time. The firm of Carrere and Hastings submitted a design, but its plans were rejected and in modified form their plans became the main branch of the New York Public Library at 42nd Street and Fifth Avenue.

The Chapel, just a few years after its completion, is pictured on this post card.

This is one of a collection of 17 photographs obtained by The Green-Wood Historic Fund in 2005 that show the chapel being built in 1910 and 1911. Green-Wood Historic Fund Collection.

Ultimately, Green-Wood chose the plans of the architectural firm of Warren and Wetmore for its chapel. That firm built some of the most prestigious buildings in New York City, including Grand Central Station, the Commodore Hotel, the Yale Club, and the New York Yacht Club. Its hiring demonstrated that, several generations removed from its founding, Green-Wood Cemetery still occupied an eminent position in New York.

The Chapel was built near the main gates, in an area that until then had been occupied by a pond, Arbor Water. A reduced version of Christopher Wren's Thomas Tower at Christ Church, Oxford, it is built of Indiana limestone.

Due to a lack of demand for a facility in which to hold funeral services at the cemetery, the chapel was closed early in the 1980's. The cemetery restored the chapel's interior and exterior in 2001, and it has since seen regular use as a place of contemplation as well as for cemetery board meetings, dinners, theatrical and dance performances, movies, concerts, book signings, gallery exhibitions, and even weddings.

The interior of Green-Wood Cemetery's Chapel is shown in this circa 1920 photograph.

AZRAEL, THE ANGEL OF DEATH

IN MARCH, 1915, CHARLES ADOLPH SCHIEREN (1842–1915), former mayor of Brooklyn and a national leader in the leather belting industry, and his wife, MARIE LOUISE SCHIEREN (1839–1915), died within a day of each other of pneumonia. He was ill the last two years of his life, and ultimately caught pneumonia. She, who had suffered from heart disease for many years, tried to nurse him back to health and also was stricken with pneumonia. As Charles Schieren lay on his deathbed, he was told that his wife was ill, but was not informed how serious her condition was. She was never apprised of the seriousness of his condition nor of his death. They were interred together at Green-Wood Cemetery in a double funeral.

The Schieren plot contains Azrael, the Angel of Death, *who called twice on the Schieren family within a day. For Jews and Muslims, Azrael is the angel who separates the soul from the body at the moment of death. A low stone in front of Azrael's figure bears the names of Charles Adolph Schieren and Marie Louise Schieren, the dates of their lives, and this inscription: "In their lives they were lovely and in their death they were not divided."*

Brooklyn Mayor Charles A. Schieren, in a circa 1895 portrait.

[189]

Their monument at Green-Wood is the work of sculptor Solon H. Borglum. Born in Utah in 1868, Borglum grew up on the American frontier, studied sculpture in Paris, and was known for his figures of Indians and cowboys. His best-known works are the five colossal busts of Civil War generals at Vicksburg National Park and *The Pioneer*, which was exhibited at the San Francisco Exposition of 1915. He was the brother of sculptor Gutzon Borglum, whose greatest work was the carving of the Presidents on Mount Rushmore. At the time of his death in 1922, Solon Borglum was running a school for sculptors in New York City.

THAT TIFFANY TOUCH

CHARLES LEWIS TIFFANY (1812–1902), founder of Tiffany & Company, was born in Killingly, Connecticut, where he received little formal education before going to work managing his father's general store. He came to New York City in 1837, and with $1000 borrowed from his father, he established a bric-a-brac and stationery store on Broadway near City Hall. Things did not go well at first: total sales for his first three days in business were $4.98. However, Tiffany & Co. soon became synonymous with fashionable shopping for jewelry, silver, glass, and porcelain. Its showrooms followed New York City's most fashionable shopping areas as they moved uptown to Broadway near Spring Street, then to Union Square, on to Fifth Avenue and 37th Street, and finally to their current location on Fifth Avenue at 57th Street. Branches were established in Paris in 1850 and London in 1868.

Charles Tiffany, who made his Tiffany & Company store famous. Courtesy Tiffany & Co. and Dictionary of American Portraits, *Dover Publications.*

Tiffany & Company's artisans have produced a treasure of fine pieces, including this Magnolia Vase which was exhibited at the Columbia Exposition in 1893. Courtesy of The Metropolitan Museum of Art.

One of Charles Tiffany's many skills was as a promoter. In 1858, when the Atlantic Cable was laid, connecting America and England by telegraph for the first time, it created a sensation. Tiffany quickly bought up scraps of the cable and sold them with his golden label. When one of P. T. Barnum's elephants was destroyed for acting up, Tiffany bought its hide to make bags. The crowd that gathered outside Tiffany & Co. to buy those bags was so large that the police had to be called out. And, when Diamond Jim Brady decided that the only appropriate gift for Lillian Russell was a chamber pot with a large diamond target on the bottom, Tiffany was only too willing to oblige. Upheavals in Europe were opportunities for him to buy and sell the world's great crown jewels.

A piece of the Atlantic Cable, with the Tiffany label attached.

Tiffany's stationery business has always been for the best of the best. Whether you wanted to send out invitations for the opening of the Brooklyn Bridge or the *Statue of Liberty*, Tiffany was the company to do your printing. This invitation to the inauguration of the first bridge between the cities of New York and Brooklyn invites ALBERT W. BAILEY (1865–1927) to the festivities. Bailey is buried at Green-Wood Cemetery, about a quarter of a mile from the Tiffanys.

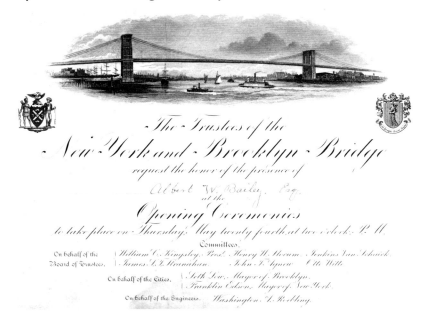

For over fifty years Tiffany led the jewelry trade in America; by the time of his death, Tiffany & Company was the greatest jewelry firm in America.

His son, LOUIS COMFORT TIFFANY (1848–1933), was one of the most talented artists America has ever produced. He studied painting in Paris, then traveled throughout North Africa and the Near East to study exotic designs. Tiffany excelled in many fields: painting, interior design (he decorated the White House for President Chester Arthur), art glass (patenting his hand-blown Favrile glass in 1894), mosaics, and jewelry. Tiffany was also one of the first artists to use electric lights in his work. In 1885, he collaborated with Thomas Alva Edison on lighting New York City's Lyceum Theatre, the first public building to be entirely lit by electricity.

But Louis Comfort Tiffany's pioneering work in stained glass is undoubtedly his greatest legacy. Beginning in the 1870's, he rejected the practice of creating stained glass by painting clear glass with enamels and then firing it, and instead created new kinds and colors of glass. His glass was colored through, and some pieces were folded, rippled, or threaded with contrasting glass, so that it seemed that twigs, sunsets, and draperies were in the glass itself.

Stained glass artist and designer Louis Comfort Tiffany. Courtesy Tiffany & Co. and Dictionary of American Portraits, *Dover Publications.*

Louis Comfort Tiffany's Pink Lotus Lamp sold at auction in December, 1997, for $2,807,500, the highest price ever paid for a twentieth century decorative arts piece. It was made circa 1905 for Ada Wrigley, the wife of William Wrigley, Jr., who founded Juicy Fruit and Doublemint gums, and was the longtime owner of the Chicago Cubs. Courtesy of Alastair Duncan.

The Tiffany Glass Company was established in 1885 to supply stained glass windows to churches and homes. From his studio in Corona, Queens, Tiffany and his workers, experimenting with new techniques and mixtures, created over 5,000 colors, textures, and varieties of opalescent glass. This glass was used to create color, shading, and layering in stained glass windows, to "paint" with glass.

Tiffany decided to use the scraps of glass left over from his windows to make shades for his lamps. Those lamps typically featured Art Nouveau-style flower or geometric forms. His lamp shades, ultimately available in over five hundred patterns, were first sold in 1895. Shades could be purchased separately from the bases, and the purchaser could choose any base from the Tiffany catalog to pair with it. Tiffany lamps continued to be sold well into the 1920's, but then lost their popularity. Tiffany, who considered himself the first American industrial artist to design for the modern age, was by then considered outdated.

Louis Comfort Tiffany, the man who was once a world-renowned artist, died in 1933, by then largely forgotten. In the ensuing years, modernists belittled his work. Many of Tiffany's lamps, scorned as "fussy and silly," were sold at rummage sales or thrown out with the trash. But, by the 1950's, there was a renewal of interest in his work; exhibits were held and collections begun. Since then, Tiffany items have become "hot" again. In June, 1995, a Tiffany lamp in the Virginia Creeper pattern, made as a special order around 1910, sold at auction for $1,102,500, the first Tiffany lamp to top $1 million. At that same auction, seventy-four Tiffany lamps from a collection put together in the late 1970's and early 1980's, sold for a total of almost $8 million.

One of the Louis Comfort Tiffany stained glass windows that adorn Green-Wood Cemetery.

The term "Tiffany lamp" is today applied to any lamp with a colored glass shade, and Louis Comfort Tiffany is most widely remembered today for his lamps. That his lamps, made from scraps, rather than his windows, his glass, or his paintings, are now his greatest legacy, would have disappointed him.

The Tiffany family's polished black marble monuments seem to be unique. The simplicity of design and elegance suggest that they may well have been designed by Louis Comfort Tiffany. Despite his fame, there is only the slightest bit of bragging here. His great accomplishments as an artist are only hinted at in a roundabout way. On his wife's stone, she is identified as having been married to "Louis Comfort Tiffany, N.A.," "N.A." being a reference to his membership in the prestigious National Academy of Design.

The monuments to Charles and Louis Comfort Tiffany and family.

A BRILLIANT CAREER, CUT SHORT

Painter George Wesley Bellows.

THE PAINTINGS of GEORGE WESLEY BELLOWS (1882–1925) are quintessentially American: big, full of energy, and immediate. His work ranks with the most significant artists of the early twentieth century. To his contemporaries, he was "one of the most powerful personalities in American art;" today, he is widely regarded as the best realist of his generation. When Bellows was elected an associate of the National Academy of Design, he was the youngest member ever to achieve that distinction, and it was predicted that he would be the foremost painter of his time. He taught at the Art Students League in New York from 1910 to 1911 and the Art Institute of Chicago in 1919 and was a founding member of the Society of Independent Artists. Bellows often won prizes at major exhibitions, and his works, including his scenes of contemporary urban life, prize fights, Maine seascapes, and portraits, are in the collection of virtually every important American art museum.

As New York City emerged as an industrial and commercial center in the 1820's and 30's, the increasing density of its population and the evils attending industrialization and urbanization became a concern. Underlying the 1838 founding of Green-Wood Cemetery was a romantic and nostalgic view of nature that, in contrast to the city, was seen as the home of all that was good and godly.

Almost a century later, George Bellows emerged as one of the finest American painters of the twentieth century. Bellows, born and raised in Ohio, came east to paint seascapes, landscapes, boxing scenes, and portraits, as "the apotheosis of the 100 per cent American artist." An important part of his work were his canvasses of New York City. Bellows broke with the artistic convention of painting the ideal, instead choosing to paint scenes from everyday life. He painted what was real to him, what captured the energy of his adopted city: "I paint New York because I live in it and the most essential thing for me to paint is the life about me, the things I feel to-day and that are part of the life of to-day."

One such painting of New York City is *Cliff Dwellers*, done in 1913. In it, Bellows turned his attention to rising immigration, the resulting crowding, and the consequent evils. This painting catalogs the ills caused by such

Cliff Dwellers, 1913, *by George Bellows, reflects antiurban attitudes. Courtesy of the Los Angeles County Museum of Art, Los Angeles County Fund. Photograph © 2008 Museum Associates/LACMA.*

overcrowding: children playing unsupervised in the street, children raising children (the young blonde woman holding a baby in the center foreground), and people idling the day away. Henry McBride, critic for the *New York Sun*, was taken aback by what he saw:

This is the only memorial to George Wesley Bellows.

> George Bellows' "Cliff Dwellers" is appalling. Can New York really be like that in summer? The dreadful people crowding the street, like naked urchins, the vendors of unhygienic lollipops, the battalion of mothers nursing their infants near the footlights where you have to see them, the street car clanging its mad way through the throng, the gentlemen on the fire escapes doing their toilets and the housewives hanging out the wash, can anything in Bedlam or Hogarth's prints equal this?

Other critics, however, were impressed by what they felt was the truthfulness and power of this work.

Cliff Dwellers, purchased by the Los Angeles County Museum of Art in 1916 as the first painting in its collection, remains to this day one of its most popular pictures.

Bellows was a blunt man who disdained pretension and loved baseball, music, and reading. When his life was suddenly cut short by appendicitis at the age of forty-two, his family was unprepared for his burial. Emma, his wife of fifteen years who had married him in the simplest of ceremonies, chose the music and the church (the Church of the Ascension at Fifth Avenue and 10th Street in Manhattan) for the funeral, but left the other details to their friends. They chose a ceremony full of pomp: twenty-four pallbearers were selected from the who's who of artists, musicians, and collectors who crowded the church.

And the world noted Bellows's passing. The newspapers of Columbus, Ohio, where Bellows grew up, ran banner headlines, "George Bellows Dead." The *New York Sun* editorialized: "This country has lost one of its foremost artists and the most eminent of the younger academic painters." *The New York Times* lamented:

> It is a misfortune not only for his many friends but for America and art that George Bellows should have died before his work was done. . . . There is no one to fill precisely his place in his generation, so there is more than customary significance in saying that his loss is one to be mourned.

Emma Bellows, suddenly a widow, recalled the day of her husband's burial:

> The service they all say was impressive. To me it was the longest twenty minutes I ever hope to put in. I saw no one, heard nothing, and then there was that trip through Brooklyn . . .

George Bellows was buried in his in-laws' lot at Green-Wood Cemetery. Without pretension in life, his monument is equally modest: rising just above ground level, it bears only his initials, G.W.B.

John La Farge, an artist of great versatility, circa 1895.

D ESCRIBED AS "nineteenth century America's most innovative and diversified artist," JOHN LA FARGE (1835–1910) excelled as a mural, still life, and landscape painter, stained glass artist, designer, and writer. La Farge was the first American master to join decorative art and architecture.

Born in New York City, and raised there in a cultured French Catholic family, La Farge graduated from St. Mary's College of Maryland at eighteen, then went to Paris and London to study art. In 1858, he moved to Newport, Rhode Island, where he studied with painter William Morris Hunt.

When La Farge was rejected for service during the Civil War because of his nearsightedness, he decided to devote himself to painting, and became a versatile artist. He painted landscapes, flowers, and figures; his watercolors brought him his greatest popularity. At a time when there was virtually no mural decoration in the United States, he painted the murals for Henry Hobson Richardson's Trinity Church in Boston, and later executed panels for New York City's Church of the Incarnation, Church of the Ascension, St. Thomas's Church, Whitelaw Reid's music room, and the Supreme

In 1899, John La Farge was awarded the French Government's Legion of Honor as "the great innovator, the inventor of opaline glass." La Farge, unlike Louis Comfort Tiffany, often fused paint on glass for his windows. This window, Dawn Comes on the Edge of Night, *dates from 1903, and has a history of ownership in Brooklyn. It was first purchased by wealthy Brooklyn businessman Frank L. Babbott, who donated it to the Packer Collegiate Institute in 1934. At that time, the* New York Herald Tribune's *critic called it one of La Farge's masterpieces. It was at the Packer Institute until 1982; since then it has been in a private collection. Courtesy of Mr. and Mrs. Willard G. Clark.*

The La Farge hillside mausoleum is an unusual, perhaps unique, design.

Court room of the Minnesota State Capitol.

A close friend of writers Henry James and Henry Adams, La Farge traveled with the latter to Japan and the South Seas to create impressionist paintings, arriving only days before painter Paul Gauguin. A frequent and leading writer and lecturer on art, his *An Artist's Letters from Japan* (1897) and *Reminiscences of the South Seas* (1912) showed off his literary skills and were illustrated with his paintings and drawings.

La Farge was also a leader in stained glass design. He invented opaline glass, which was made with opaque particles suspended in transparent glass, and pioneered in stained glass design. He produced thousands of stained glass windows for residences and churches, including Trinity Church in Boston, New York City's Church of the Ascension, Wellesley College Chapel, Memorial Hall at Harvard University, and Rhode Island's Newport Congregational Church.

THE LAW IS THE LAW

THE ONLY PERSON who ever served as mayor of both of the then-separate Cities of New York and Brooklyn is SETH LOW (1850–1916). Low was a man with a strong sense of right and wrong. As a leader of the reformers, he fought against rampant bribery of the police, championed the merit-based awarding of municipal franchises, and was the first mayor in New York State to introduce a competitive examination system for appointments to municipal offices.

During Low's term as New York City's mayor, a young fireman died in the line of duty. However, because this fire fighter had not yet completed a

Seth Low, the only man elected mayor of the Cities of New York and Brooklyn, in a circa 1884 engraving.

year of service, his family was not entitled by law to any insurance money. Sympathetic friends soon got a special act approved in the State Legislature which allowed Low to waive the one year requirement for this case. Low met with a delegation that urged him to approve the waiver, but he refused, telling them that the law required one year of service as a prerequisite to insurance coverage. They left, cursing Low as they went.

Low then went to his desk, wrote out his personal check for the full amount of the insurance, and had it delivered to the deceased fireman's family. Low refused, despite the urgings of his aides, to allow any word of his generosity to be made public.

SHAKING THE FAMILY TREE

BORN IN NEW YORK CITY, the daughter of wealthy sugar refiner George Elder, LOUISINE WALDRON ELDER (HAVEMEYER) (1855–1929) was educated at a fashionable boarding school in Paris. There she met American painter Mary Cassatt, who introduced her to the emerging Impressionists. Louisine Elder became Edgar Degas's first American patron, using her pin money to purchase one of his paintings for $100 at a time when his work and that of his compatriots was generally considered undesirable.

In 1883, she married HENRY OSBORNE HAVEMEYER (1847–1907), later head of the American Sugar Refinery. Their mansion, at 66th Street and Fifth Avenue in New York City, was exotically decorated by LOUIS COMFORT TIFFANY, and housed their eclectic art collection. That collection included many paintings, including European masterpieces and modern French works, which they purchased under the guidance of their art adviser Mary Cassatt. Louisine Havemeyer was awarded the rosette of the Legion of Honor for her support of French art.

Louisine Havemeyer and Henry O. Havemeyer, in an 1890 photograph taken in Paris. She wears a dress newly-purchased from the designer Worth. Courtesy of Harry W. Havemeyer.

Louisine Havemeyer holds the Torch of Liberty aloft while addressing a male audience in New York City.

When her husband died in 1907, Louisine Havemeyer added a new cause to her life: woman suffrage. In 1913, she helped to found the Congressional Union for Woman Suffrage, and exhibited her collection of paintings (the only time during her lifetime that she allowed them to be shown to the public) for the benefit of that organization. She also gave speeches for the cause, parlaying her famous name and social prominence into publicity for her message. She effectively brought attention to the movement with the "Torch of Liberty," which was passed through the States, a model of the *Mayflower* lit by light bulbs powered by her car battery at the climax of her speeches, and her arrest on the White House Lawn after she tried to set fire to an effigy of President Woodrow Wilson. While spending three days in jail for her trespass, rather than pay a $5 fine, she received less-than-congratulatory telegrams from her relatives, and later reflected sardonically:

> If you intend doing anything out of the ordinary, you better take a look at the "family tree" first. If you have not any family tree, why, go ahead; but if you have one of those wide-spreading, interlocking branching affairs with shallow, wabbly roots, look out; it may give you a lot of trouble. Mine gave me trouble. . . . From them I gleaned I had stripped the family tree, I had broken its branches, I had torn up its roots and laid it prostrate in the sorrowing dust. What had the whole treeful of innocents ever done that I should treat them thus? Did I realize I had lost my citizenship? That telegram forgot that citizenship (real citizenship) was what I was fighting for—and theirs as well as mine!

Undeterred, Louisine Havemeyer toured the country on a train that was dubbed the "Prison Special" with other suffragists who had "served terms."

Her great legacy is her bequest to The Metropolitan Museum of Art in New York of many of her and her husband's collections, including porcelain, pottery, glass, sculpture, and paintings. That museum, which up until her bequest had been criticized for its refusal to purchase "modern" works, suddenly possessed one of the finest collections of Old Masters and Impressionist paintings in America, including dozens of canvasses by Degas, Cezanne, Manet, Courbet, Corot, and Monet. Her gift was perhaps the greatest ever given to The Metropolitan Museum.

A LANDMARK COURTHOUSE

JAMES BROWN LORD (1858–1902), the grandson of JAMES BROWN (founder of the private banking firm of Brown Brothers) on his mother's side and lawyer DANIEL LORD (senior partner and founder of the law firm of Lord, Day, and Lord) on his father's side, was trained in architecture by prominent church architect William A. Potter of New York City. Lord designed two Delmonico restaurants, Babies' Hospital, many homes in Tuxedo Park, New York, and the New York City Branch Library at 222 East 79th Street.

The entrance to the Havemeyer family's underground vault, which stretches beneath Orchard Hill.

The Havemeyer's daughter, Electra Havemeyer Webb, was also a collector. But she preferred to collect Americana, including cigar store Indians, quilts, toys, and the like, much to her mother's consternation. Electra's legacy is the "collection of collections" that makes up Vermont's Shelburne Museum.

The Appellate Division Courthouse, shown here in a photograph taken just a few years after its completion, is one of New York's great buildings.

Architect James Brown Lord's monument.

The splendors of the Appellate Division Courthouse, architect James Brown Lord's greatest work, are shown in these views of its magnificent lobby and courtroom. Photographs courtesy of Presiding Justice Francis T. Murphy, Appellate Division of the Supreme Court of the State of New York, First Judicial Department.

Lord's last and greatest work was the Appellate Division, First Department, Courthouse at Madison Avenue and 25th Street in Manhattan. Opening in 1900, it is still in use today. In this remarkable building, an unheard-of one-third of its construction budget was devoted to sculpture decorating its exterior and murals and stained glass adorning its interior, all by the leading artists of the time. JOHN LA FARGE, Kenyon Cox, Karl Bitter, and Daniel Chester French are just a few of the prominent artists who worked on this project. Both the exterior and important sections of the interior have been designated New York City landmarks.

AN EARLY SCREEN STAR

Screen star Florence LaBadie died from injuries she suffered in an automobile accident.

BORN IN CANADA to a well-known French-Canadian family, FLORENCE LaBADIE (1894–1917) studied art, painting and sculpture there before coming to New York City with her family. By her mid-teens she was working as a model and in the theatre. She soon became a screen star, acting in twenty releases in 1915 (most of which were "two-reelers") and six feature films the next year. Because of her on-screen stunts and her off-screen exploits, she quickly developed a reputation as a young daredevil. Movies were promoted for the star appeal of this young beauty; in all she appeared in over one hundred productions, including *The Million Dollar Mystery*, *Cinderella*, and *Dr. Jekyll and Mr. Hyde*. When World War I began, she entertained Canadian troops who were camped outside Montreal, undergoing training for combat in Europe.

In September, 1917, Florence LaBadie was a passenger in a car driven by Daniel Carson Goodman, her fiance and an author-screenwriter, in Ossining, New York, when its brakes failed on a hill. She was thrown from the car, severely injured, and died six weeks later.

THE MILLIONAIRE DADDY

EDWARD WEST BROWNING (1875–1934), a New York City real estate tycoon, had a fortune estimated at $6 or $7 million (the equivalent of $70 to $80 million today). Often in the news for his involvement in legal disputes stemming from adoption and marital problems, his nickname of "Daddy" was nationally known. Over two million letters, many addressed simply to "Daddy, New York" or "The Millionaire Daddy, U.S.A.," were displayed, tied in bundles, in his office. Known for his contributions to children's charities, he established the Browning Foundation, which operated playgrounds for children throughout New York City and gave toys and play devices to hospitals for use by young patients. In 1928, "Daddy" Browning offered New York City $1 million to convert the reservoir in Central Park into a beach, swimming pool, and playground, but the city declined the offer.

"Daddy" Browning in his office, surrounded by just a few of the letters he received from children. Daily News *L.P. Photo.*

But Browning was often in the news for more controversial matters involving children. In 1926, at the age of fifty-one, he married a fifteen-year-old schoolgirl, Frances (Peaches) Heenan. They lived together for less than a year before she sued for divorce, making "sensational allegations." When she failed to obtain either the divorce decree or the money she was seeking, she took to the stage as "Peaches Browning."

Several years later, supposedly in an effort to satisfy his adopted daughter, Dorothy Sunshine (who was nine at the time), and her desire for a playmate, Browning advertised for a "pretty, refined girl about 14 years old" for adoption. As *The New York Times* reported, "hundreds of poor children applied for the position of daughter in a luxurious home." This was something of an understatement; in fact, "Daddy" Browning received 12,000 letters from young girls who wanted to be his daughter. The "girl" who was chosen, Mary Louise Spas of Astoria, Queens, claimed to be sixteen, but turned out to be twenty-one; her adoption was later annulled.

The last few years of his life, "Daddy" Browning ate only uncooked vegetables and fruit, boasted of his 46 inch chest (expanded) and 26 inch waist, and lived by the slogan, "Do good, help others, keep fit. Get back to nature and you'll get back to health." At the time of his death, four nurses, two orderlies, a butler, several housemaids, two doctors, and several members of his family were present. Neither his first nor his second wife were there; they were apparently resting up for the ensuing years of court battles over his fortune.

"Daddy" Browning and Mary Louise Spas are surrounded by the losing entries in the contest to be adopted by him. Though she was the winner, her triumph was short-lived; when it turned out that she was twenty-one years old, not sixteen as she had claimed, the adoption was annulled. Daily News *L.P. Photo.*

THE TRAVELLING BUILDING FACADE

GENERATIONS of visitors have come away from the American Wing of The Metropolitan Museum of Art impressed by a centerpiece of the collection: the facade of an early-nineteenth century building. But few are aware of the story behind it.

MARTIN EUCLID THOMPSON (1789–1877) was one of New York's leading architects during the first half of the nineteenth century. One of his

The United States Assay Office on Wall Street, circa 1865; its facade is now the focal point of the Charles Engelhard Court of The Metropolitan Museum's American Wing.

greatest works was the landmark Branch Bank of the United States, built with Tuckahoe marble on the north side of Wall Street, just east of Broad and Nassau Streets, between 1822 and 1824. In 1854, that building became the United States Assay Office, which it remained until 1915, when its facade was disassembled, marked and stored by The Metropolitan Museum to await re-erection in a wing to be devoted to Colonial art. Eventually it was rebuilt by architect GROSVENOR ATTERBURY (1969–1956) as the facade for the American Wing, which opened in 1924. When The Metropolitan Museum rebuilt its American Wing in the 1970's, reopening it in 1980, it made this facade the focal point of the courtyard.

LOST ON THE *LUSITANIA*

THE ARCTIC MONUMENT in the Brown family plot is not the only memorial at Green-Wood Cemetery to individuals lost in a shipwreck. This monument is to the memory of two who died on May 7, 1915, when the British passenger ship, the S.S. *Lusitania*, was torpedoed by a German U-boat off the coast of Ireland. Nearly 1200 lives were lost, including 128 Americans.

THE *ANGEL OF DEATH*

WILLIAM WETMORE STORY, the expatriate American sculptor whose father served as a Justice of United States Supreme Court, is buried with his wife in the Cimitero degli Inglesi (the English Cemetery) in Rome, Italy. They rest under the *Angel of Death*, the funerary monument that Story designed for their final resting place.

Virtually the same monument was recreated by the Leland Company, "Workers in Stone" at 557 Fifth Avenue in New York City, for the Cassard family at Green-Wood Cemetery in 1909 or 1910. It is of lightly veined

This stone honors two passengers who were lost at sea when the Lusitania *went down.*

The Angel of Death, *from a design by sculptor William Wetmore Story. It was cleaned recently.*

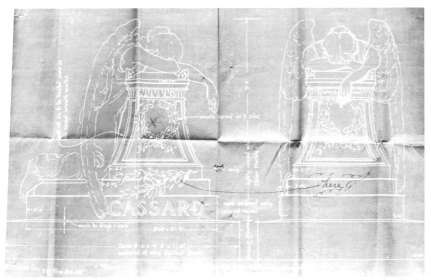

The working drawing used by the Leland Company to build the Cassard family's Angel of Death.

Italian marble, with a Barre granite base. Unfortunately, the angel's left hand has broken off, and though it lay on the ground for years, it is now gone.

MURDER ON LOVER'S LANE

On September 14, 1922, Edward Wheeler Hall (1881–1922) and Eleanor Mills were found dead under a crabapple tree on a lover's lane in New Brunswick, New Jersey. His arm was around her waist and his calling card leaned against his shoe. A scarf was around her neck; when investigators removed it, they discovered that her throat had been cut. Their love letters were scattered over them. Edward Wheeler Hall, until his demise, had been the rector of the Episcopal Church of St. John the Evangelist in that town. Eleanor Mills was the wife of the church's sexton and sang in the choir. Both were married, and they had apparently been having an affair for some time.

Four days after the murders, Rev. Hall was interred in the Stevens family vault at Green-Wood Cemetery. But he reposed there for only a few weeks; on October 5, by court order, his body was exhumed and taken to the Kings County Hospital's morgue for an autopsy. Later that same day, Rev. Hall's remains were returned to the Stevens vault.

Press coverage of the murders was sensational. Hall's widow, Frances Noel Hall (1874–1942), one of the wealthiest and most socially-prominent women in town, was summoned for questioning by the police. But she drove to the police station only to find that the crush of reporters and cameramen made it impossible for her to gain entry. Thrill-seekers packed the field near the crabapple tree, looking for souvenirs as vendors hawked balloons, peanuts, and refreshments. Though a grand jury was soon convened to investigate the murders, no one was charged.

It was not until four years later, with the *New York News* and the *New York Mirror* locked in a circulation battle, and each running front page

Drawings of the murder victims, Rev. Edward Wheeler Hall and Eleanor Mills. Daily News *L.P. Photo.*

The defendants in the Hall-Mills murder case: (left to right) William Stevens, Frances Stevens Hall (widow of the Rev. Edward Wheeler Hall), and Henry Stevens. Daily News *L.P. Photo.*

headlines about the unsolved case and demanding action, that pressure built to reopen the investigation. On October 30, 1926, Rev. Hall's remains were again removed from Green-Wood Cemetery and a second autopsy was conducted. This time the grand jury charged Frances Hall, the Rev. Dr. Hall's widow, along with her brothers Henry and WILLIAM C. STEVENS (1872–1942), with the murders.

The sensational trial that followed was covered by three hundred reporters who had come from throughout the United States and Europe. Telegraphers for Western Union and the Postal Telegraph were stationed in the courthouse, ready to wire any news instantaneously to the world. A New York radio station covered the trial from across the street, with a reporter sprinting from the courtroom to the microphone to report the latest proceedings.

Mrs. Hall's team of attorneys was known as "the million dollar defense," and the prosecutor's name was Simpson. The star witness for the prosecution was Mrs. Jane Gibson, popularly known as "The Pig Woman" (she raised pigs on her farm near where the bodies were found), who claimed to have seen the defendants committing the murders. Ill at the time of the trial, she was wheeled into the courtroom in a hospital bed, and gave her testimony lying down. After a one month trial, the jury acquitted Mrs. Hall and her brothers.

Radical lawyer William Kunstler wrote the definitive account of these murders and the trial, *The Minister and the Choir Singer.* In it, Kunstler hypothesized that Ku Klux Klansmen, intent on punishing adultery and promiscuity, committed the murders.

The murdered Edward Wheeler Hall, along with his acquitted wife Frances and brother-in-law William Stevens, now repose together in the Stevens family vault.

The Van Ness-Parsons Pyramid. Albert Parsons, who was responsible for this Egyptian Revival tomb, married ALICE VAN NESS. Note the mix of Old Testament, Christian, and Egyptian symbolism across the front: Jochebeth, cradling her son Moses, Jesus holding a lamb (symbolic of innocence), and the Egyptian sphinx. The decoration above the doorway is a winged eye, the symbol decreed by the Egyptian god Osiris to protect temple doorways. Hieroglyphics and a representation of Jesus on the cross adorn the entrance to the tomb. A plaque of the Egyptian Sun God was formerly on the wall at right; though it has disappeared, the sun has burnt the shadow of the plaque into the stone.

Detail of the entrance to the Van Ness-Parsons tomb.

ALBERT PARSONS'S PYRAMID

IN 1798, Napoleon conquered Egypt. His massive *Description de L'Egypte,* published between 1809 and 1822, brought worldwide attention to the architecture, artifacts, plants, and animals of the Nile Valley. Pictures of ancient tombs and tomb paintings were circulated around the world.

The pyramid, obelisk, and other forms of Egyptian Revival architecture soon became popular choices for cemetery decorations. Though critics in the 1830's criticized Egyptian Revival buildings as pagan and unchristian, and one critic even went so far as to describe that style as "the architecture of cats and deified crocodiles," it was used widely for cemeteries and prisons. The entrances to Mount Auburn Cemetery in Cambridge, Massachusetts, Touro Cemetery in Newport, Rhode Island, and Grove Street Cemetery in New Haven, Connecticut, are all Egyptian Revival. The Tombs (Prison) in New York City, built in the 1830's, got its name because of its Egyptian Revival design.

It is therefore not surprising to find a pyramid in Green-Wood Cemetery; what is surprising is the late date of this tomb. Most of the Egyptian Revival tombs at Green-Wood Cemetery date from the 1830's and 1840's; this one was apparently built in the twentieth century. It is the inspiration of ALBERT ROSS PARSONS (1847–1933). Born in Sandusky, Ohio, Parsons early-on showed an aptitude for music, and by the age of thirteen was playing the organ in an Indianapolis church. He studied piano in New York City and abroad, then taught music for the rest of his life. In 1885, Parsons was named head of the piano department of the Metropolitan Conservatory of Music, and continued in that position for many years. He was an organist at Holy Trinity Church and the Fifth Avenue Presbyterian Church, and served as president of the Music Teachers' National Association and the American College of Musicians of the State of New York.

Parsons was also an Egyptologist. His book, *The New Light From the Pyramids*, attracted international attention. Though his pyramid may not have achieved international fame, it contributes to the variety of architectural styles at Green-Wood Cemetery.

NEW YORK'S FIRST BLACK FEMALE DOCTOR

Susan Smith McKinney-Steward (1846–1918) was born Susan Maria Smith in Weeksville, Brooklyn, and grew up on her father's pig farm at the corner of Fulton Street and Buffalo Avenue. As a child, she studied with the leading organists in Brooklyn, then taught music in the public schools of Washington, D.C., and later led the choir and played the organ for twenty-eight years at the Bridge Street A.M.E. Church in Brooklyn.

But she saw greater challenges ahead. Deciding to be a pioneer, she applied for and was admitted to the newly-created New York Medical College for Women. In 1870, she graduated as valedictorian and became the first black female doctor in New York State, and only the third in the country. Practicing medicine from her offices on DeKalb Avenue in Brooklyn and from an office in Manhattan, she helped to found the Brooklyn Women's Homeopathic Hospital and Dispensary at Myrtle and Grand Avenues in 1881. In 1882, she served on the medical staff of her alma mater, the New York Medical College and Hospital for Women, and pursued postgraduate studies at the Long Island Medical College in Brooklyn from 1887 to 1888. She also worked as the resident physician at the Brooklyn Home for the Colored Aged, and served on its governing board from 1892 to 1895.

Dr. McKinney-Steward became resident physician and a faculty member at Wilberforce University in Xenia, Ohio, in 1898, and she remained there until her death. She married twice: to Rev. William McKinney (who died in 1895), and to U.S. Army Chaplain Theophilus G. Steward. She was also active in the temperance and woman suffrage movements.

In 1974, Brooklyn's Junior High School 265 was renamed Dr. Susan Smith McKinney Junior High School in her honor.

Susan Smith McKinney-Steward, pioneer female doctor. Courtesy of the Brooklyn Historical Society.

Susan Smith McKinney-Steward's monument.

Gospel singer Ira David Sankey.

Detail of the monument to Ira David Sankey, featuring a lyre in tribute to his musical career.

THOMAS HASTINGS (1784–1872) began his career in music as the leader of the village choir in Clinton, New York. Shortly thereafter, he took charge of a singing school, and developed a reputation as a church choir instructor. In 1832, he came to New York City, where for many years he directed the choir at Dr. Mason's Church on Bleecker Street. Hastings devoted himself to collecting sacred music, composing tunes and hymns, and editing musical periodicals. He wrote the music for *Rock of Ages* and *Majestic Sweetness Sits Enthron'd*, and the words for *Hail to the Brightness* and *Ye Disconsolate*.

ATTENDING the international convention of the Young Men's Christian Association (Y.M.C.A.) in 1870, IRA DAVID SANKEY (1840–1908), the singing evangelist, met Dwight L. Moody, and joined him in his religious work in Chicago. For many years thereafter they led sensational evangelical meetings throughout the United States and Europe. Though Sankey's tenor voice was sometimes described as unexceptional, its sweetness, emotion, and power in Gospel singing invariably moved his huge audiences. Collections of his hymns, such as *There Were Ninety and Nine*, *Pull for the Shore Sailors*, and *Sweet Bye and Bye*, were popular worldwide. His monument at Green-Wood Cemetery is decorated with a lyre, a tribute to his musical career.

POPULAR (BUT NOT CRITICAL) ACCLAIM

THOUGH largely forgotten today, LAURA JEAN LIBBEY (1862–1925) was one of the most popular writers of her time. In the early 1880's, while in her twenties, Laura Jean Libbey wrote her first romance story. Walking her manuscript across the newly-completed Brooklyn Bridge, she took it to a Manhattan publisher who immediately bought it for $25. Laura Jean celebrated by spending her new-found fortune on five pounds of marshmallows, eating half and giving the other half to her friend; they both got sick.

Laura Jean Libbey wrote prolifically during the 1880's and 1890's, often penning her romantic novels at the rate of a chapter a day. Each was the story of a virtuous and virginal heroine who married the villain, but remained a virgin because her evil husband was almost immediately jailed, kidnapped, or forced to flee from the police, or because she quickly slipped into a fever-induced sleep. And they all ended the same way, with the young woman rescued from the villain by her hero, whom she married at the end of the novel.

Usually her work appeared in magazines and was then reprinted in inexpensive paperbacks which sold for fifteen to twenty-five cents each. She claimed that she was the first author of paperbound novels. Though her writing was not well-received by the critics, who found it to be melodramatic and repetitious, she was enormously popular, sold millions of books, and made a fortune.

Typical of Laura Jean Libbey's writing is this passage from *Junie's Love Test*:

> "I believed so truly in our marriage," she sobbed, piteously, "that when he came to me that day at the hotel, and told me it was only a mock marriage we had gone through, I fell on my knees and begged him to take then and there the life he had so cruelly destroyed; but he turned on his heel, and, with a mocking laugh on his lips, left me alone, to live or to die of a broken heart."

Representative of the sixty titles that she penned were *A Fatal Wooing*

(1883), *All for Love of a Fair Face; or, A Broken Betrothal* (1885), *He Loved Her But Was Lured Away*, *The Abandoned Bride*, and *Little Leafy, the Cloak-maker's Beautiful Daughter*. Her chapter titles were long and fervent; in *The Girl He Forsook*, Chapter 1 was entitled "Why should Heaven let those meet who might learn to love each other, if there is an insurmountable barrier between them which can never be beaten down? I say it is cruel—it is unjust!"

Laura Jean Libbey "wrote from the heart" for working class teenage girls. Her success, she said, was due to the "happy ending of all my books, and the fact that I write directly to the heart." Only one of her stories had an unhappy ending; it was greeted with such a barrage of protest letters that she never repeated that blunder again.

Raised in Brooklyn in a family dominated by her mother, Laura was devoted to her. Virtually all of her novels were written while her mother was alive and Laura Jean was unmarried. Though she revered her mother, she regretted the demands her mother placed on her, including that she remain single.

Shortly after her mother's death in 1898, Laura Jean Libbey married Van Mater Stilwell, a Brooklyn lawyer. Abandoning romance-writing, she tried her hand as a playwright, penning over one hundred plays in a year. In fully half of those she used the same joke: a widower was chided for remarrying so soon after his first wife's death. He responded, "Well, isn't she as dead now as she ever will be?" She named her plays by writing out title pages and then randomly attaching them to the already-completed plays. None of her plays made it to the stage.

Laura Jean Libbey made a brief appearance, without success, as a vaude-ville performer. Later she wrote an advice column for the *New York Mail* called "Cupid's Red Cross: First Aid to Wounded Hearts." Her advice was well behind the times, and the column, over a period of a few months, made its way farther and farther toward the back of the newspaper, until it reached the last page and then disappeared.

When she died, only one newspaper, the *Brooklyn Daily Eagle*, carried any mention of her passing, and even that was a brief notice. At her request, her monument at Green-Wood Cemetery bears her maiden name, and the bulk of her estate was left to her sisters, not her husband.

PAINTING PROSPECT PARK

A NATIVE of Indiana, WILLIAM MERRITT CHASE (1849–1916) studied painting in New York City, then went to St. Louis to work. When a group of businessmen there offered to finance his art studies in Europe, Chase was ecstatic: "My God, I'd rather go to Europe than go to heaven."

Chase, known to his contemporaries as "The Dean of American Painters," was the quintessential painter and instructor of his time. He led the movement to enhance appreciation of American artists, was a prolific

Laura Jean Libbey (1862–1925), the romance novelist who wrote "to the heart." Dictionary of American Portraits, *Dover Publications.*

Laura Jean Libbey's monument reflects her life story. Her mother, the most important person in her life, is memorialized on the central obelisk, and it bears Laura's maiden name. Laura Jean Libbey is buried beside "mother," with no trace of her husband in sight.

William Merritt Chase posed, circa 1886, in the costume that had been used in his painting The Smoker. *Courtesy of the William Merritt Chase Archives, The Parrish Art Museum, Southampton, N.Y.*

painter, a fine technician who continuously experimented with new approaches, a consummate teacher, and a skilled publicist. He served as president of the Society of American Artists, was a leader of the famed Tile Club, and was president and a member of The Ten (a group of painters). It was said of him that "[n]o other artist or critic had so much influence on America's idea of art."

In 1878, Chase taught the first painting class at New York's Art Students' League, and opened his own New York School of Art in 1896. He has been called the most important teacher of American artists ever, having taught during thirty-eight years more students than any other prominent painter. Chase is remembered also for the great artists who studied with him: Charles Sheeler, Joseph Stella, Georgia O'Keeffe, Marsden Hartley, Edward Hopper, Charles Demuth, and ALFRED MAURER (1868–1932). His art school at Shinnecock, Long Island, was fashionable long before the Hamptons were. Chase led unprecedented tours of Europe, during which he introduced his students to his prominent artist-friends there.

Painting in a remarkable range of styles, Chase borrowed from the French impressionists, Japanese prints, and fellow artists such as John Singer Sargent and James McNeil Whistler. His work was characterized by broad brush strokes and rich pigmentation. Chase developed a reputation in Europe and America for his portrait and figure paintings. But it was

Prospect Park, Brooklyn, *by William Merritt Chase, circa 1887. Courtesy of The Parrish Art Museum, Southampton, N.Y., Littlejohn Collection.*

his paintings of dead fish that were his best known subject and which were most avidly collected by American museums during his lifetime.

Chase feared that these dead fish would be his legacy. Fortunately, they are not. In 1878, Chase took space in New York City's famous Tenth Street

Studio, hoping to make his living painting American landscapes. At the time, most American painters were working on European scenes. Chase focused his energies on painting urban scenes, particularly the parks and waterfronts of Brooklyn and New York City. This was a daring choice of subject, for even the American landscape painters who had chosen to paint their own country had usually devoted themselves to scenes of unspoiled forests and bucolic farms. Instead, Chase wanted to paint the prosperity and gentility of the new urban "leisure class," a modern subject.

Many of his paintings were scenes from Brooklyn where his parents lived, and featured his wife or other members of his family in novel outdoor scenes in Prospect Park and along Brooklyn's shore. As Chase said of Brooklyn, "Along the docks and wharves there is every bit as good material as that on the banks of the Thames, which the English artists have made immortal." Chase became, as one critic noted, "the first metropolitan artist to appreciate the hitherto almost untouched field of landscape in and about the city." He painted *plein air*, outside at the scene, and advised artists not to "meddle" with changes or refinements after they brought their work back to the studio.

Chase's paintings were controversial; some critics objected to their snapshot quality, portraying real scenes of contemporary life without any allusion to the past or any moral lesson. Chase defended his work: "If one can paint a fence rail well, it is far better than an unsuccessful attempt at the most sublime scenery, for it is not what one does, but the way it is done."

From 1886 until 1890, Chase did most of his painting in Brooklyn's Prospect Park. However, when he made his annual late spring trip to Prospect Park in 1890 to paint rhododendrons, he was stopped by the park's superintendent who advised him that professional artists were not permitted to paint in the park without a permit. Though Chase objected, he nevertheless applied by mail for a permit, but when he did not receive it, he shifted his work to Central Park. It was not until later that he learned that the permit had not been sent to him because he had failed to enclose a self-addressed envelope with a 2 cent stamp.

Chase's landscapes were largely ignored by buyers and critics of his time. But at least one editorial writer understood the remarkable contribution Chase made when he eulogized him: "Whistler disowned us and made a joke of the city of Lowell, his birthplace; Abbey accepted Knighthood, but the *New York Post* finds it pleasant to think of the late William M. Chase, who died October 25, as 'belonging wholly' to America."

Today, Chase's paintings are in the collections of the leading museums in the United States, are at the very top of the American art market, and often sell for more than $1 million.

In 1886, William Merritt Chase married ALICE GERSON (1866–1927), his favorite model and the daughter of a Brooklyn friend. Their home was a "veritable museum of contemporary art." This photograph of them dates from around 1911. Courtesy of the William Merritt Chase Archives, The Parrish Art Museum, Southampton, N.Y.

Chase lived in a grand and flamboyant manner, strolling New York's streets adorned with top hat, cane, spats, monocle and boutonniere, accompanied by his wolfhound. This humble monument to him and his wife shows none of that flamboyance.

William F. Howe, lawyer to the famous and infamous.

I N 1861, WILLIAM F. HOWE (1821–1900) established his law firm in New York City. Two years later, Abraham Hummel went to work for him as an office boy, and soon became the junior partner. For the rest of the century the firm of Howe and Hummel dominated the New York legal scene. Their client list was a who's who of the famous and the notorious, the entertainer and the criminal.

During the Civil War, Howe became known as "Habeas Corpus Howe" for his ability to get soldiers released from the army on writs, usually arguing that their enlistments were invalid because they were drunk when they signed up.

Howe, known as the "father of the criminal bar," defended six hundred and fifty murder cases. He convinced one jury that his client, Ella Nelson, had accidentally fired six shots. His knowledge of the law was legendary; the Chief Justice of New York's highest court said that Howe was "perhaps without peer at the criminal bar," and another observer wrote that "he left an imprint upon the records of the criminal courts of New York City that no one has ever equaled."

A large man, weighing nearly 250 pounds, Howe filled the courtroom with his presence and his booming voice. He dressed in flashy clothes, including many-colored waistcoats and checkered trousers, and as many diamonds as he could wear, except on the last day of a murder trial, when he always wore black. Ever-prone to theatrics, his courtroom specialty was weeping. His offices were strategically placed across the street from the jail (known as "The Tombs"), and even the dimmest of criminals could spot the forty foot-long billboard that advertised Howe and Hummel. It was no coincidence that their cable address was "LENIENT." If Howe or Hummel won a trial, they distributed free copies of the minutes as advertising to attract new clients. Reporters at New York City's major newspapers did their bidding.

Another Howe and Hummel specialty was the breach-of-promise blackmail suit. They represented showgirls who had had affairs with prominent New Yorkers and prominent New Yorkers who had had affairs with showgirls. Gangs, such as "General" Abe Greenthal's national pickpocket ring, the Sheeny Mob, and the Whyos, had them on retainer. Their client list included the abortionist Madame Restelle, Tammany Boss Richard Croker, concert saloon owner Harry Hill, "Man-Killing Race-Track Girl" Annie Walden, "Hackensack Mad Monster" Dr. Jacob Rosenzweig, and EDWARD STOKES, who killed Colonel Jim Fisk. Civil clients included exotic dancer Little Egypt, Brooklyn Bridge jumper Steve Brodie, Ned Harrigan of the Harrigan and Hart song and dance team, feminists Victoria Woodhull and Tennessee Claflin, eccentric GEORGE F. TRAIN, and entertainers P. T. Barnum, Edwin Booth, John Barrymore, and Lillie Langtry.

The firm of Howe and Hummel remained at the forefront of the legal profession until Howe died in 1900. Hummel did not remain in practice long after that; he was driven from the country by the reformer, District Attorney WILLIAM TRAVERS JEROME (1859–1934).

William F. Howe's final resting place at Green-Wood Cemetery is unmarked.

CASEY AT THE BAT

ONE NIGHT in 1888, DE WOLFE HOPPER (1858–1935), a popular actor, was performing at Wallack's Theatre on Broadway in New York City. Between acts he was approached by a patron, who told him that members of baseball's New York Giants and Chicago White Stockings were in the audience, and asked him to recite a poem, *Casey at the Bat*, by Ernest Lawrence Thayer, which only recently had been published in the *San Francisco Examiner*. Hopper took the copy and, mustering all of his dramatic skills, built to the climax. With two runners on, two outs, and the home team trailing in the bottom of the ninth, the game hung in the balance:

> Oh! somewhere in this favored land
> the sun is shining bright;
> The band is playing somewhere,
> and somewhere hearts are light,
> And somewhere men are laughing,
> and somewhere children shout;
> But there is no joy in Mudville—
> mighty Casey has struck out.

DeWolfe Hopper, early in his career, when he still had thousands of recitations of Casey at the Bat *yet to come.*

Both Hopper's rendition and Thayer's poem became instant hits; Hopper went on to perform it 10,000 times during his career. The poem introduced the baseball phrases "hope springs eternal" and "kill the umpire." It inspired many books, tapes, television shows, an opera, and movies starring Wallace Beery, an animated Disney character, and Elliott Gould.

At the turn of the century, Hopper tracked Ernest Thayer down and insisted that the author of *Casey at the Bat* recite his version of it. Thayer obliged, but Hopper was keenly disappointed: "Fond mommas have brought their sons to me to hear their childish voices lisp the poem, but Thayer's was the worst of all. He was rotten."

"THE GREAT AMERICAN CRANK"

FEW MEN have led as full, colorful, and bizarre a life as GEORGE FRANCIS TRAIN (1829–1904). A man of tremendous energy, intelligence, ambition, and vanity, a gifted speaker and iconoclast, Train championed many causes and pioneered in many fields. For several decades of the nineteenth century, if there was history to be made, this brilliant oddball was there to make it. Aptly named "Train," he was a locomotive who knew only one speed: full steam ahead.

Orphaned as a boy, Train managed to talk his way into his uncle's merchant shipping firm in Boston. At the tender age of twenty, Train realized

A Thomas Nast cartoon of George Francis Train. Train joined Nast to lead the attack on the Tweed Ring.

that ships trading with Liverpool were returning to America with few passengers. He hired Irish-American longshoremen and stevedores to write home in praise of their adopted country, created a prepaid passage certificate, and arranged for immigrants to send money back to their families to finance their trips. Soon his uncle's firm was collecting $1,000,000 a year to bring immigrants to America.

Train went to Australia during its gold rush, and introduced canned goods, Fourth of July celebrations, and bowling there. When miners rebelled against the British Crown in 1854, they offered Train, a respected and popular merchant, the presidency of their newly-proclaimed Five Star Republic. Train, only twenty-five years old, declined the honor, and took off for Europe. In 1855, he convinced Queen Maria Cristina of Spain to finance the Atlantic and Great Western Railroad in America. He spent 1856 and 1857 at the court of Napoleon III, studying German, French, Portuguese, and Spanish, and doing some writing. His book, *Young America on Wall Street* (1857), a collection of his foreign correspondence, sold well in America and Europe, and his fame spread.

It was Train who, over vehement opposition, introduced the first street railway ("horse tramway") to the British Isles in 1860. During his sojourn there, as the Civil War raged in his homeland, Train defended the Union, speaking at public meetings, addressing champagne breakfasts, and publishing the *London American*. Though many in England considered him a spy for his monitoring of Confederate blockade runners, he was hailed back home in a petition signed by Philadelphia's citizenry as "The Eloquent Champion of the American Union."

When Train left England, apparently fed up with lawsuits against him filed by those who wanted to see his tramways fail, he returned to Boston, where he was greeted everywhere by approving crowds. With his customary modesty, he observed, "I had returned to my country the most popular American in public life." But popularity was not Train's game: within days he stormed into the lion's den, interrupting Senator Charles Sumner's speech at an abolitionist meeting in Faneuil Hall before being arrested. Soon Train was debating slavery with Senator Cassius M. Clay of Kentucky and was being received in the White House by President Abraham Lincoln.

It was time for Train to move on, and his next career was as chief cheerleader for the Union Pacific Railroad. Train organized the Credit Mobilier to finance this wonder (he was no longer associated with it when scandal struck a few years later), wielded the symbolic shovel at Omaha, Nebraska, with which the Union Pacific was launched, and gave the oration there that the *Nebraskan* described as the "most tip-top speech ever delivered west of the Missouri."

Then Train was off to other causes. He was a conspicuous presence at the 1864 Democratic convention. By 1867, he was in Kansas, addressing large and enthusiastic crowds on behalf of woman suffrage. This was not his only effort on behalf of unpopular causes: he would later speak on behalf of Chinese immigrants and Fenians (Irish revolutionaries). The next year, he went to Dublin, and was immediately arrested by authorities who feared that he was there to cause trouble. The *Cleveland Leader* felt that his arrest was a "good cause for war." Train was quickly released, only to be arrested again for an old debt. Insisting that he had already paid that debt, he was taken back to jail, where he spent the summer. From his cell (one of the fifteen jail cells he would occupy in his busy life; the *Boston Globe* would one day editorialize that Train was the most interesting prisoner the Charles Street Jail had ever held), Train proclaimed his candidacy for President of the United States:

> I am that wonderful, eccentric, independent, extraordinary genius and political reformer of America, who is sweeping off all the politicians before him like a hurricane, your modest, diffident, unassuming friend, the future President of America—George Francis Train.

Released from jail ten months later, still steadfastly refusing to pay up, Train returned to the United States. By 1870, he was ready to travel as no man had ever traveled before: around the world in record time. No ordinary traveler, Train interrupted his global race to stir the French Communards in Marseilles, addressing them daily for a week, and leading the crowds through the streets singing *The Marseillaise*. Train was in the front ranks when National Guard fortifications were captured without a shot being fired. When the Guard Mobile came to get him, ready to end his meddling with their lead, he wrapped himself in the French and American flags and dared them to shoot. Instead, they beat a hasty retreat. Train was jailed as a spy, then expelled from France, and completed his trip in what he claimed was eighty days (not including the month or so he spent shaping French history). Two years later, the French novelist Jules Verne, fascinated by Train's story, used him as his model for Phileas Fogg in *Around the World in Eighty Days*.

George Francis Train, about 1860. Train led a busy life; the Louisville Courier-Journal, *in his obituary, described him as having "the brains of 20 men, all pulling in different directions."*

Train decided that 1872 would be his year to win the Presidential election. He set out on the campaign trail with an ingenious financing scheme: he charged admission to his speeches. Train urged the 2,000,000 citizens whom he addressed in over eight hundred meetings (what he called his "Presidential Conventions") to "Get aboard the express train of George Francis Train." His campaign literature hailed him as a man who

> ... does not drink, smoke, chew, swear, gamble, lie, cheat, steal, who never held public office, never played the demagogue, who has always been right on great national questions, and who believes he is an instrument in the hands of some mysterious power, to emancipate the people from the slavery of Party and the Fanaticism of ages, and who challenges anyone to find a blemish on his reputation.

Train finished last in the election, behind even the prohibitionist and free-love candidates. But, for his efforts, he pocketed $90,000 from admissions to his campaign speeches.

Train was also an avid inventor, particularly by his own account. He claimed to have invented the coal chute (coal had been delivered a bag at a

A more likely candidate for the first one to put the eraser on the pencil is EBERHARD FABER (1822–1879). Born in Bavaria to a family that had been in the pencil business since 1761, he came to New York City soon after the Revolution of 1848, and went into business as agent for his family's pencil factory. In 1861, Faber opened his own factory in New York City on the East River at 42nd Street, the first lead pencil factory in the United States. His business prospered, and when his 42nd Street factory was destroyed by fire in 1872, he built a bigger factory in Greenpoint, Brooklyn. Faber was the first pencil manufacturer to put rubber erasers on his pencils and to add metal point protectors to them. His factory turned out gold pens, pen holders, pencils, slates and slate pencils, India rubber goods, tracing cloth, and pencil cases. He also operated a factory in Newark, New Jersey, for making rubber bands and erasers. His son, Eberhard Faber, took over the family business upon his death and headed it for 66 years. In 1992, 2 billion pencils were manufactured in the United States; one-third of those were made by the Eberhard Faber Company.

JOHN MACKAY immigrated to New York from Dublin with a dream: to save $25,000 and return to Ireland as a gentleman of leisure. But after eight years of digging in the California Gold Rush, he was virtually penniless. Undeterred, he moved on to Virginia City in the Nevada Territory, and struck it rich, very rich, hitting "The Big Bonanza," a mine with unprecedented deposits of gold and silver ore. At the height of his success, Mackay was making $800,000 a month (the equivalent of about $13.5 million today) and became one of the richest men in the world. He always felt a particular affinity for miners; during his lifetime he gave away $9 million (about $150 million in today's money) to men who approached him man-to-man and asked him for "loans" which they never repaid.

time), perforated stamps (young women had worked cutting the sheets), steps attached to carriages (eliminating the need for men to stand by with steps in their hands as carriages approached), the lip on ink bottles, and the eraser on pencils.

When Victoria Woodhull and Tennessee Claflin were jailed in 1872 on obscenity charges for publishing the details of the Beecher-Tilton affair, Train sprung to their defense, publishing in his newspaper, *The Train Ligne,* excerpts from the Old Testament which he maintained "were worse than anything published by these women." Law enforcement authorities, led by the infamous witch-hunting Anthony Comstock, apparently agreed with his analysis; they arrested him for obscenity.

Brought before a judge, Train insisted that "I am guilty of publishing an obscene paper composed of Bible quotations." The court entered a not guilty plea on Train's behalf, and he was taken off to jail. Over Train's protest, his attorney, WILLIAM F. HOWE, argued that Train was not guilty of obscenity, but if he was, he was insane. The court offered to free Train if he would plead insanity, but Train said he would rather die in jail: "Take me back to the Bastille! Away with me to the donjon." Train was held in the Tombs for fourteen weeks, and passed the time greeting visitors, writing to newspapers, and finally winning a presidential election (that of Murderers' Row). A jury found Train sane, the prosecution stalled rather than prosecute, and Train was offered chances to just walk away from the jail. But Train would not be dismissed, and a jury was directed to find him insane. Finally released, Train protested the obscenity laws by walking out of jail wearing nothing but an umbrella. But a cloud hung over him because of the confused sanity proceedings.

After setting up trusts for his wife and children, Train gradually withdrew from contact with his family. When he needed money he made a speech, often on behalf of the working man, sometimes in support of Jacob Coxey, the "General" of Coxey's Army. And he reveled in the role of the eccentric, dubbing himself "The Great American Crank." Introduced to gentlemen, he refused to shake their hands, believing that to do so would rob him of his energy. Instead, he shook hands with himself. More and more he could be found on a park bench in Madison Square Park, feeding the pigeons and squirrels and entertaining the children. He gave out candy to youngsters and hired horsecars for their picnics in Central Park. He began to date his letters from the date of his birth: "P.E. 47" was 1876, the 47th year of the Psychological Era. Hauled into court by creditors, he testified that his assets were $100, including his clothes and watch, but that his outstanding claims against others were $14 million.

In 1890, Train circled the globe in sixty-seven days, a record that he broke two years later with a sixty day trip. Ten years later, still in a rush, he dictated his autobiography to a stenographer in thirty-five hours; it was published and sold well. As he approached the age of seventy, he boxed exhibitions with Professor Mike Donovan, the pugilist and physical fitness idol. He published *Train's Penny Magazine,* "On News Stands 2 cents, on Trains 5 Cents," "The work of cranks for the instruction of wise men and the amusement of fools." A contemporary described him as "a man who might have built the Pyramids, or been confined to a strait-jacket for his eccentricities."

A visitor to Green-Wood Cemetery could wander its paths and roads without ever finding any trace of George Francis Train. There is no monument there to this phenomenal man. He is interred near Sylvan Water in the hillside mausoleum of Colonel GEORGE TURNBULL MOORE DAVIS (1810–1886), his father-in-law. Davis was an aide to General Winfield Scott during the Mexican War, later chief clerk of the War Department in Washington, and was a newspaper editor in Louisville, Kentucky.

TURN ON THE HEAT, THE PARTY'S OVER

ONE OF THE most elaborate tombs anywhere is that of JOHN WILLIAM MACKAY (1831–1902). Mackay made his fortune in mining, banks, railroads, and cable companies. A Scotch-Irish immigrant, he came to New York City in 1840. When gold was discovered in California, he went west and became the most successful miner there. In 1860, Mackay moved to Nevada to mine, and by 1872 had established the gold and silver "Bonanza" mines under what was to become Virginia City. His company, in which he had a 40% interest, controlled the principal mines of the Comstock Lode; from one of his mines alone $150,000,000 in gold and silver were removed. He was one of the founders of the Bank of Nevada at San Francisco, and was a director of the Southern Pacific Railroad.

Mackay, his wife, and two sons moved to New York City in 1876. He lived abroad for the rest of his life in palatial homes in London and Paris. In 1883, he founded the Commercial Cable Company with James Gordon Bennett, Jr., and the next year it laid cables across the Atlantic from the United States to England and France. Over the next year and one-half Mackay engaged in a bitter fight with Jay Gould and his telegraph monopoly before emerging victorious. He created the Postal Telegraph Cable Company, and took on the Gould-Western Union land monopoly. The final step in his cable plans was to lay a cable across the Pacific; he was working on that project when he died.

Mackay's life was more widely covered by the press than that of any other millionaire of his time. Stories of his battle to break Jay Gould's telegraph and cable monopoly, of a disgruntled speculator's attempt to assassinate him in 1895, of vast sums spent by his wife on jewelry, and of their extravagant life-style, kept him in the public eye for years.

Though Mackay was known for his lavish life-style, he really outdid himself with the extravagance of his tomb at Green-Wood Cemetery, spending $250,000, a huge sum in those days (and equal to about $4.8 million today), on his final residence. With neither desire nor need to scrimp, he installed a heating system and electrical lighting inside, recognizing that eternal comfort is worth any price. Four bronze sculpture groups adorn the corners of the tomb, and Italian marble walls enclose a Pieta and altar.

"Silver Bonanza King" John Mackay and his wife, MARIE LOUISE MACKAY, knew how to live extravagantly. After he hit pay dirt in 1873 with the Comstock Lode, she had almost half a ton of silver shipped from his Virginia City mine to Tiffany & Company, where 200 men worked for two years to fashion their "Dinner Service for Twenty-four Persons." The 1350 pieces were decorated with Irish shamrocks and Scottish thistles, symbols of Mrs. Mackay's heritage. They were shown at the Paris Exposition of 1878, and helped Tiffany's win the grand prize for its silverware display. In 1998, the punch bowl and ladle from that set sold at auction for $222,500.

The fabulously wealthy John Mackay.

John Mackay's tomb has a unique feature: it is heated.

CIVIL ENGINEER OLE SINGSTAD (1882–1969) was the designer or consultant on an entire generation of motor vehicle tunnels, including the Holland, Lincoln, Queens Midtown, and Brooklyn-Battery Tunnels, twin rapid transit tubes under the East River in New York City, the Baltimore Harbor Tunnel, the Hudson Tubes from New Jersey to Manhattan, the tube between Oakland and Alameda, California, the Callahan and Sumner Tunnels in Boston, and the West Virginia Memorial Tunnel at Wheeling.

Singstad felt that his greatest accomplishment was the three-tiered ventilation system that he designed for the Holland Tunnel. When that tunnel opened, it was the first underwater automobile highway in the world. On November 12, 1927, at 4:00 p.m., President Calvin Coolidge, aboard the Presidential yacht, pushed a button that rang a brass bell at the tunnel's entrance to signal its opening. Officials, however, wary of disaster, held up all traffic until midnight in the hopes that the fewer cars at that hour would limit the strain on the tunnel.

Singstad recalled the opening day:

> I couldn't wait to enjoy my tunnel and so when the speeches were over, I set out to walk through it alone. Soon I heard a rumbling, shuffling sound in the distance. "Good God!" I thought, "it sounds like an ocean, like the tunnel's caved in!" I jumped up to the elevated sidewalk. My fears were happily unfounded. The noise came from hundreds of people who, prevented from driving through the tunnel, had parked their cars and were walking—some pushing baby carriages—through what I don't mind calling a new wonder of the world.

Late in his life, Singstad regretted that so many of the tunnels that he helped to build were for cars and so few were for mass transit.

Ole Singstad's headstone is on a hillside near Border Avenue which was opened for burials in the twentieth century.

Former New York Governor Al Smith (left) and former New Jersey Governor A. Harry Moore (right) shake hands across their States' borders, celebrating the underwater link provided by Ole Singstad's Holland Tunnel. Daily News *L.P. Photo.*

ON SEPTEMBER 8, 1934, as Captain ROBERT L. WILLMOTT (1892–1934) of the *Morro Castle* began to partake of the farewell dinner traditionally held on incoming liners on their last night at sea, he must have been in a triumphant mood. A thirty-year veteran of the Ward Line, and a captain since 1916, it appeared that he had once again guided his ship on a safe and successful cruise.

The *Morro Castle, smoldering and aground just off Asbury Park, New Jersey, as crowds gather on the beach to take in the spectacle.* Daily News *L.P. Photo.*

Captain Willmott had a long and proud association with the *Morro Castle*. It was Willmott who had supervised the construction of the *Morro Castle* at Newport News, Virginia, and who took command of her in 1930. Only a year before this cruise, he had stayed on the *Morro Castle's* bridge for three days, guiding her through a hurricane off Cape Hatteras. But Captain Willmott routinely refused to hold boat and fire drills for his crew and passengers; he believed those drills excited the passengers, and made them subject to panic. Anyway, he was of the opinion that "You're safer here than crossing Times Square or South Street." On this cruise, he had brought the *Morro Castle* safely from Havana to just off the New Jersey coast on a Labor Day holiday trip, and would soon dock in New York City. Each of the 562 passengers and the crew would have stories to tell when they made shore. Little did Willmott know what awaited him and his charges.

As Captain Willmott ate his melon, the first course of his meal, he collapsed. Before the evening was over, he lay dead, the victim of acute indigestion and a heart attack courtesy of what was indeed his farewell dinner.

As the evening wore on, one of the worst disasters in marine history began to unfold. Within hours after Captain Willmott's death, and only four hours before the *Morro Castle* was scheduled to dock, its S.O.S. went out. The ship, in a heavy gale, rough seas, and a driving rain, was on fire amidships, just off the New Jersey coast, and many passengers were trapped in their cabins. No one thought to close the door to the writing room where the fire started, and it quickly spread. No hose or fire station was available to fight the flames; a month earlier, a passenger had sprained her ankle when she slipped on water from a leaky station, and had sued for $25,000. Captain Willmott had responded by ordering the hoses removed and stations capped to avoid any further liability for falls. Now the fire raced unchecked through the ship.

Four lifeboats were successfully lowered, but many passengers were trapped aft by the flames, and sang songs such as *Hail, Hail, the Gang's All Here* to shore up their courage. Five wives jumped into the sea, each holding her husband's hand. Though all five of these women were either rescued from the water or swam to shore, only three of the men survived. As rain fell in torrents, other ships raced to the scene, plucking up survivors who had been in the water up to six or seven hours.

The once-proud ship continued to burn just two hundred feet off Asbury Park's beach, grounded in only fifteen feet of water, as a crowd of over 100,000 gathered to watch. Business boomed for hot dog vendors, renters of binoculars, and photographers. For twenty-five cents, anyone could walk out on the jetty to get closer to the wreckage. The Asbury Park City Council approved a resolution directing the City Manager to press a claim for the ship, hoping to turn it into a tourist attraction and supersede Atlantic City as New Jersey's top resort. There was talk of building a gangplank out to the wreck, and charging admission to cross it.

In all, 182 lives were lost. It was at first believed that Captain Willmott's body had been consumed by the flames. Early efforts to locate his remains

The monument to Captain Robert Willmott.

had to be called off because the smoldering hulk was too hot to permit a search. However, on September 11, searchers found a badly-burned body on the floor of the captain's cabin. The intense heat from the fire had apparently melted the legs of the metal bed upon which his body had been placed. Near his body was a key ring that read "Captain."

Captain Willmott and his wife, whom he met in 1931 when she was a passenger on a cruise aboard the *Morro Castle*, were to have celebrated their first anniversary on October 7. Mrs. Willmott was preparing her husband's welcome home meal when she heard on the radio that he was dead.

Angel atop a Border Avenue tomb.

CHAPTER EIGHT

More Recent Additions
(1936 to today)

HITTING THE CEILING

THOUGH ALONZO B. SEE (1849–1941) was the moving force behind A. B. See Elevator Company, one of the giants of that industry, few people had ever heard of him before 1922. That year, however, he became "suddenly famous" when, in reply to a request from Adelphi College for funds to educate young women, he stated that "all women's colleges should be burned." This pronouncement, which sparked a national controversy, caused many readers, as *The New York Times* observed, to "hit the ceiling faster than they ever ascended in one of the See elevators." But by 1936, See had seen the light, announcing that he had changed his views and women did indeed deserve an opportunity for higher education.

Perhaps in apology for his sin, Alonzo B. See's monument features this idealized female figure.

CHARLES EBBETS AND HIS SON

WHEN Charles Ebbets's son was born in 1878, everything seemed possible. But it soon became apparent that the boy, named for his father, was not healthy. So in 1883, Charles, Sr. took a job as bookkeeper, clerk, and scorecard-hawker with the new Brooklyn baseball club, hoping that he could save enough money to move his sickly son out to the country.

CHARLES EBBETS (1859–1925) was soon promoted to business manager of the baseball team, and his real involvement with day-to-day baseball matters began. He was now responsible for players' contracts, payroll, and the logistics of road trips. Ebbets wanted to build a business that his son could inherit, and knew that that business was baseball. Saving for years, he bought the ball club, naming it first the Brooklyn Superbas, then later the Brooklyn Dodgers.

As the years passed, Charley Ebbets became even more ambitious. He dreamt of building a modern ballpark way out in the countryside of Brooklyn, on the site of a shanty-town known as Pigtown. His steel and concrete structure would have two tiers, and would seat 25,000 fans. It would be called Ebbets Field, in honor of himself and his son. Building plans went ahead despite the efforts of friends who tried to talk Ebbets out of his dream. He had a ready reply for them:

> I'm building this new ballpark for my son. Mark my words, some day Ebbets Field will be in the heart of Brooklyn, and thousands of fans will come to see the team play baseball. Some day, the Brooklyn club will be so famous that Ebbets Field will be too small to handle the crowds!

Charles Ebbets, Sr., the man behind the Brooklyn Dodgers. Courtesy of the National Baseball Hall of Fame and Museum, Inc., Cooperstown, New York.

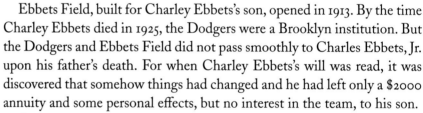
Beloved Ebbets Field, 1913–1960. Rest in peace.

These gravestones memorialize Charles Ebbets, Sr., who died on April 18, 1925. His funeral was held a week later, on a cold and rainy day, and new Dodger Club President Ed McKeever caught the flu and died four days later. On the day of Ebbets's funeral, all National League baseball games were cancelled.

Ebbets Field, built for Charley Ebbets's son, opened in 1913. By the time Charley Ebbets died in 1925, the Dodgers were a Brooklyn institution. But the Dodgers and Ebbets Field did not pass smoothly to Charles Ebbets, Jr. upon his father's death. For when Charley Ebbets's will was read, it was discovered that somehow things had changed and he had left only a $2000 annuity and some personal effects, but no interest in the team, to his son.

CHARLES EBBETS, JR. (1878–1944) tried for the rest of his life to collect his legacy. But he never succeeded in that battle. A news report of his death, appearing on May 16, 1944, tells the story:

> Charles Ebbets, Jr., sixty-five-year-old son of the founder of the Brooklyn Baseball Club, died yesterday, penniless and forgotten after nineteen years of fighting to collect his share of his father's million-dollar estate.

His body was found in a little room not far from Ebbets Field. He is buried in a Green-Wood Cemetery lot not far from his father's.

Ebbets Field, where eight World Series were played, closed in 1957, when da Bums deserted Brooklyn. It was torn down three years later, and the Jackie Robinson Apartments now occupy the site.

LIFT EVERY VOICE AND SING

JAMES WELDON JOHNSON (1871–1938), writer, diplomat, and civil rights activist, was born in Jacksonville, Florida. He studied at Atlanta University, earning bachelor and masters degrees there, then taught school and studied law, becoming in 1897 the first black attorney to be admitted to the Florida bar since the Civil War.

In 1901, Johnson came to New York City, and collaborated with his brother, J. Rosamund Johnson, in writing popular songs, including *Lift Every Voice and Sing*, which became the unofficial black national anthem. He served as a U.S. diplomat, stationed in Nicaragua and Venezuela, from 1906 to 1914.

Johnson left his mark on many aspects of American culture. His first book, which some consider to have been his best, was the fictional *Autobiography of an Ex-Colored Man*. It appeared anonymously in 1912. Johnson also edited *The Book of American Negro Poetry* and collected two books of spirituals. His English libretto for the opera *Goyescas* was presented at the Metropolitan Opera in 1915. For many years he was the executive secretary of the National Association for the Advancement of Colored People (N.A.A.C.P.), and he led the fight for passage of the Dyer Anti-Lynching Bill of 1921. He believed that blacks should look to their racial heritage for inspiration, and was a key figure in the Harlem Renaissance of the 1920's. In 1930, he was appointed professor of creative writing at Fisk University, and was named visiting professor of literature at New York University in 1934. His most famous written work was *God's Trombones* (1927), a series of sermons in verse. His autobiography, *Along This Way*, was published in 1933.

On June 26, 1938, while driving near his summer home in Dark Harbor, Maine, Johnson's car was struck by a train, and he was killed instantly. Within days of his death, he was brought to Green-Wood Cemetery, but his stay there was brief; a few months later his remains were removed to Fresh Pond Crematory in Middle Village, Queens, New York. It was not until 1976 that his ashes were returned to Green-Wood, where they were buried with those of his just-deceased wife.

The James Weldon Johnson Houses of the New York City Housing Authority, named in his honor, are on Lexington Avenue in Manhattan.

James Weldon Johnson, writer, diplomat, and civil rights activist, in a photograph taken in the 1920's. Daily News *L.P. Photo.*

Almost sixty years after his death, this granite stone was placed in honor of James Weldon Johnson.

William Surrey Hart's simple monument. He is buried alongside his parents, two sisters, and his baby brother. His brother died in the Dakota territory, and was at first interred alone, because there was no cemetery in that frontier area, on a bluff overlooking the Mississippi River.

T*HE WESTERN*, a book by George N. Fenin and William K. Everson, is dedicated to William S. Hart, "the finest Western star and director of them all, and the best friend the West ever had." A native of Newburgh, New York, WILLIAM SURREY HART (1865–1946) grew up in Kansas, Minnesota, and the Dakota territory. He saw Texas cattle being driven across the West, and played with Sioux children who taught him their language and customs. After working as a cowboy in Kansas, Hart came back east and worked for the post office in New York City, then studied acting, but thought of himself as a "white Indian boy." Turning to acting, he toured playing Shakespeare, then took to the New York stage where he performed from 1898 until 1912, playing western heroes such as the lead in *The Virginian* (1907).

Obsessed with making western movies, Hart went off to Hollywood in 1913 and began acting in films, appearing in *The Fugitive*, then starring in at least one western feature each year through 1925, and almost always directing his feature films. At the height of his career, Hart earned $1000 a day (the equivalent of $9000 today), a huge sum for that time. He was the personification of the he-man of the West to a generation of moviegoers. His horse, "Paint," was almost as famous as Hart. Hart rarely worked after 1925, spending most of his time at his ranch in California.

Hart played a major role in the creation of Hollywood's western movies. Outraged at the historical license that other moviemakers had taken, he

William Surrey Hart, center, in The Gun Fighter, *1916. Hart was fascinated by the West; he owned Billy the Kid's six shooters, and was a friend of legendary lawmen Bat Masterson and Wyatt Earp.*

brought a gritty authenticity to his westerns with worn clothing and ramshackle sets. "The truth of the West," he wrote, "meant more to me than a job." His trademark was a dusty, down-at-the-heels look which served as background for melodramatic plots in which he, as the stone-faced "good bad man," was redeemed by the love of a virtuous woman. Many of his films, including *Hell's Hinges* (1916), *The Dawn Maker* (1916), *The Aryan* (1916), *The Narrow Trail* (1917), *Wagon Tracks* (1919), *The Toll Gate* (1920), *Wild Bill Hickok* (1923), and *Tumbleweeds* (1925), are considered silent film classics. Known internationally as the "Two Gun Man," Hart, in his prime, was, along with Charlie Chaplin, Mary Pickford, and Douglas Fairbanks, one of the most famous screen stars in the world. He also wrote many books during his heyday, including *Told Under a White Oak Tree* (1922), *Hoofbeats* (1933), and his autobiography, *My Life East and West*.

When *Tumbleweeds* was filmed in 1925, at the huge cost of $312,000, Hart was sixty years old. By then, the public had little enthusiasm for him playing the young romantic lead, and was tiring of the rigid formula, slower pace, and increasing sentimentality of his work. *Tumbleweeds* was a box office failure, and Hart retreated to his Horseshoe Ranch in Hollywood, where he lived for the next twenty years, and where he died. He left an estate of $1,000,000, with generous bequests to various charities, and was brought east to be buried.

His 253-acre ranch, where many of his films were shot, was left to the County of Los Angeles as a free park, along with an endowment of $150,000. Hart had explained that "I am trying to do an act of justice. I'm trying to give back to the American people what the American people so generously gave to me." He specified that no business of any kind could be conducted there. It is now open to the public as the William S. Hart County Park and Museum, and features nature trails, corrals, grazing buffalo, and his mission-style home filled with western artifacts.

WE'RE OFF TO SEE THE WONDERFUL WIZARD OF OZ

BORN Francis Philip Wupperman in New York City, he took the stage name FRANK MORGAN (1890–1949) and starred in vaudeville, on stage, screen, and radio. In 1916, he launched his movie career. Under contract to Metro Goldwyn Mayer (M.G.M.) for twenty years, Morgan appeared in dozens of movies for that studio, often playing the role of the affable absentminded professor, the bumbling chortler. Best known for his performance as the inept Wizard in *The Wizard of Oz* (1939), he was nominated for an Oscar as Best Supporting Actor for his performance in *Tortilla Flat* (1942) and as Best Actor for his performance in *Affairs of Cellini* (1934).

Buried a few feet from him is his brother, RALPH MORGAN (1883–1956). Though Ralph was thinner, older, and a more versatile actor than his brother Frank, he was less famous. He appeared in over one hundred

The monument to Frank Wupperman, better known as actor Frank Morgan.

movies, usually in small roles, from 1930 to 1952. His most famous parts were in *Rasputin and the Empress* (as Czar Nicholas II) and in *The Power and the Glory*. He also appeared in four serials, playing the villain in *Dick Tracy vs. Crime, Inc.* and *Gang Busters* and the upstanding father in *The Great Alaskan Mystery* and *The Monster and the Ape*. Ralph Morgan was also featured in *Wells Fargo*, *The Life of Emile Zola*, and *Anthony Adverse*, and served as president of the Screen Actors Guild.

Samuel Chester Reid, who designed the American flag. Dictionary of American Portraits, *Dover Publications.*

Samuel Chester Reid's creation, the American flag, decorates his grave.

Some have credited JOSEPH WILLIAM KAY (1845–1928), a water-meter manufacturer, with coining the phrase "Old Glory" as a reference to the American flag; others say Captain William Driver of Salem, Massachusetts coined that phrase in 1824.

HE DESIGNED THE AMERICAN FLAG

IN 1955, Tom Manning, an employee at Green-Wood Cemetery doing research on famous people buried there, discovered that Captain SAMUEL CHESTER REID (1783–1861), war hero and designer of the American flag, was interred there in an unmarked grave. Through the efforts of Manning, local veterans groups, and Congressman Frank E. Dorn, an act of Congress was passed authorizing a granite monument and flag pole to honor Reid.

On October 28, 1956, with Secretary of the Navy Charles S. Thomas and two of Reid's descendants, Col. Louis Sanders (a great-grandson) and Samuel Chester Reid IV (a great-great-grandson), in attendance, Samuel Chester Reid finally got the monument he had done so much to deserve. The Granite Craftsmen's Guild of New York, a group of monument dealers, paid for Reid's memorial. The stone bears this legend:

> Samuel Chester Reid 1763–1861. Designed the flag of the United States of America with thirteen stripes and one star for each state. Approved by Congress April 4, 1818. First flag of this design, made by Mrs. Reid, flown over the Capitol at Washington, April 12, 1818.

Reid's epitaph goes on to describe his other great contribution to his country: during the War of 1812, he commanded the frigate *General Armstrong*, which, vastly outgunned and outmanned, engaged three British men-of-war at Fayal in the Azores on September 26, 1814, thereby preventing them from delivering reinforcements and military supplies to the British troops at New Orleans. Those British troops, deprived of that help, soon lost the Battle of New Orleans to General Andrew Jackson. As Jackson later said, "If there had been no Battle of Fayal, there would have been no Battle of New Orleans." Had not Reid and Jackson triumphed, all of Louisiana and the Northwest Territory might have remained British.

BETTER VERY LATE THAN NEVER

STARTING IN THE 1820's, GEORGE CATLIN (1796–1872) was a man on a mission: to paint and record American Indians and their customs before what he was convinced was their imminent destruction. The first professional painter to go West, Catlin sketched many Indian tribes, including the Sioux, Osage, and Comanche, and was the only outside artist to draw several other tribes before they became extinct. His *Letters and*

Notes on the North American Indians, published in 1841, is a classic study of the traditions of these great peoples.

In January, 1837, Catlin, long sympathetic to Indians, learned that Osceola, the young leader of the Seminoles, had been captured while carrying a white flag of truce. Catlin was so outraged by this treachery that he went to Fort Moultrie, South Carolina, to visit and paint Osceola. Imprisoned there with Osceola were 250 men, women, and children of the Seminole and Euchee tribes, who had been seized by the United States Army during the war that had raged for five years in Florida. Typical of Catlin's feelings toward the Indians is this sympathetic description:

> Among [the prisoners] the most conspicuous is Os-ce-o-la, commonly called Powell as he is generally supposed to be a half-breed, the son of a white man (by that name) and a Creek woman.

> I painted him precisely in the costume in which he stood for his picture, even to a string and trinket. He wore three ostrich feathers in his head, and a turban made of a vari-colored cotton shawl. His dress was chiefly of calicoes, with a handsome bead sash or belt around his waist, and his rifle in his hand.

> He is looked upon by the Seminolees as the master spirit and leader of the tribe, although he is not a chief. From his boyhood, he led an energetic and desperate sort of life, which secured for him a conspicuous position in society. When war came to his country, he took a conspicuous and decided part. In some way, whether he deserved it or not, he acquired an influence and a name that soon sounded to the remotest parts of the United States, especially among the Indian tribes.

> This gallant fellow was captured a few months ago and brought in to Fort Mellon, Florida. Then he was sent to this place for safe-keeping, where he is grieving with a broken spirit and ready to die, cursing white men, no doubt, to the end of his breath.

Osceola died just five days after Catlin painted him. The cause of death was listed as malaria, but it seems likely that he died of a broken heart, of loss of the will to live. As a final indignity, Osceola's head was cut off, and put on display in the "Medical Museum" at Fort Moultrie.

Catlin was internationally famous as a painter and chronicler of Indians. The first American to present a Wild West show, he exhibited his paintings and toured with Indians throughout this country and Europe, and became a celebrity in London and Paris. The showman P. T. Barnum, his partner on a venture in England, said of Catlin, "I find him a very kind, sociable and excellent gentleman."

But none of this impressed Catlin's in-laws. When Catlin married Clara Gregory, her parents held out hope that he would settle down and return to the practice of law. That, however, was not to be. Instead, Catlin went west in 1832, leaving his wife behind, and spent years without her, painting and observing. When Clara died in Paris from pneumonia, the Gregorys traveled there, and brought her remains and George and Clara's young children back with them.

Painter George Catlin. Dictionary of American Portraits, *Dover Publications.*

Osceola, The Black Drink, A Warrior of Great Distinction, *George Catlin's 1838 painting of the Indian leader. Courtesy of the National Museum of American Art, Smithsonian Institution, Gift of Mrs. Joseph Harrison, Jr.*

This plain stone, marking George Catlin's grave, was placed on the edge of the Gregory plot almost a century after his death.

After his death, George Catlin paid a further price for his estrangement from his in-laws. When he died in 1872, his remains were brought to the Receiving Vault at Green-Wood Cemetery. They stayed there for a year, as the Gregory family debated whether they wanted him in their family plot. Finally relenting, they put this famous man off in a far corner of their lot.

The monument to Clara Gregory, imported from France, is the central monument in the Gregory's family plot. The plain Barre granite stone that now marks George Catlin's grave was not put in place until 1961, almost a century after his death. Arrangements for it were made by publisher Clarkson N. Potter, and it was paid for by the Society of Westerners and the Gregory family.

PIONEERING RADIO AND TELEVISION REPORTER

RADIO AND TELEVISION journalist EDWARD ROSCOE MURROW (1908–1965) was born in Greensboro, North Carolina. In 1935, he was hired by the Columbia Broadcasting System (CBS), and two years later became the director of its European news bureau, where he trained correspondents Eric Sevareid and Howard K. Smith. His broadcasts from London during the German blitz in 1940 brought the war in Europe home to Americans. In 1954, he courageously presented an exposé of McCarthyism on CBS television. He was appointed head of the U.S. Information Agency by President John F. Kennedy, and served in that position from 1961 to 1964. His remains were cremated at Green-Wood Cemetery.

Edward R. Murrow on the set of his television show, Person to Person, *in 1954.* Daily News *L.P. Photo.*

NEVER RELAX

JOHNNY TORRIO (1882–1957), Al Capone's boss and the brains behind the Chicago Syndicate, retired as the ruler of Windy City organized

Johnny Torrio's tomb.

Albert Anastasia, courtesy of the police photographer, 1936. Daily News *L.P. Photo.*

crime in 1925. He spent the rest of his life living off his fortune in Brooklyn, occasionally acting as elder statesman for the Mob. But old habits die hard. When he went to have his hair cut in a Brooklyn barber shop in April, 1957, he sat Chicago-style: eyes open and chair turned so he could see anyone who approached the door. His vigilance, however, could not protect him from a fatal heart attack.

Several months later ALBERT ANASTASIA (1902–1957), the "Lord High Executioner" of organized crime, was also in a barber shop. He, however, threw caution to the wind, sitting with his eyes closed and facing away from the door. Anastasia never saw his assassins coming through the door. Either the shooter or the planner of this assassination was JOEY GALLO (1929–1972), widely known as "Crazy Joe." Gallo was gunned down on April 7, 1972, his forty-third birthday, at Umberto's Clam House in Little Italy, apparently the victim of a war for control of New York City's rackets.

Joey Gallo in custody. Daily News *L.P. Photo.*

This monument was commissioned and installed after the 1909 murder of Rose Merello Guarino. She was killed by the family's disgruntled caretaker.

ONLY IN NEW YORK COULD THEY STEAL
A BUILDING (TWICE)

IN 1848, JAMES BOGARDUS (1800–1874) erected the world's first cast iron building on the west side of Manhattan, at Washington and Murray streets. Known as the Laing Stores, its two street fronts were brought to the site in pieces, then bolted together like a large Tinker Toy to create the building's walls. More than a century later, when an urban renewal project (which included the construction of Manhattan Community College) was planned for the site, the Laing Stores facades were taken apart. Stored away in 1971 by the Landmarks Preservation Committee, the facades were to be reassembled when an appropriate location was found.

Eventually it was decided that the appropriate place was at the corner of

James Bogardus's portrait appears on his obelisk.

Cast iron architecture achieved great popularity in the second half of the nineteenth century, and the Architectural Iron Works, founded and managed by DANIEL BADGER (1806–1884), became one of the largest fabricators of cast iron building fronts in the world. Cast at his foundry at the corner of 14th Street and Avenue C in Manhattan, these building parts were shipped throughout the United States and the world, and were then assembled on site.

Badger worked for many architects who are buried at Green-Wood Cemetery, including GAMALIEL KING, JOHN KELLUM, GRIFFITH THOMAS, JOHN SNOOK, and JAMES RENWICK. He erected buildings for many businessmen who repose at Green-Wood, among them PETER GILSEY, CHARLES TIFFANY, CORNELIUS ROOSEVELT, JOHN LA FARGE, A. A. LOW, WALTER HUNT, and PETER COOPER.

Several of Badger's buildings survive today in New York City, including the Cary Building, which was built in 1856 on Church Street, with identical facades along Chambers and Reade Streets, and the Haughwout Building at the corner of Broome Street and Broadway.

The cast iron Cary Building, erected by Daniel Badger's Architectural Iron Works, is today little-changed from its original appearance.

Cannon Walk at South Street Seaport, an ode to the stolen Laing Stores Building.

Fulton and Front Streets, as a part of the South Street Seaport Restoration. There was only one problem with this plan: the pieces of the Laing Stores were gone. It had been stolen by thieves, and not once but twice. At first the cast iron pieces were stored in a lot. When most of them disappeared one day, the Commission had the remaining pieces locked in a warehouse. Those also soon disappeared.

At the corner of Fulton and Front Streets now stands a building, Cannon Walk, on the site where the Laing Stores building was to have been reassembled. Cannon Walk was erected from new materials, as a tribute to the stolen building.

A VERY LONG CAREER

EUBIE BLAKE (1883–1983), born James Hubert Blake, first showed an interest in music at the age of six, when he discovered an organ in a department store and picked out tunes while his mother shopped. Young Eubie made such an impression on the store manager that he sent a $75 organ to the Blake home, to be paid for at 25 cents per week. Though Eubie's mother warned her youngster that no "ungodly music" was to be played, he soon discovered ragtime.

Beginning his career as a musician at the age of fifteen, Eubie Blake played piano in a "sporting house," then moved on to saloons and clubs, playing Atlantic City in the summers. In 1915, he joined with Noble Sissle to form a pianist-singer team; after World War I, they worked in vaudeville as the elegantly-dressed Dixie Duo, one of the first black teams to work without darkening their skin with burnt cork.

Blake retired at the age of sixty-three and worked at transcribing the songs that he had long ago committed to memory, as well as writing new ones. At the age of eighty-six, his album *The 86 Years of Eubie Blake* was released, and he came out of retirement to give concerts and make appearances. The Broadway musical *Eubie*, first staged in 1978, added to his fame, and he was awarded the Medal of Freedom by President Reagan in 1981. His last professional appearance occurred in 1982, just one week before he turned ninety-nine; he lived to be one hundred. His remains were cremated at Green-Wood Cemetery.

OPENING JAPAN TO THE WEST

TOWNSEND HARRIS (1804–1878) rose to the presidency of the New York City Board of Education and almost single-handedly founded

Townsend Harris, who opened Japan to the West. Dictionary of American Portraits, Dover Publications.

Townsend Harris's new memorial was paid for, in part, by Japanese organizations and individuals.

the Free Academy (later known as the College of the City of New York), the first tuition-free college in America, despite the vehement opposition of local colleges which charged for schooling. But his greatest contribution was opening Japan to American trade.

In 1855, Harris was appointed American consul general to Japan, and the next year he raised Old Glory over the first foreign consulate in that country. His influence in Japan was tremendous, and he was able to negotiate the Treaty of Amity and Commerce with Japan in 1858, opening it up to foreign residents and to world trade. It has been said that Harris knew the Japanese better than any other foreigner has ever known them. The Japanese delegation that visited America in 1860 to ratify this treaty caused a sensation in New York and other eastern cities.

This monument to Harris was dedicated at Green-Wood Cemetery in July, 1986, by Japanese organizations, individuals, and City College.

A FEW WHO GOT AWAY . . .

WHEN ENTERTAINER Mae West, a native of Brooklyn, died on November 22, 1980, word quickly spread that she would be buried at Green-Wood Cemetery. However, it turned out that that word was put out to mislead the press and the public, which waited at Green-Wood while Mae West was quietly interred at nearby Cypress Hills Cemetery.

On May 7, 1849, Major General William J. Worth, a hero of the Mexican War and Commander of the Department of Texas, died of cholera in San Antonio, Texas. A month later, New York City's Common Council appointed a committee to make arrangements for his body to be brought back to New York for burial, and he was interred at Green-Wood Cemetery. But in 1854, New York City's Board of Alderman approved the erec

Ragtime pianist Eubie Blake, tickling the ivories at his Brooklyn home. Daily News L.P. Photo.

tion of a monument to Worth on the triangle of public land at Broadway, Fifth Avenue, and 25th Street, just to the west of Madison Square Park. On November 23, 1857, General Worth's remains were removed from Green-Wood and taken to City Hall, where he lay in state for two days. Then, with a military escort, he was taken to his final resting place next to the Worth Monument, which had been built in his honor. He has the distinction of being the only individual buried at a New York intersection.

Well-known painter Jasper Cropsey (1823–1900) has many relatives who are interred at Green-Wood Cemetery. Even several of his namesakes are there. He is not.

Two recent books have reported that Margaret Sanger, the birth control advocate, is interred at Green-Wood Cemetery. There is a Margaret Sanger at Green-Wood, but it is not *that* Margaret Sanger.

. . . AND ONE WHO STAYED

AUGUSTUS CHAPMAN ALLEN (1806–1864) and his brother, John Kirby Allen, left New York in the early 1830's to seek their fortune in the wilds of Texas. In August, 1836, soon after the Republic of Texas was established, they founded the City of Houston, Texas. Their efforts also resulted in Houston being named Texas's capital.

Augustus Allen was appointed United States Consul to Mexico in 1852, and kept himself busy trading and championing an interoceanic canal across the Isthmus of Tehuantepec. But Allen's health deteriorated, and on January 11, 1864, he died at the Willard Hotel in Washington, D.C. His remains were sent to Green-Wood Cemetery, and he was interred there.

Augustus Allen reposed near Green-Wood Cemetery's Cypress Avenue and Vernal Path for more than a century. But as the 150th anniversary of Houston's founding drew near in 1986, his heirs, with the support of Houston's City Council and its Mayor's Office, petitioned New York's courts, asking that his remains be disinterred from Green-Wood Cemetery and reinterred in Houston.

Ultimately, the petition was withdrawn, and Augustus Allen's remains continue to lie undisturbed at Green-Wood.

THE MAESTRO

BORN in Lawrence, Massachusetts, to Jewish immigrants from Russia, LEONARD BERNSTEIN (1918–1990) resisted his father's efforts to steer him into the family's beauty-supply business, instead choosing a music career. After studying music and graduating from Harvard, he spent the summers of 1940 and 1941 working at Tanglewood with Serge Koussevitzky, who became his mentor. Bernstein was appointed the New York Philharmonic's assistant conductor in 1943, and became an overnight sensation on November 14 of that year, when he stepped in for the ailing Bruno Walter to conduct.

Leonard Bernstein, rehearsing for a Central Park concert. Daily News L.P. Photo.

For nearly fifty years, Leonard Bernstein was one of the leading figures in the music world. His *First Symphony* (*Jeremiah*) was voted the best new American orchestral work by the New York Music Critics' Circle for 1943–44. His musical *On the Town* (1944) ran for over a year on Broadway. In 1957, he collaborated with Stephen Sondheim on his masterpiece, *West Side Story*. That same year he was named co-conductor of the New York Philharmonic, and the next year he was named its music director and chief conductor, positions he held until 1969.

Bernstein was for many years one of the most sought-after guest conductors in the world, and served as conductor laureate of the New York and Israel Philharmonics. At the same time that he was winning new respect for American music, he also became the most influential music teacher in history through his *Young People's Concerts* which were televised to millions in the 1960's, was a gifted pianist, and was a theatrical conductor. He wrote several books, perhaps the best of which was *The Joy of Music* (1959). He was also an early champion of the fight against AIDS and raised millions of dollars for AIDS research and care.

Green-Wood Cemetery was founded as a nonsectarian Christian cemetery. However, over the years a few Jews have been buried there. Certainly the most prominent of those is Leonard Bernstein.

It is not surprising that Bernstein would choose Green-Wood, rather than a predominantly Jewish cemetery, as his final resting place. Bernstein was long interested in diverse religions. He maintained a lifelong involvement with Judaism, writing several works of music, including *Kaddish*, which were derived from the Old Testament. But he also had a great interest in Catholicism, and wrote *Mass* for the opening of the Kennedy Center in Washington, D.C., in 1971. The services at his burial were from the Jewish religion.

It is a Jewish tradition, dating back centuries, to leave a small stone at graveside as a token of a visit to pay respects to the deceased. The accompanying photograph, taken shortly after Bernstein's death, shows several such stones. The one with a paper strip across it is marked "Vienna Philharmonic," an orchestra which Bernstein often led.

Publicity photograph of actor-songwriter Paul Jabara. Photograph courtesy Claudie Jabara Hadad. Carved into Jabara's granite monument is this: "Beloved son, sweet brother & uncle, our love forever."

PAUL JABARA (1948–1992), songwriter, singer, and actor, was born in Brooklyn. He made his Broadway debut in the original cast of the rock musical *Hair,* created the role of King Herod in the original London production of *Jesus Christ Superstar,* appeared in movies such as *Midnight Cowboy, The Lords of Flatbush, The Day of the Locust,* and *Star 80,* and in several television series, including *Starsky and Hutch* and *Mary Hartman, Mary Hartman.*

Moving to Los Angeles in the 1970's, Jabara achieved his greatest success there with his songwriting. He wrote the disco hit *Last Dance,* which was featured in the 1978 movie *Thank God It's Friday* and won an Oscar for best original song, captured a Grammy Award, and went platinum and gold on the record charts with the Donna Summer rendition. He also wrote *The Main Event,* a hit for Barbra Streisand, *Enough is Enough,* performed as a duet by Barbra Streisand and Donna Summer, *Work that Body,* a big seller for Diana Ross, *It's Raining Men,* sung by the Weathergirls, and *Two Lovers,* performed by Julio Iglesias. His own albums included *Paul Jabara and Friends,* which featured Whitney Houston, and *Paul Jabara's Greatest Hits and Misses.*

DO AS I SAY, NOT AS I EAT . . .

BORN in Brooklyn, Dr. STEPHEN BERGER (1953–1994) was a health-advice columnist for the *New York Post* from 1984 until 1994, and wrote several books in which he championed nutritional dieting to improve the body's immune system. He promised those who followed his advice that their longevity was assured. Berger authored several bestselling books, including *Dr. Berger's Immune Power Diet* (1985) (which spent sixteen weeks at number one on *The New York Times'* best-seller list in the advice category, in which he told how he, at 6 feet 7 inches, reduced his weight from 420 to 210 pounds), *How to be Your Own Nutritionist* (1987), and *Forever Young—20 Years Younger in 20 Weeks: Dr. Berger's Step-by-Step Rejuvenation Program* (1989).

For several years prior to Berger's death, the New York State Board of Professional Medical Conduct was investigating charges against his Central Park West diet practice, where he treated such notables as Liza Minnelli, Sally Jessy Raphael, and Irving "Swifty" Lazar. Apparently his license to practice medicine was about to be taken from him when he died.

At the time of his death, at the age of forty, Berger weighed 365 pounds; the medical examiner attributed his death to cocaine and extreme obesity. Dr. Berger, known to employees for his fondness for French fries with gravy and knockwurst topped with potato salad, was apparently not a follower of his own strict diets. One doctor who knew Dr. Berger insists that he saw him, at one lunch, order a double pastrami with extra fat.

WHEN HE was found dead on August 12, 1988, in his East Village apartment, from what friends described as a heroin overdose, JEAN MICHEL BASQUIAT (1960–1988) was only twenty-seven years old. *The New York Times*, a few days after his death, looked back:

> In a city that exalts successful artists in the fashion of rock stars, Jean Michel Basquiat seemed blessed. When he burst on the art scene in 1981, his paintings of anguished figures were hailed by some critics as works of genius. Admirers besieged him at Manhattan's hottest night clubs. Sales of his art grossed millions of dollars.

The son of middle class Haitian and Puerto Rican parents, Basquiat quit school and left home at the age of seventeen to join a friend in the graffiti movement, writing cryptic social commentaries, under the name "Samo," on walls that would be seen by trendsetters throughout Soho and the East Village. Some were parables, others phrases such as "Playing Art With Daddy's Money" and "9 to 5 Clone."

Playing guitar in a band in clubs frequented by artists, Basquiat befriended Andy Warhol, and became his protegé and companion. He became the best known of the few young black artists who developed international followings in the 1980's. His angry, primitive figures, painted on canvasses, doors, or refrigerators, were popular among collectors. By the age of twenty-four, he had sold paintings for $10,000 to $25,000 to the Whitney Museum of Art, the Museum of Modern Art, and to collectors S. I. Newhouse, Richard Gere, and Paul Simon. His works went at auction in the $30,000 to $100,000 range.

Spending money as fast as he made it, Basquiat entertained lavishly, gave money away, painted new works wearing designer suits, and became hooked on drugs. When Warhol died in February, 1987, Basquiat became something of a recluse, painting more while doing more drugs.

On November 6, 1988, a memorial service to the young artist was held at St. Peter's Lutheran Church on East 54th Street in Manhattan. More

Jean Michel Basquiat's monument, decorated for Christmas. Many elaborate Christmas wreaths are left at graveside in the newer areas of the cemetery.

than two hundred of Basquiat's friends and contemporary art enthusiasts attended. On the altar was a color photograph of Basquiat and one of his paintings bearing the phrase, "Nothing to be gained here."

The New York Times eulogized him with this: "Regarded by many contemporary art experts as a genius, Jean Michel Basquiat was remembered as a man who pursued every aspect of his life with drive and devotion, including those that were destructive." One longtime friend recalled, "He could be a jerk. But he was a jerk with such incredible energy." Another friend remembered him as someone "who knew every White Castle hamburger joint in the five boroughs."

In 1996, the life of the young artist who was described by one observer as "the art world's closest equivalent to James Dean" was recreated in the movie *Basquiat.* Jeffrey Wright played the title role, with David Bowie as Warhol, and Dennis Hopper, Gary Oldham, and Courtney Love in supporting roles.

HOME RUN TO HEAVEN

IN THE LAST decade or so, Green-Wood Cemetery has removed some roads and paths, replacing them with concrete slabs as footings for the placement of low granite monuments. Those monuments, by cemetery regulation, must all be the same size and shape. However, those regulations have not prevented creative expression. Many of these monuments are dedicated to recent immigrants, and the practice of placing a photographic image of the deceased, which until recently was only rarely seen at the cemetery, has now become very popular. Here, baseball imagery is used in this original tribute.

"Home Run to Heaven."

Selected Bibliography

Appletons' Cyclopaedia of American Biography, edited by James Grant Wilson and John Fiske. New York: D. Appleton and Company, 1887.

Appletons' Dictionary of New York and its Vicinity. New York: D. Appleton & Co., 1891.

Asbury, Herbert. *The Gangs of New York: An Informal History of the Underworld*. New York: Alfred A. Knopf, 1927.

Barnum, Phineas Taylor. *Struggles and Triumphs, or Forty Years' Recollections of P.T. Barnum, Written by Himself.* Buffalo, N.Y.: Warren, Johnson & Co., 1873.

Berger, Meyer. *Meyer Berger's New York*. New York: Random House, 1960.

Boatner, Mark M. *The Civil War Dictionary*. New York: David McKay Company, Inc., 1959.

Brower, Effie. *Greenwood Leaves*. Brooklyn: Printed privately for the author, 1878.

Cleaveland, Nehemiah, and Smillie, James. *Green-Wood Illustrated*. New York: 1847.

Cleaveland, Nehemiah. *A Hand-Book For Green-Wood*. New York: E. B. Tripp, 1873.

Dictionary of American Biography, edited by Allen Johnson. New York: Charles Scribner's Sons, 1936.

Historical Times Illustrated Encyclopedia of the Civil War, edited by Patricia L. Faust. New York: Harper Perennial, 1991.

Koykka, Arthur S. *Project Remember: A National Index of Gravesites of Notable Americans*. Algonac, Michigan: Reference Publications, 1986.

Livingston, E. A. (Bud). *President Lincoln's Third Largest City: Brooklyn & The Civil War*. New York: Bud Press, 1994.

Notable New Yorkers of 1896–1899, edited by Moses King. New York: Moses King, 1899.

Pike, Martha V., and Armstrong, Janice Gray. *A Time to Mourn: Expressions of Grief in Nineteenth Century America*. Stony Brook, New York: The Museums at Stony Brook, 1980.

Poppeliers, Chambers, and Schwartz. *What Style Is It? A Guide to American Architecture*. Washington, D.C.: Preservation Press, 1983.

Sears, John F. *Sacred Places; American Tourist Attractions in the Nineteenth Century*. New York: Oxford University Press, 1989.

Stiles, Henry R. *A History of the City of Brooklyn, N.Y.* Volumes II and III. Brooklyn: Published by Subscription, 1869, 1870.

The Diary of George Templeton Strong, edited by Allan Nevins and Milton Halsey Thomas. New York: The Macmillan Company, 1952.

The New York Times Obituary Index. New York: *The New York Times*, 1970, 1980.

The New York Times. New York: *The New York Times*, various years.

Index of Names

All names except those in small caps are of individuals who were buried, cremated, or have a monument, at Green-Wood Cemetery.